Interior Castle

The Classic Text
with a Spiritual
Commentary

CLASSICS with COMMENTARY, a series in the Christian Classics line devoted to rediscovering classic Christian literature, mines the depths of the rich tradition of Christian spirituality. Critical translations accompanied by timely and accessible commentary and probing questions revitalize these works for another generation of spiritual pilgrims.

Books in the CLASSICS with COMMENTARY series

- *The Imitation of Christ* by Thomas a Kempis
- *Interior Castle* by Teresa of Avila
- *Visits to the Most Holy Sacrament and to Most Holy Mary* by Alphonsus de Liguori
  (Coming September 2007)

CLASSICS
with
COMMENTARY

Interior Castle

**The Classic Text
with a Spiritual
Commentary
by Dennis J. Billy, C.Ss.R.**

Teresa of Avila

Christian Classics ✠ *Notre Dame, Indiana*

© 2007 by Ave Maria Press, Inc.

Founded in 1865, Ave Maria Press is a ministry of the Indiana Province of Holy Cross.

www.christian-classics.com

ISBN-10 0-87061-241-7   ISBN-13 978-0-87061-241-1

Cover and text design by John Carson

Printed and bound in the United States of America.

In loving memory of
Katherine Mazuryk
"Cha Cha Katherine"
(1910–2005)

✛

I began to think of the soul as if it were a castle made of a single diamond or of a very clear crystal, in which there are many rooms, just as in Heaven there are many mansions.

—Teresa of Avila

Contents

Introduction............................9

How to Read *Interior Castle*.......21

Prologue 33

First Mansions...........................37
    Chapter 1 39
    Chapter 2 47

Second Mansions 59
    Chapter 1 61

Third Mansions 71
    Chapter 1 73
    Chapter 2 81

Fourth Mansions.........................91
    Chapter 1 93
    Chapter 2 103
    Chapter 3 111

Fifth Mansions 123
    Chapter 1 125
    Chapter 2 133
    Chapter 3 143
    Chapter 4 151

Sixth Mansions 159
    Chapter 1 161
    Chapter 2 171
    Chapter 3 177
    Chapter 4 187
    Chapter 5 197
    Chapter 6 205
    Chapter 7 215
    Chapter 8 227
    Chapter 9 235
    Chapter 10 245
    Chapter 11 251

Seventh Mansions 259
    Chapter 1 261
    Chapter 2 269
    Chapter 3 277
    Chapter 4 287

Epilogue................................297

Notes...................................301

Suggested Readings...............315

Introduction

✛

Saint Teresa of Avila (1515–1582) was a contemplative nun, religious reformer, monastic foundress, spiritual writer, and gifted poet. She was also one of the great Christian mystics of all time. She lived during the period of early modern Catholicism, a period of reform and bitter religious rivalry in Western Europe, and when Spain, her native land, was an expanding colonial power and arguably the most powerful nation on earth. She wrote *Interior Castle* at the request of her trusted and learned confessor, Jerome Gratian[1], during a six-month period in 1577 in order to explain to the nuns of her Discalced Carmelite reform the various kinds of prayer they might experience on their journey to God. This work contains her mature spiritual doctrine and is considered by many her masterpiece.

Plan and Purpose

The types of prayer contained in this work range from the most basic of the ascetical life to the highest and most rarefied of mystical states. Although Teresa writes in a practical, spontaneous, easy-to-read style, and makes good use of images and metaphors to convey her teaching, she is still sometimes very difficult to understand. The reason for this comes, in part, from the nature of the mystical experiences she describes and the inherent limitations of human language to adequately convey a person's face-to-face encounter with the divine. Even those experienced in the ways of prayer have a hard time penetrating Teresa's intense yet deeply elusive thought; beginners in the spiritual life struggle with it even more.

My purpose in writing this spiritual commentary is to make the teaching of this Christian classic more accessible to today's readers. I do so, chapter by chapter, by examining Teresa's thought making relevant distinctions, and restating her teaching in a way that makes it less dense and easier to grasp. I do this without diluting Teresa's spiritual doctrine. I have used E. Allison Peers' English translation so that readers can enjoy the classic translation of this text.[2] I also pose pertinent questions to Teresa's readers to help them probe her thought still further and discover the relevance of her teaching for their own lives. By breaking open the work in this way, I hope to encourage readers to recognize the intrinsic worth of Teresa's teaching and see it as a viable way of understanding the interior life and interpreting one's experience of God.

Teresa's Life and Writings

Teresa was born in Avila on March 28, 1515. Her father, Alonso of Cepeda, was the son of a wealthy Jewish merchant from Toledo who had recently converted to the Christian faith. After the death of his first wife in 1507, he entered a second marriage to Teresa's mother, Beatrice of Ahumada, some two years later. Teresa's mother came from an aristocratic Christian family of Avila. She bore her husband ten children and died when Teresa was fifteen years old.

As a child, Teresa had a deep desire to give her life to Christ. At the age of seven, she even tried to run away with her brother to convert the Moors and become a martyr for the faith. In time, however, this early enthusiasm began to wane. Teresa took her mother's death very hard and gradually set aside her pious interests. To correct this tendency and to offer her sound Christian instruction, her father sent her away to be educated as a lay boarder at the Augustinian convent at Santa María de Gracia. It was there that Teresa first felt the call to enter religious life. She received this inspiration largely through the influence of Mary of Brinceño, who was charged with the lay students at the convent, and by reading the letters of Saint Jerome.

Upon her return home, her father was happy that his daughter had once more regained her Catholic piety, but was adamantly against her becoming a nun. In the face of this opposition, Teresa ran away on November 2, 1535, and entered the Carmelite Monastery of the Incarnation in Avila. In time, her father acquiesced to his daughter's wishes and gave his consent for her to become a nun.

The following year, Teresa received the Carmelite habit and professed her vows. She became deathly ill shortly thereafter and was sent to Becedas to receive treatment from a woman known throughout Castile for her healing remedies. Her health did not improve, and it was during this time that she read and was deeply influenced by Gregory the Great's *Morals* and Francis of Osuna's *Third Spiritual Alphabet*, a treatise on prayer in which she took great delight. Teresa's health steadily declined, so much so that on August 15, 1539, she went into a coma and was presumed dead. She regained consciousness some four days later, but was paralyzed in her legs for the next three years. When she finally recovered, she attributed her healing to the intercession of Saint Joseph and continued her life at the Monastery of the Incarnation.

All during this time, Teresa continued her life of prayer and even learned to move beyond discursive meditative practices and to simply rest in contemplative silence before the Lord. Although she had sporadic mystical experiences, she entered a period of dryness that lasted for almost eighteen years. In addition, she was held back by her desire to please and win the approval of others.

In 1554, at the age of thirty-nine, Teresa had two experiences that touched her deeply and changed her entire outlook about her spiritual journey. One was an experience of Christ's healing and redeeming power while praying before a statue of the suffering Christ. The other was a deep sense of the Lord calling her as she read the account of Saint Augustine's conversion in his *Confessions*. These experiences gave her deep peace and a sense of the Lord's abiding presence in her life that helped her let go of her fears and worldly attachments and give herself entirely over to the service of the Lord. As Teresa's mystical communion with God deepened, she had great difficulty explaining her experiences to her friends and confessors. Some of them even became suspicious of her and told her outright that her mystical ecstasies were the work of the devil. She continued her quest for sound guidance from learned and holy confessors and eventually found comfort from such men as Saint Francis Borgia (1510–1572) and Saint Peter of Alcántara (1499–1562). These and other learned and saintly men encouraged her in her trials and affirmed that the Lord was working in her.

Teresa's reputation as a reformer began with these intense experiences of personal conversion that led to her desire to change her life and bring it more fully in conformity with God's will. A sense of dissatisfaction over life at the Monastery of the Incarnation led a small group of nuns to gather in her cell in September of 1560 and dream of initiating a reform in their order. This reform took root gradually and in the midst of great opposition within the monastery, the Carmelite order, and the local townspeople. With the support of Peter of Alcántara, Teresa gained permission from Rome and established a reformed monastery of Carmelites dedicated to Saint Joseph in Avila on August 24, 1562. Her close friend and associate Saint John of the Cross (1542–1591) helped her bring the reform to the male branch of the order and, like Teresa, met staunch resistance at nearly every turn. Teresa spent the rest of her life crisscrossing Spain to further the cause of her reform. She established a total of fourteen reformed Carmelite monasteries in her lifetime and left behind a large literary corpus, the most important of which include *The Book of Her Life* (1562–65), *The Way of Perfection* (1562–69), *Meditations on the Song of Songs* (1567), *The Book of Foundations* (1573), and *Interior Castle* (1577). She died at Alba de Tormes on October 4, 1582, was beatified in 1614, proclaimed patroness of Spain in 1617, canonized in 1622, and declared a doctor of the Church in 1970.[3]

Teresa's Spiritual Doctrine

Even this brief (and admittedly limited) sketch of Teresa's life tells us that she had intense suffering in her life, had periods of both dryness and deep mystical experience, and felt deeply called to a life of conversion. Her teaching on prayer reflects each of these themes and is found mainly in her *Life*, *The Way of Perfection*, and *Interior Castle*. Because these works were written at different times, for diverse audiences, and for distinct purposes, it is difficult to formulate an overall synthesis of her spiritual doctrine.

Teresa, moreover, spiritually matured over time. Her insights into mystical prayer deepened as she herself drew closer to God and experienced the lasting inner peace of spiritual marriage. When reading her works, therefore, we must allow for growth and expect certain inconsistencies between her earlier and later writings. That said, her teaching on prayer, while not uniform in every point, possesses a remarkable degree of coherence. She assumes the classical distinctions between *oratio* (i.e., vocal prayer), *meditatio* (i.e., meditation or mental prayer), and *contemplatio* (i.e., contemplation) and uses them to develop not a scholarly treatise on prayer, but one rooted in experience and explained through metaphor.[4]

Nowhere in her writings does Teresa lay out the various grades of prayer in a systematic and fully integrated way. Because of limited space, I list them here in an abbreviated and adapted form to help her readers grasp the general contours of her teaching. This strategy will be of help, provided one remembers that Teresa merges some categories at times and, in some places, does not specifically identify the kind of prayer she is discussing. We summarize these grades of prayer as follows:[4]

1. *Vocal Prayer* uses words to express our hearts and minds to God. It can follow prescribed formulas, as in the Lord's Prayer and the Hail Mary, or be a spontaneous outpouring of the heart. It can be done in private or in a group. It also plays an important role in liturgical prayer. Because it is simple and easy to learn, it is usually the first kind of prayer to which people are introduced. Vocal prayer is "embodied prayer." Through it, a person makes use of the body as a way of giving honor and glory to God. The greatest strength of vocal prayer is the way it can involve the whole person—body, mind, and spirit—in prayer. Its greatest weakness is the way it can degenerate into a mechanized, external display that is void of inner meaning. Vocal prayer is important at every stage of the spiritual life. Even though it is simple and easy to learn, it should in no way be denigrated. Jesus himself encouraged his disciples to pray with meaningful words from the heart when addressing their Father in heaven (Mt 6:7–13).

2. *Meditation or Mental Prayer* for Teresa is "nothing but friendly intercourse, and frequent solitary converse, with him who we know loves us."[6] It is a discursive type of prayer that focuses the mind on a particular gospel story or mystery of the faith. Through it, a person probes the meaning of a particular belief and makes it an integral part of his or her life. It is practiced in silence and normally for an extended period of time (twenty to thirty minutes). It can be done both privately and in common. There are many methods of mental prayer. Most of them include a period of preparation, some reflection on a particular aspect of the faith, an application of that reflection to one's life, a resolution to do something about it, and a concluding prayer. Through mental prayer, a person is able to consider "in-depth" the meaning of his or her faith. When practiced regularly, it enables one to delve beneath the surface of one's beliefs and to participate with more awareness in the ongoing conversion of life.

3. *Affective Prayer* brings meditation from the level of the head to that of the heart. Although Teresa discusses this grade of prayer in her writings, she does not use the phrase to specifically identify it.[7] For her, "affective prayer" is merely a deeper kind of meditation. What has

begun as a sustained reflection on a particular aspect of the faith gradually begins to penetrate a person's will and to manifest itself in heartfelt prayers of love and affection. In affective prayer, a person's will functions as the predominant faculty. However, since both reason and will must be present in any genuine act of mental prayer, what we are really talking about here is a matter of emphasis. At this stage, the person praying has become so absorbed in the object of meditation that deep sentiments and inner longings of love for God swell up within the heart and find expression. Affective prayer is mental prayer that has come to term. It is the prayer of mind and heart, but with the heart playing the dominant role. Such prayer must be spontaneous and should not be forced. It is to be judged by the fruits it produces in a person's life and not by the sensible consolation that often accompanies it.

4.   *Acquired Recollection* is a simple, loving gaze upon a concrete representation of the divine (e.g., an icon, the tabernacle, the consecrated host). As such, it moves beyond the discursive level of prayer that involves the deliberated movement of the intellect and the will in mental prayer. This grade of prayer is the dividing line between the ascetical and mystical stages of the spiritual life. During it, the person at prayer acts under the influence of grace but is still the primary agent involved in the action. This form of prayer subsumes all the fruits of mental and affective prayer into itself. Unlike these earlier forms of prayer, however, there is no specific "method" or way of going about it. It simply happens. In this prayer, one's spirit has become awakened to the divine and is content with doing nothing else but sitting in the divine presence. A person who prays in this way leads a simple life and shows visible signs of steady progress in the life of conversion.

5.   *Infused Contemplation* marks the beginning of the mystical prayer in the life of the believer. Here, the person praying receives an intimate, experiential knowledge of God. This knowledge comes in the form of an intellectual light that illumines the mind and enables the person to have an intuitive, connatural knowledge of the divine. Infused contemplation is a pure gift from God. The person praying can do nothing to instigate its coming or to prolong its stay. At this stage of prayer, the person praying opens his or her mind to God in a vulnerable stance of passive receptiveness. Being open in this way to the illuminating light of the divine is itself a special gift from God and given to those specially chosen for it. Those blessed with the experience of

infused contemplation receive an obscure but assured knowledge of the divine and are given the moral certitude that they are in a state of grace. They are moved to devote themselves more deeply to the interior life and normally need to place themselves under the care of a holy, learned, and experienced director.

6. *The Prayer of Quiet* takes the person praying into an even deeper experience of God. Whereas infused contemplation fills the intellect with the illuminating light of the divine, the prayer of quiet allows that light to penetrate the will. The result is an experience of intense joy and inner consolation. At this stage, the will is captivated and totally absorbed in God. The person praying in this way is given great freedom of spirit, a filial respect and deep confidence in God, a love of suffering, uncommon humility, detachment from worldly pleasures, and the desire to grow in the virtues. At this level, it is normally very difficult for the person to describe his or her experiences of God. As the name suggests, the person blessed with this experience tends toward solitude and repose, but is able to actively engage the other faculties of the soul. The experience of quiet may last for a long time or only a few moments. The person who receives this experience should be grateful when it occurs and, when it passes, should be encouraged to continue to pray in other ways.

7. *The Prayer of Union* brings the person praying to an even deeper experience of the divine. In the prior two stages of contemplation, only the intellect and will are captivated by the illuminating light of God. Here, all the internal faculties become absorbed in this intense, penetrating light. The memory and imagination are particularly affected at this stage. They become totally focused on God and, as a result, leave the person praying free of all distractions and weariness. Those blessed with this experience are certain of their intimate union with God. They experience him with such intensity that they can easily become "beside themselves" by falling into ecstasy. Being absorbed in God in this way can last for a few fleeting moments or a period of hours. During such times, the person can sometimes feel a sensible "touch," an intense "fiery dart," or a longer-lasting "wound of love" in the soul. These experiences are not essential to the prayer of union, but are often associated with it. They reveal the heights of mystical experience and indicate an intense relationship of love between God and the person praying.

8. *Spiritual Betrothal* occurs when the divine light captivates the soul's external senses. This stage is an extension of the prayer of union. Now not only the internal sense, but also the external senses of hearing, sight, smell, taste, and touch are distanced, either totally or in part, from their ordinary functioning. The person's internal and external senses are so absorbed in God that he or she finds it exceedingly difficult to become involved in external activity. At this stage, mystical ecstasy (in the sense of standing "outside of one's senses") is part and parcel of a person's experience of the divine. It can be gentle and pleasing to the person praying or intensely violent and painful. In spiritual betrothal, the person praying enters into a deep covenant with God. The soul is pulled up out of its senses and becomes totally awake to the divine world. This state of betrothal or conforming union leads the soul to the threshold of perfect, mystical union with God.

9. *Spiritual Marriage* brings about the total absorption of the soul into God. Although the distinction between creator and creature remains, the soul's subjective experience is such that a complete identification with the divine love has taken place. This transformation of the soul into the Beloved is permanent and involves a complete surrender of self. The person seeks God in all things and is willing to undergo the greatest of trials for the love of God. At this stage, the intense spiritual ecstasies of the previous stages greatly diminish—and even disappear. Instead, the person is blessed with a vivid awareness of God's deep, abiding love. It is here, in this inner sanctum, that the person communes with the Trinity in a way that, in this life, cannot be equaled. Only the beatific vision can take the soul further into the mysterious depths of the Godhead. People who experience God in this way possess a deep spirit of detachment and have a strong desire to serve God. They put others before themselves and are willing to undergo great suffering for the coming of the kingdom.

These nine grades of prayer generally correspond to the purgative (grades one to four), illuminative (grades five and six), and unitive (grades seven through nine) ways. It must be remembered, however, that these "stages" of the spiritual journey do not always occur in strict succession. More often than not, they are mingled in a person's life and are very difficult to isolate. Detachment from worldly things, for example, while typically associated with the purgative way, is also necessary for growth in self-knowledge and the acquisition of wisdom, normally associated with the illuminative way. Each, in turn, is necessary for the intimate communion with God associated with the unitive way. For this and other reasons, it is usually better to ask which of these stages is the dominant emphasis in a person's life at any particular moment and in which general direction he or she is moving, toward or away from union with God. Such a determination is usually a good indication of person's spiritual state.[8]

Interior Castle

Another way of looking at these grades of prayer is to understand them in terms of the seven spiritual mansions of Teresa's spiritual masterpiece, the *Interior Castle*, known in Spanish as *Moradas* ("mansions" or "dwelling places"). Teresa uses the metaphor of the soul as a castle of diamond or clear crystal as the organizing image for her work. Although she recognizes that there are many mansions or dwelling places variously arranged within this castle, she focuses on seven, of which she has some little knowledge. The seventh mansion lies in the very heart of the soul and is the place where God has chosen to make his abode. For Teresa, the spiritual life is all about entering the castle of the soul through prayer and making one's way successively through the various mansions until one enters God's abode and becomes totally one with him. The book consists of twenty-seven chapters of varying lengths and distributed unequally across the various mansions.

Although it will not do justice to Teresa's depth and complexity, a brief description of these mansions will give a general sense of how she organizes and approaches her teaching. In the First Mansions (two chapters), Teresa introduces her organizing image of the interior castle and speaks of the great beauty and dignity of the soul. She also identifies prayer as the gate to this castle, describes the great misery of a soul deformed by serious sin, and emphasizes the importance of self-knowledge for growth in the spiritual life. In the Second Mansions (one chapter), she explains the great importance of perseverance for those wishing to reach the last mansions. In the Third Mansions (two chapters), she speaks of how little security there is in the state of exile, even for those who have reached a high degree of perfection. In the Fourth Mansions (three chapters), she distinguishes between spiritual sweetness and spiritual consolation, discusses the difference between the imagination and understanding, and explains the prayers of infused recollection and quiet, and their effects. In the Fifth Mansions (four chapters), she describes how the soul unites

itself with God in prayer and says what she means by the prayer of union.
To illustrate her point, she offers the image of a silkworm spinning a
cocoon, dying, and then being transformed into a beautiful white butterfly. In the Sixth Mansions (eleven chapters), she deals with the state of
spiritual betrothal by speaking of certain ways by which the Lord awakens
the soul and emphasizing the troubles that come to the souls upon whom
the Lord bestows this favor. She further explains how God suspends the
soul by ecstasy and emphasizes the courage needed by souls who receive
such a great favor. She points out the effects of spiritual betrothal on the
soul and tells of the intense grief such a soul feels for its past sins. She
distinguishes spiritual betrothal from the prayer of union and shows how
God speaks to the soul through intellectual and imaginative visions. In the
Seventh Mansions (four chapters), she tells of the great favors bestowed
on those who enter the state spiritual marriage. She uses comparisons to
distinguish this state from the prayer of union and spiritual betrothal. She
speaks of the effects of spiritual marriage on the soul and concludes by
mentioning what the Lord has in mind by conferring such favors on the
soul.

Although Teresa is more concerned with the later mansions and says
little about the kind of prayer that goes on in the first three, we can generally assume that the believer is slowly making progress in vocal prayer,
mental prayer, affective prayer, and acquired recollection, those stages
normally referred to as "the four degrees of ordinary prayer." In the fourth
mansion the believer experiences infused contemplation and the prayer of
quiet; in the fifth, the prayer of union; in the sixth, spiritual betrothal; and
in the seventh, spiritual marriage. The first three mansions refer to what
is typically called the "ascetical" life, while the final four mansions are
concerned with the "mystical."[9] The understanding that there were various levels of both the ascetical and mystical states would have been very
familiar to the Catholic mindset of the time.

As stated earlier, Teresa wrote the *Interior Castle* with the nuns of her
Carmelite reform in mind as her audience. She was convinced that the
Lord would bless many of them with mystical favors, and she wanted them
to have an awareness of what to expect on their inner journey. When she
finished the work, she gave it to her confessor, Jerome Gratian, for correction and safekeeping. The original manuscript still exists and is housed
today with the Discalced Carmelite nuns in Seville. It bears Gratian's corrections and those of other censors.[10] The text first appeared in print in
the Spanish edition of Teresa's writings published six years after her death
in Salamanca in 1588. There are a number of critical Spanish editions of

Teresa's masterpiece.[11] There are also a number of English translations of varying qualities.[12] E. Allison Peers's English translation of the *Interior Castle*, the one used in this commentary, is generally considered the standard version.[13]

How to Read Interior Castle

✤

To get the most benefit out of reading the *Interior Castle*, today's readers need some guidelines (interpretative filters, if you will) to help them find the work's relevance for their lives. Without these guidelines, Teresa's readers will have a difficult time distilling the work's meaning in a way that has concrete application to their own experience. The following list, while in no way exhaustive, covers some of the most important areas of concern that should touch their awareness as they read the work.

1.   To begin with, it is important to keep in mind what kind of book we are dealing with. The *Interior Castle* is neither a prayer book nor one of academic theology. It represents an attempt on Teresa's part to give her readers a glimpse of the kinds of prayer they might experience as they make their way to God. She does not claim to be comprehensive in what she says and readily admits that there are many other mansions or states of prayer that she does not treat directly. She focuses, moreover, much more on the later grades than on the earlier ones, partly because she had already treated the earlier in her autobiography and *The Way of Perfection*. Teresa speaks mainly from her own experience and, in effect, gives her readers a personal tour of the various mansions or dwelling places that she has encountered within her own soul. She assumes that, if God so blesses them, her readers will have similar experiences in their spiritual lives. When going through the *Interior Castle*, we should not be disturbed if it seems overwhelming or difficult to understand the first time through. Readers should first try to get a sense of the whole and then go back to those sections that were difficult to understand or of particular interest to them.

Teresa's effort should also encourage them to think about how they would go about giving a tour of the interior life to others.

2.   When reading the *Interior Castle*, we also need to be conscious that Teresa was writing out of obedience to her confessor and spiritual guide, faced unwelcome interruptions, and was very sensitive to the watchful eye of the Spanish Inquisition. The role of a spiritual director in Teresa's day was generally much more directive than today, in part because of the heavy emphasis many spiritual authors of the time placed on obedience and the director's capacity to discern God's will. Since the manuscript of her autobiography had already been confiscated by Church authorities, Teresa's director, Jerome Gratian, asked her to write another work specifically for her sisters, rather than simply expanding her autobiography and running the risk that it too might be confiscated. Not having a copy of her earlier work before her, Teresa constantly apologizes to her readers for possible repetitions and quickly passes over other material that she knows she has treated elsewhere in depth. It is a good idea, therefore, to read the *Interior Castle* in the light of the many concrete references that Teresa makes to her other works, especially her autobiography and *The Way of Perfection*.[1] Although she wrote quickly, finishing the work in six months despite intermittent interruptions of various kinds (including one lasting almost four months), Teresa was very careful in what she put down and says numerous times that she submits everything she has written to the Holy Catholic Church. Her self-deprecating manner, repeated confessions of her own ignorance, avowals of humble submission to her confessors, affirmations of loyalty to the Church, strong stance against its enemies, and occasional denigrating remarks about the inferior nature of women are due, at least in part, to her desire to calm any suspicions about her teachings on the part of Church authorities. That is not to say that Teresa was insincere in her beliefs or in what she wrote, but she knew what it took for a woman to survive in what was still very much a man's world. The fact that she submitted her completed work to her confessor for correction and further emendation further underlines this reality.

3.   When reading the *Interior Castle*, we should also bear in mind the particular audience Teresa is addressing. Although it is possible that she knew her work would, at some point, attract a much larger readership, she directs herself specifically to the nuns of her Carmelite reform. These were contemplative nuns living a life of strict enclosure.

Upon entering Carmel, they broke off contact with the outside world and entered the desert of cloistered life, where their physical movements were highly restricted and where they followed a strict daily regimen of work, prayer, and spiritual reading. Teresa's controlling metaphor of the soul as a spacious interior castle with many mansions taps directly into the spiritual longings of such contemplatives. She is telling them, in effect, not to be troubled by their inability to move about freely in the outside world, for they have a much larger world to explore within themselves. The image of an interior castle reinforces the cloistered life by encouraging those specifically called to the contemplative vocation to explore their own inner worlds. When reading the *Interior Castle*, we should be aware of the work's primary audience and not be disturbed if the controlling image does not have as deep an impact on us as it would on the nuns of Teresa's Carmelite reform. At the same time, readers should be conscious of the universal value the metaphor holds and allow it to speak to the contemplative side of their lives. While relatively few are called to enter the cloister, all are called to foster a contemplative outlook toward life.

4. Coupled with the above, we should also be aware of the privileged place Teresa gives religious life in the hierarchical order of sanctity, making it the standard according to which other states of life must ultimately conform. She accepted, in other words, the "two-tiered" understanding of holiness prevalent throughout the Catholic world of her day and which held great sway right up to the dawn of the Second Vatican Council. According to this outlook, "the way of the commandments" comprises the basic call of all baptized Christians (especially the laity) and "the way of the counsels" that of a chosen elite (especially religious and clergy). Only recently has this deeply entrenched outlook begun to change. The documents of the Second Vatican Council recognize a unique way to God in each vocational state and steer clear of any undue hierarchical comparisons.[2] When reading the *Interior Castle*, we should be conscious of both the audience for which it was originally intended and the understanding of holiness that supports its claims. Readers should also try to distill from its pages those points concerning growth in the Spirit and the walk of Christian discipleship that would be pertinent to their present situation. In this volume, the brief introduction to each chapter and

the reflection questions that follow should be particularly helpful in this regard.

5. We should also be conscious of the distinction between the ascetical and mystical states and be ready to distinguish where the first ends and the second begins. This is especially important in a work that spends so much time on the different mansions or states of prayer. Everyone needs grace in order to pray. In the early stages of prayer, however, the person praying receives God's grace and is the primary subject in the act of praying. For this reason, these stages are normally referred to as ascetical prayer. Vocal prayer, mental prayer, affective prayer, and acquired recollection are normally categorized as such. Mystical prayer begins a certain union between the human and the divine, sets in, and God becomes the primary subject in the act of praying. For this reason, infused contemplation, the prayer of quiet, spiritual betrothal, and spiritual marriage are typically identified as varying states of mystical prayer. With this distinction in mind, it is important for us to bear in mind that, when moving from the third to the fourth mansions, a person is leaving ascetical prayer behind and entering into the mystical state. This fundamental distinction will help readers keep their bearings as they read the work. It will also give them a sense of what they can achieve by cooperating with God's grace (the first three mansions) and what depends totally on God (the final four mansions).

6. When reading the *Interior Castle*, we must also take into account Teresa's strong, combative posture toward the world. The reasons for this attitude go deep into roots of European culture. Part of it has to do with an antagonistic understanding of the relationship between the sacred and the profane, a current that goes back to the origins of Christianity itself. Another part of it concerns a deep suspicion of the material world and the temptations of the flesh, which manifested itself in a desire to flee from the influence of the world, lest it have an inordinate influence in the circumstances of daily life. Yet another reason looks to the philosophical and theological underpinnings which support a vision of reality where the "world of spirit" is constantly at war with the "world of the flesh." All of these reasons (and many more) can help us to appreciate why Teresa often presents the world in a considerably derogatory light. If that is not enough, theology now provides us with not one, but a variety of different models through which we can understand the relationship between Christ

and culture. In addition to the "Christ against the world" posture promulgated in the *Interior Castle*, we now see that Christianity has, at times, identified itself with the world, sought to rise above it, been in paradoxical relation to it, and even tried to transform it.[3] As they read Teresa, readers need to be conscious of the attitude toward the world placed before them and ask some probing questions about how they relate to the culture they live in.

7. We must also be aware of Teresa's assumptions about the human person and make allowances for how they shape her thought in both positive and negative ways. Teresa's understanding of the human person was typical of the Catholicism of her day. Although she maintains the essential metaphysical unity of body and soul, her discourse and manner of speaking often exalt the soul at the expense of the body. In doing so, she introduces a subtle form of dualism in its spiritual outlook that permeates much of what it says about the nature of Christian discipleship and does not sit well with our current sensitivities. Teresa does not demonstrate great concern for the body and at times even exhorts her readers to disregard it to the point of neglect. As the title *Interior Castle* suggests, she is much more concerned with the inner life of the soul in its quest for sanctity than with the health of the body. The soul, for Teresa, is the person's essential form; the body, its essential matter. The soul has rational faculties or powers (e.g., reason and will), certain internal senses (e.g., imagination and memory), and communicates with the outside world through the five external senses (hearing, sight, touch, taste, and smell). She also draws a distinction between "spirit" and "soul," with the spirit being the highest (or deepest, depending on one's point of view) dimension of the soul. For Teresa, the human spirit has the capacity to be elevated by grace so that it can commune with the Spirit of God. This intimate communion will eventually overflow throughout the rest of the soul and, in Teresa's mind, also have a transformative effect on the body. Without knowing such basic assumptions about the human person, it would be difficult for most readers to grasp the nuances of Teresa's thought, thus making it even more difficult to evaluate her teaching.

8. When reading the *Interior Castle*, we should also keep in mind that Teresa's primary image of God is that of a beloved spouse. Teresa is one of the Church's major proponents of spousal mysticism. All of her other images of God (e.g., Humble Servant, Majestic King,

the Crucified One) serve the notion that God wishes to enter into an intimate relationship with his beloved. While Teresa is quick to point out the limitations of the marriage metaphor, she insists that it is still the best way to understand the nature of the relationship that God passionately desires to share with the soul. Whether this relationship reaches its fulfillment in this life or the next is beside the point. Teresa's position is clear: God offers human beings a gift more precious than they could ever imagine. God, the Majestic King and Creator of the Universe, wishes to make his abode deep within the human soul. Teresa's spousal mysticism is centered on both Christ and, since he shares everything with the Father and the Spirit, the Most Holy Trinity. When going through the *Interior Castle*, readers should keep in mind this underlying desire of God. If God did not wish to relate to the soul in this way, Teresa's teaching would be seriously undermined.

9. In addition to the underlying image of God used in the *Interior Castle*, we should also keep an eye out for the other images employed by Teresa to convey her thought. Teresa was an excellent teacher and had a unique gift for coming up with the right image to express complex ideas in a way that touched her readers' experience. In addition to the image of the interior castle itself, which she uses as the controlling metaphor for the entire work, she uses myriad images to illuminate a number of different states in which the soul may find itself during its spiritual journey. She describes a soul steeped in sin as a pool of black, fetid water or a black cloth covering a crystal in sunshine. She says that the works of a soul in the state of grace are like pure springs flowing from a single source. She explains the difference between meditation and contemplation, saying that the former is like a large basin that is filled from a distance through an ingenious system of man-made channels, while the latter is like a basin that is easily filled because it has been constructed at the very source of a spring. One of her most memorable images is when she compares the transformation taking place in the prayer of union to the silkworm that spins its cocoon and turns into a beautiful white butterfly. Teresa fills the *Interior Castle* with these and other images to communicate her spiritual experiences as clearly as possible. She is at her best in such instances. Readers should pay close attention to the way images carry her thought and convey her deepest insights about the spiritual life.

10. Finally, when reading the *Interior Castle*, we should try to be conscious of how mysticism can be used as an alternative source of authority, especially for women. Teresa wrote at a time when women had very little voice in spiritual and religious matters. While she is very careful to submit her teaching to Church authorities, she is also very conscious of the power her spiritual experiences have unleashed. The success of her Carmelite reform bears witness to the way God's power and authority can be made manifest in someone who otherwise would have gone through life largely unnoticed. Mysticism, for Teresa, was not only a way of sharing an intimate union with God, but also a means by which God uses weak human beings to transform the world. The mystic is someone who is blessed with a power and authority that comes directly from God. During the history of the Church, some individuals invoked mystical authority to subvert Church authority (the very reason why the Spanish Inquisition was so wary of it). Teresa wielded its power to transform herself, her order, the Church, and society. Readers should be aware that the *Interior Castle* is about the transformation not only of the human soul but also of the world in which they live.

Conclusion

It would not be a realistic expectation on our part to think that we will be able to fully assimilate Teresa's spiritual doctrine as she understood and intended it herself. It is difficult enough to understand our own thoughts and motivations, let alone someone who lived more than four centuries ago. The best we can hope for is to establish a dialogue with her words that will enable us to enter her world and come to a partial understanding of what the journey to God meant for her. In doing so, we will come to know Teresa's teaching in a way that gives us access to her world (limited though it may be) and has relevance for our own journey to God.

We should approach the *Interior Castle*, therefore, with minds that are open to what Teresa has to say, yet critical of what its implications might be for our own sojourn through time. The work is itself a metaphor for the spiritual journey and, regardless of how we receive it, challenges us to discover those metaphors for the spiritual journey that have relevance for us today. Some of us may become captivated by Teresa's teaching. Others may find it helpful in only a partial or ancillary sense. Still others may find it bound so closely to the worldview of another era that it hardly speaks to us at all. However we receive it, the *Interior Castle* asks us to take the spiritual journey seriously and to find ways of articulating our experience of God that make sense to us today and move us further along the path of radical gospel conversion.

This spiritual commentary seeks to help beginners gain access to Teresa's rich spiritual heritage. It does so by offering summaries of her thought, making appropriate distinctions, and posing relevant questions for today's believers. In doing so, it hopes to help its readers to initiate commentary and formulate their own questions, not only on Teresa's teachings, but also on their own spiritual lives.

Readers can use this commentary in any number of ways and should make use of it as it fits their own spiritual needs. Since Teresa's teachings in the *Interior Castle* build on what comes before it, the way to benefit from it most would probably be to read this work from beginning to end in order to gain a sense of the whole and then return to the beginning and study each chapter carefully (reading it again and again) until Teresa's teaching becomes clear before moving to the next chapter. It goes without saying that some chapters will be much easier to understand than others. By going through the *Interior Castle* in this way, readers will build a cumulative knowledge of the work and be well situated to penetrate the more difficult material in the later mansions.

Dennis J. Billy, C.Ss.R.

✛

Interior Castle

Teresa of Avila

Translated by E. Allison Peers

✛

Interior Castle[1]

✠

Introduction

Teresa of Avila's *Interior Castle* is one of the great spiritual classics of all time. Written in obedience to the expressed command of her confessor and spiritual guide, it represents her most mature attempt to capture through written words the rarefied mystical experiences of the soul's inner journey to God. For Teresa, intimacy with the divine is the whole purpose of the Christian life. A person reaches this goal through an ongoing process of detachment from worldly allurements and a growing attachment to the things of God. Prayer is the means by which a person enters into this process and eventually becomes an intimate friend of God.

Using the image of the soul as a translucent, crystalline castle with many mansions or dwelling places within, Teresa sets out in this book to describe the various types of prayer that lead one into the very heart of divine love. All in all, she describes seven interior mansions or dwelling places that a person must travel through if he or she wishes to experience the mystical throes of divine friendship. She is quick to point out, however, that there are many other mansions (perhaps thousands) in the soul's interior castle and that she focuses only on those of which she has some little knowledge and experience. In no way does she wish to impose her approach on others or suggest that it is the only way to conceive of the spiritual life.

At the outset of this commentary on this great spiritual classic, one other very important distinction should be kept in mind. Although one cannot pray without the help of God's grace, Teresa points out that the person praying is more active in the earlier stages of prayer (the first three mansions) and becomes increasingly passive and under the influence of the Holy Spirit in the later ones (the final four). This change in activity—where God, not the person praying, increasingly becomes the primary agent in prayer—is the line of demarcation between ascetical and mystical prayer. Although Teresa describes all the various levels of prayer, it is evident from the amount of space given to each of the seven mansions of dwelling places that her main concern in this work is with the later stages of mystical prayer, especially with what she calls "spiritual betrothal" and "spiritual marriage." For this reason, her teaching on the earlier degrees or stages of prayer needs to be complemented by material on those topics found in her earlier works.

NB: Peers' translation is presented here, with changes made to conform it with American rather than British spelling and punctuation. Peers' original footnotes are retained, although they have been adjusted to contemporary biblical citation and now appear as endnotes. The titles of Teresa's original subdivisions have also been maintained and appear in italics at the beginning of each chapter. According to Peers, Teresa's first intention was simply to divide the work into seven main sections. By the time she completed the manuscript, however, she had changed her mind and decided to divide each of the seven major sections into smaller units. To effect this change, she used the margins of the manuscript to subdivide her work and then wrote the titles of these subdivisions on a separate sheet. Although this original sheet has been lost to posterity, the nuns of her Toledo convent had fortunately made a copy of the entire book, along with the various chapter titles. Peers maintains that the style of these chapter headings reflects Teresa's style so closely that their authenticity cannot be seriously questioned.

Prologue

✦

Introduction

Teresa opens her work with some introductory remarks about why she
has taken pen to hand and embarked on writing yet another work
on prayer. She underscores the difficulty of this task, since she believes
she has neither the spiritual depth nor the actual desire to accomplish it.
She also complains of poor health, which hinders her ability to accomplish even the basic administrative tasks. Only obedience to her superiors
has brought her to sit down at her desk and commence this work. From
this obedience, she hopes to find the strength to overcome her physical
impediments and rise to the occasion.

Obedience, she believes, has a way of making even the most complicated of tasks simple. She places her complete trust in the Lord and asks for
help in making this work see the light of day. Conscious of her own weaknesses as an author and spiritual guide, she asks the Lord to strengthen
her memory and to show her what she should write down. Left to her own
resources, she knows she will add nothing new to what she has already
written on the topic. Only the Lord will prevent her from repeating herself.
Only the Lord will help her to write things that will draw people closer to
him. She writes out of obedience, knowing that, even if the Lord does not
grant her request for help, her willingness to take up the task will still help
her on her spiritual journey.

In the closing paragraphs of her prologue, Teresa notes the date and
place where these initial efforts are taking place, affirms her loyalty to the

Church, and states that anything that might appear against its teaching is due only to her own ignorance. She also identifies her specific audience as the nuns of her Carmelite reform. To them, she wishes to explain her doctrine of prayer in a way that will be clear, practical, and truly useful. She asserts that her efforts will have been worthwhile if her words help just one of these nuns draw closer to God. She concludes by attributing any good stemming from this work to the Lord alone and that whatever ability she has in spiritual matters has its origin and destiny in him.

Of note, Teresa begins both the prologue and epilogue to the book with the letters JHS. Because the Latin-alphabet letters *J* and *I* were not systematically distinguished until the seventeenth century, Teresa's JHS is equivalent to IHS, both of which are monograms of the name of Jesus, derived from the first three letters of his name in Greek—IHΣ.

Text

JHS.

F ew tasks which I have been commanded to undertake by obedience have been so difficult as this present one of writing about matters relating to prayer: for one reason, because I do not feel that the Lord has given me either the spirituality or the desire for it; for another, because for the last three months I have been suffering from such noises and weakness in the head that I find it troublesome to write even about necessary business. But, as I know that strength arising from obedience has a way of simplifying things which seem impossible, my will very gladly resolves to attempt this task although the prospect seems to cause my physical nature great distress; for the Lord has not given me strength enough to enable me to wrestle continually both with sickness and with occupations of many kinds without feeling a great physical strain. May He who has helped me by doing other and more difficult things for me help also in this: in His mercy I put my trust.

I really think I have little to say that I have not already said in other books which I have been commanded to write; indeed, I am afraid that I shall do little but repeat myself, for I write as mechanically[1] as birds taught to speak, which, knowing nothing but what is taught them and what they hear, repeat the same things again and again. If the Lord wishes me to say anything new, His Majesty will teach it me or be pleased to recall to my memory what I have said on former occasions; and I should be quite satisfied with this, for my memory is so bad that I should be delighted if I could manage to write down a few of the things that people have considered well said, so that they should not be lost. If the Lord should not grant me as much as this, I shall still be the better for having tried, even if this writing under obedience tires me and makes my head worse, and if no one finds what I say of any profit.

And so I begin to fulfill my obligation on this Day of the Holy Trinity, in the year MDLXXVII[2] in this convent of Saint Joseph of Carmel in Toledo, where I am at this present, submitting myself as regards all that I say to the judgment of those who have commanded me to write, and who are persons of great learning. If I should say anything that is not in conformity with what is held by the Holy Roman Catholic Church[3] it will be through ignorance and not through malice. This may be taken as certain, and also that, through God's goodness, I am, and shall always be, as I always have been, subject to her. May He be forever blessed and glorified. Amen.

I was told by the person who commanded me to write that, as the nuns of these convents of Our Lady of Carmel need someone to solve their difficulties concerning prayer, and as (or so it seemed to him) women best understand each other's language, and also in view of their love for me, anything I might say would be particularly useful to them. For this reason he thought that it would be rather important if I could explain things clearly to them and for this reason it is they whom I shall be addressing in what I write—and also because it seems ridiculous to think that I can be of any use to anyone else. Our Lord will be granting me a great favor if a single one of these nuns should find that my words help her to praise Him ever so little better. His Majesty well knows that I have no hope of doing more, and, if I am successful in anything that I may say, they will of course understand that it does not come from me. Their only excuse for crediting me with it could be their having as little understanding as I have ability in these matters if the Lord of His mercy does not grant it me.

Exploring the Interior Castle

- Have you ever taken on a task that seemed too big to handle, almost impossible to achieve? If so, how did you fare? What hindrances or impediments did you encounter along the way? Were they internal or external to you? What fears did you have? How did you deal with them?

- Were you able to see this task through? If not, what prevented you from doing so? What role did God play in your efforts? Did you ask him for help? Did you turn to him in a time of need? Is God an active partner in your life or merely a distant and detached observer?

- What is your understanding of obedience? How would you describe it? Is it similar to Teresa's? Do you associate it with spiritual maturity or immaturity? Do you hold it as a deep spiritual value? What do these words from the Our Father mean to you: "Thy will be done on earth as it is in heaven"? How do you implement them in your life?

- Do you believe that all of your gifts and talents come from God? If so, do you readily acknowledge this belief to others? Do you believe that God teaches you things about life and about your relations to others? Do you believe, like Teresa, that he leads and guides you? If so, does he do so only in general or in very specific ways? Do you actively seek guidance from God? Can you think of any instances in your life when God has pointed out the way for you?

First Mansions

✛

Introduction

Teresa devotes two chapters to her treatment of the first mansions. In them, she introduces the metaphor of the interior castle and reveals how she came upon it when asking the Lord for help. Because the soul is created in God's image and likeness, it possesses many noble qualities that distinguish it from all other creatures.

The soul is God's paradise, being made by God and for God. He takes delight in dwelling within its innermost sanctum. Teresa laments humanity's general lack of self-knowledge and the decision many make not to embark on the inner journey that will lead them to God. People are so caught up with worldly cares that they are content simply with remaining in the outer courtyard of the castle and do not desire to enter into the soul's first interior mansions.

Teresa also laments the darkness that comes over souls that are completely separated from God. She wishes they knew how much God desired to commune with them and share in their friendship. In this section of her book, she underscores the importance of prayer as the key to the spiritual life. It is the gate leading into the castle and the means by which the soul deepens its relationship with God. For Teresa, these first mansions are the beginning of the spiritual life. Because one can easily turn back at this early stage, she advises extreme caution against the wiles of the evil one.

Chapter One

✛

Introduction

In this chapter, Teresa puts forth the operative image for the entire work. She says that, as she was praying to God and seeking guidance from him about what to write, a thought came to her that would lay the foundation for everything else to come. She began to think of the soul as a castle made out of diamond or very clear crystal. This is a fitting image for something made according to God's image and likeness and that represents the summit of creation. The soul, she says, is very beautiful to God and is something in which he takes great delight. It is so sad that people do not have a greater awareness of their origin and the purpose for which they were created. Such ignorance is tantamount to not knowing one's parentage or one's country of origin.

To follow the image of the soul as a castle made of diamond still further, she says that many people seem to be more interested in the castle's outer walls and external setting than in the luxurious and richly decorated rooms of its interior. In the same way, she says many people are so caught up in worldly concerns that they have little interest in embarking on the inward journey that will ultimately lead them to a face-to-face encounter with God. To possess such a castle and never explore its rich interior is a great human tragedy, for this castle, she maintains, has many inner rooms in a variety of arrangements.

At the very center of this interior castle lies the chief mansion, where God communes with the soul, shares with it the secrets of his inner

Trinitarian life, and bestows many blessings upon it. God grants these favors to whomever he likes. It is a great consolation to know that such favors are possible and that God bestows them on weak and very limited human beings. He confers such favors not because of a person's holiness, but to manifest his power in the eyes of the world.

A person enters the castle through prayer. She says a wise man once told her soul without prayer is like a person whose arms and limbs are paralyzed. Without it, the soul is limp and unable to move along in its spiritual journey. Prayer, for Teresa, is the door and point of entry into the castle. Those who pray can gain access to the first interior mansions of the soul. She reminds her readers that there are many ways of "being" present in a place. Through prayer, a person can be interiorly present to his or her soul. Vocal prayer and meditation are the main ways of prayer for those at this beginning stage of the spiritual life. For Teresa, there is a close connection between the two. Vocal prayer that does not include some modicum of quiet reflection is not really prayer at all.

This initial level of spiritual self-awareness is very fragile and easily lost. Those who refuse to enter the soul's interior castle through the door of prayer live in great danger. Those who make it into these outer rooms are still very much concerned with worldly affairs, but have good intentions and commend themselves to God from time to time. Unfortunately, when they finally enter these rooms, many distractions and worldly allurements get in with them and can create great havoc and confusion for them.

Teresa tells her readers that they are most likely far more advanced in their spiritual journey than those who are either outside the castle or only in the outer rooms. She tells them, however, that she needed to explain this beginning stage in order to develop her later thoughts on prayer and the interior life. She begins this chapter beseeching the Lord in prayer and, in doing so, subtly emphasizes the importance of bringing all of one's needs to God wherever they occur and whenever they come to mind.

✛

Text

Treats of the beauty and dignity of our souls; makes a comparison by the help of which this may be understood; describes the benefit that comes from understanding it and being aware of the favors that we receive from God; and shows how the door of this castle is prayer.

While I was beseeching Our Lord today that He would speak through me, since I could find nothing to say and had no idea how to begin to carry out the obligation laid upon me by obedience, a thought occurred to me that I will now set down, in order to have some foundation on which to build. I began to think of the soul as if it were a castle made of a single diamond or of very clear crystal, in which there are many rooms[1] just as in Heaven there are many mansions.[2] Now if we think carefully over this, sisters, the soul of the righteous man is nothing but a paradise, in which, as God tells us, He takes His delight.[3] For what do you think a room will be like that is the delight of a King so mighty, so wise, so pure and so full of all that is good? I can find nothing with which to compare the great beauty of a soul and its great capacity. In fact, however acute our intellects may be, they will no more be able to attain to a comprehension of this than to an understanding of God; for, as He Himself says, He created us in His image and likeness.[4] Now if this is so—and it is—there is no point in our fatiguing ourselves by attempting to comprehend the beauty of this castle; for, though it is His creature, and there is therefore as much difference between it and God as between creature and Creator, the very fact that His Majesty says it is made in His image means that we can hardly form any conception of the soul's great dignity and beauty.[5]

It is no small pity, and should cause us no little shame, that, through our own fault, we do not understand ourselves, or know who we are. Would it not be a sign of great ignorance, my daughters, if a person were asked who he was, and could not say, and had no idea who his father or his mother was, or from what country he came? Though that is great stupidity, our own is incomparably greater if we make no attempt to discover what we are, and only know that we are living in these bodies, and have a vague idea, because we have heard it and because our Faith tells us so, that we possess souls. As to what good qualities there may be in our souls, or Who dwells within them, or how precious they are—those are things which we seldom consider and so we trouble little about carefully preserving the soul's beauty. All our interest is centered in the rough setting of the diamond, and in the outer wall of the castle—that is to say, in these bodies of ours.

Let us now imagine that this castle, as I have said, contains many mansions,[6] some above, others below, others at each side; and in the center and midst of them all is the chief mansion where the most secret things pass between God and the soul. You must think over this comparison very carefully; perhaps God will be pleased to use it to show you something of the favors that He is pleased to grant to souls, and of the differences between them, so far as I have understood this to be possible, for there are so many of them that nobody can possibly understand them all, much less anyone as stupid as I. If the Lord grants you these favors, it will be a great consolation to you to know that such things are possible; and, if you never receive any, you can still praise His great goodness. For, as it does us no harm to think of the things laid up for us in Heaven, and of the joys of the blessed, but rather makes us rejoice and strive to attain those joys ourselves, just so it will do us no harm to find that it is possible in this our exile for so great a God to commune with such malodorous worms, and to love Him for His great goodness and boundless mercy. I am sure that anyone who finds it harmful to realize that it is possible for God to grant such favors during this our exile must be greatly lacking in humility and in love of his neighbor; for otherwise how could we help rejoicing that God should grant these favors to one of our brethren when this in no way hinders Him from granting them to ourselves, and that His Majesty should bestow an understanding of His greatness upon anyone soever? Sometimes He will do this only to manifest His power, as He said of the blind man to whom He gave his sight, when the Apostles asked Him if he were suffering for his own sins or for the sins of his parents.[7] He grants these favors, then, not because those who receive them are holier than those who do not, but in order that His greatness may be made known, as we see in the case of Saint Paul and the Magdalene, and in order that we may praise Him in His creatures.

It may be said that these things seem impossible and that it is better not to scandalize the weak. But less harm is done by their disbelieving us than by our failing to edify those to whom God grants these favors, and who will rejoice and will awaken others to a fresh love of Him Who grants such mercies, according to the greatness of His power and majesty. In any case I know that none to whom I am speaking will run into this danger, because they all know and believe that God grants still greater proofs of His love. I am sure that, if any one of you does not believe this, she will never learn it by experience. For God's will is that no bounds should be set to His works. Never do such a thing, then, sisters, if the Lord does not lead you by this road.

Now let us return to our beautiful and delightful castle and see how we can enter it. I seem rather to be talking nonsense, for, if this castle is the soul, there can clearly be no question of our entering it. For we ourselves are the castle: and it would be absurd to tell someone to enter a room when he was in it already! But you must understand that there are many ways of "being" in a place. Many souls remain in the outer court of the castle, which is the place occupied by the guards; they are not interested in entering it, and have no idea what there is in that wonderful place, or who dwells in it, or even how many rooms it has. You will have read certain books on prayer that advise the soul to enter within itself: and that is exactly what this means.

A short time ago I was told by a very learned man that souls without prayer are like people whose bodies or limbs are paralyzed: they possess feet and hands but they cannot control them. In the same way, there are souls so infirm and so accustomed to busying themselves with outside affairs that nothing can be done for them, and it seems as though they are incapable of entering within themselves at all. So accustomed have they grown to living all the time with the reptiles and other creatures to be found in the outer court of the castle that they have almost become like them; and although by nature they are so richly endowed as to have the power of holding converse with none other than God Himself, there is nothing that can be done for them. Unless they strive to realize their miserable condition and to remedy it, they will be turned into pillars of salt for not looking within themselves, just as Lot's wife was because she looked back.[8]

As far as I can understand, the door of entry into this castle is prayer and meditation: I do not say mental prayer rather than vocal, for, if it is prayer at all, it must be accompanied by meditation. If a person does not think Whom he is addressing, and what he is asking for, and who it is that is asking and of Whom he is asking it, I do not consider that he is praying at all even though he be constantly moving his lips. True, it is sometimes possible to pray without paying heed to these things, but that is only because they have been thought about previously; if a man is in the habit of speaking to God's Majesty as he would speak to his slave, and never wonders if he is expressing himself properly, but merely utters the words that come to his lips because he has learned them by heart through constant repetition, I do not call that prayer at all—and God grant no Christian may ever speak to Him so! At any rate, sisters, I hope in God that none of you will, for we are accustomed here to talk about interior matters, and that is a good way of keeping oneself from falling into such animal-like habits.[9]

Let us say no more, then, of these paralyzed souls, who, unless the Lord Himself comes and commands them to rise, are like the man who had lain beside the pool for thirty years:[10] they are unfortunate creatures and live in great peril. Let us rather think of certain other souls, who do eventually enter the castle. These are very much absorbed in worldly affairs; but their desires are good; sometimes, though infrequently, they commend themselves to Our Lord; and they think about the state of their souls, though not very carefully. Full of a thousand preoccupations as they are, they pray only a few times a month, and as a rule they are thinking all the time of their preoccupations, for they are very much attached to them, and, where their treasure is, there is their heart also.[11] From time to time, however, they shake their minds free of them and it is a great thing that they should know themselves well enough to realize that they are not going the right way to reach the castle door. Eventually they enter the first rooms on the lowest floor, but so many reptiles get in with them that they are unable to appreciate the beauty of the castle or to find any peace within it. Still, they have done a good deal by entering at all.

You will think this is beside the point, daughters, since by the goodness of the Lord you are not one of these. But you must be patient, for there is no other way in which I can explain to you some ideas I have had about certain interior matters concerning prayer. May it please the Lord to enable me to say something about them; for to explain to you what I should like is very difficult unless you have had personal experience; and anyone with such experience, as you will see, cannot help touching upon subjects that, please God, shall, by His mercy, never concern us.

Exploring the Interior Castle

- Do you bring your needs to God? If so, how do you do it? What do you say? How do you pray? Do you do it often? Rarely? How does it make you feel? Happy? Embarrassed? Incomplete? Subservient? Why does God wish us to express our needs to him? How does doing so benefit us?

- Do you understand Teresa's discussion on the relationship between vocal prayer and meditation? Do you ever say vocal prayers without reflecting on what you are saying? Must one always reflect on the meaning of the words when one prays vocally?

- How do you picture your inner life? Are you in touch with it? Have you ever thought about it? What does Teresa mean by the word "soul"? Does it mean the same thing to you? Does the metaphor of the soul as an interior castle speak to you? Are there other images that touch your inner experience more powerfully?

- If we follow Teresa's metaphor, where would you place yourself? Are you outside the castle? Within the first mansions? A bit further along the way, like many of the nuns of her Carmelite reform? How do you know where you are on your inner journey to God? What guidelines can you use to interpret your progress in your soul's journey to God? Do you agree with Teresa's assessment of the dangers of worldly concerns for life in the Spirit?

Chapter Two

✛

Introduction

In this chapter, Teresa gives a haunting description of a soul that has fallen into serious sin and become totally separated from God. In her mind, no deeper darkness exists in the whole universe. The actions of such people flow not from the source of all goodness, but from their own self-centeredness. They intend to please the evil one instead of God and have no share in the divine life for as long as they remain in this state of alienation.

Teresa says she knows a person (most likely herself) who was allowed to see what it was like for a soul to commit a deadly sin. If people could see the horrors of such a state, she believes they would certainly stop committing such grave offenses. A person totally separated from God is like a tree that produces rotten fruit because it purposely roots itself in a black pool of stagnant water. How much better would it be to plant oneself near a clear mountain spring? Souls that have separated themselves from God have cast a thick black cloth over their hearts that prevents God's light from shining through. The rooms of their interior castle are in a state of complete and utter disarray.

Teresa tells her readers to beg God to spare them such a fate. Referring to herself again, she says she has learned two great lessons from this vision of a soul in the state of complete alienation from God: (1) to fear giving offense to God and (2) to look into the mirror of humility. From this vision, she has come to see that she, too, is capable of doing great evil and that any good she does manage to do comes from God, not her. If her readers can remember these two simple lessons, she believes that all she has written thus far has been worthwhile. She apologizes to them for her lack of intelligence and her need to explain basic things before she can go on to more serious spiritual concerns. She asks them to be patient with her as she goes about describing the supernatural work the Lord does in the soul.

After this brief digression, Teresa returns to the metaphor of the castle with its many mansions. She tells her readers to imagine the mansions being arranged not in neat, ordered rows, but, much like the leafy palmetto bush, in a series of outer rinds that conceal a delicious fruit at its heart. She bids her readers to fix their gaze on the center room, where God makes his abode. The soul, moreover, should not be compelled to remain in a single room for an extended period of time, but be made to feel free to roam through the various mansions. Just as a bee moves from flower to flower, so too the soul should feel free to wander first through the rooms of self-knowledge and humility and then beyond, while never quite leaving them behind. It is better to walk through these mansions with care than to go about haphazardly through other rooms. Teresa asserts that nothing in the spiritual life is more important than humility. A person comes to know him or herself only when he or she begins to seek God. Knowledge of God brings self-knowledge. A person should look to God to find his or her identity. Instead of being so self-conscious about how one is perceived by others or what path one should follow, it would be much more beneficial to the soul simply to keep its eyes on Christ.

With regard to the first mansions of the interior castle, Teresa provides some useful information from her own experience. The castle, she believes, has a great number of mansions, not the mere seven that she is seeking to explain. Those who enter these initial rooms are generally still steeped in worldly concerns. Because the forces of the evil one are always at work to divert their efforts away from the path to God, it is very important that a person have recourse to God, the Blessed Mother, and the saints for help in their struggle against temptation. She also says that hardly any light makes its way from the center room where God makes his abode into these outer rooms. Those who have entered these rooms have so many preoccupations (what Teresa calls "snakes, vipers, and poisonous creatures") that they are prevented from seeing the light. For this reason, those who seek to progress in self-knowledge and humility and who truly wish to make their way into the second mansions would do well to simplify their lives and put all unnecessary business aside. While it is true that very few rooms in this castle are totally free from struggles with the forces of the evil one, those in these outer rooms need to be especially careful.

Teresa closes with some examples of how, even with the sisters in her Carmelite reform, the evil one never ceases to find new ways to tempt and divert them from their quest for holiness. She advises caution and reminds her readers that true perfection consists in love of God and neighbor. Her approach in her discussion of the first mansions or dwelling places is to describe the state of those who never bother to enter, the great struggles encountered by those who managed to get into these outer rooms, and the danger they face of relapsing. Prayer, as always, is the key for entering the castle and making progress in it. In these outer mansions, self-knowledge and humility lead the soul to focus all its attention on Jesus Christ. Only then will they be ready for entrance into the second mansions.

Text

Describes the hideousness of a soul in mortal sin, some part of which God was pleased to manifest to a certain person. Says something also of self-knowledge. This chapter is profitable, since it contains some noteworthy matters. Explains in what sense the Mansions are to be understood.

Before passing on, I want you to consider what will be the state of this castle, so beautiful and resplendent this Orient pearl, this tree of life, planted in the living waters of life[1]—namely, in God—when the soul falls into a mortal sin. No thicker darkness exists, and there is nothing dark and black that is not much less so than this. You need know only one thing about it—that, although the Sun Himself, Who has given it all its splendor and beauty, is still there in the center of the soul, it is as if He were not there for any participation that the soul has in Him, though it is as capable of enjoying Him as is the crystal of reflecting the sun. While in a state like this the soul will find profit in nothing, and hence, being as it is in mortal sin, none of the good works it may do will be of any avail[2] to win it glory; for they will not have their origin in that First Principle, which is God, through Whom alone our virtue is true virtue. And, since this soul has separated itself from Him, it cannot be pleasing in His eyes; for, after all, the intention of a person who commits a mortal sin is not to please Him but to give pleasure to the devil; and, as the devil is darkness itself, the poor soul becomes darkness itself likewise.

I know of a person[3] to whom Our Lord wished to show what a soul was like when it committed mortal sin. That person says that, if people could understand this, she thinks they would find it impossible to sin at all, and, rather than meet occasions of sin, would put themselves to the greatest trouble imaginable. So she was very anxious that everyone should realize this. May you be no less anxious, daughters, to pray earnestly to God for those who are in this state and who, with all their works, have become sheer darkness. For, just as all the streamlets that flow from a clear spring are as clear as the spring itself, so the works of a soul in grace are pleasing in the eyes both of God and of men, since they proceed from this spring of life, in which the soul is as a tree planted. It would give no shade and yield no fruit if it proceeded not thence, for the spring sustains it and prevents it from drying up and causes it to produce good fruit. When the soul, on the other hand, through its own fault, leaves this spring and becomes rooted in a pool of pitch-black, evil-smelling water, it produces nothing but misery and filth.

It should be noted here that it is not the spring, or the brilliant sun that is in the center of the soul, that loses its splendor and beauty, for they are always within it and nothing can take away their beauty. If a thick black cloth be placed over a crystal in the sunshine, however, it is clear that, although the sun may be shining upon it, its brightness will have no effect upon the crystal.

O souls redeemed by the blood of Jesus Christ! Learn to understand yourselves and take pity on yourselves! Surely, if you understand your own natures, it is impossible that you will not strive to remove the pitch that blackens the crystal? Remember, if your life were to end now, you would never enjoy this light again. O Jesus! How sad it is to see a soul deprived of it! What a state the poor rooms of the castle are in! How distracted are the senses that inhabit them! And the faculties, that are their governors and butlers and stewards—how blind they are and how ill-controlled! And yet, after all, what kind of fruit can one expect to be borne by a tree rooted in the devil?

I once heard a spiritual man say that he was not so much astonished at the things done by a soul in mortal sin as at the things not done by it. May God, in His mercy, deliver us from such great evil, for there is nothing in the whole of our lives that so thoroughly deserves to be called evil as this, since it brings endless and eternal evils in its train. It is of this, daughters, that we should walk in fear, and this from which in our prayers we must beg God to deliver us; for, if He keep not the city, we shall labor in vain,[4] since we are vanity itself. That person to whom I referred just now said that the favor which God had granted her had taught her two things: first, she had learned to have the greatest fear of offending Him, for which reason she continually begged Him not to allow her to fall, when she saw what legible consequences a fall could bring; secondly, she had found it a mirror of humility, for it had made her realize that any good thing we do has its source, not in ourselves but rather in that spring where this tree, which is the soul, is planted, and in that sun that sheds its radiance on our works. She says that she saw this so clearly that, whenever she did any good thing, or saw such a thing done, she betook herself straightway to its Source, realizing that without His help we are powerless. She then went on at once to praise God; and, as a rule, when she did any good action, she never gave a thought to herself at all.

If we can remember these two things, sisters, the time you have spent in reading all this, and the time I have spent in writing it, will not have been lost. Wise and learned men know them quite well, but we women are slow and need instruction in everything. So perhaps it may be the Lord's will that these comparisons shall be brought to our notice. May He be pleased of His goodness to give us grace to understand them.

These interior matters are so obscure to the mind that anyone with as little learning as I will be sure to have to say many superfluous and even irrelevant things in order to say a single one that is to the point. The reader must have patience with me, as I have with myself when writing about things of which I know nothing; for really I sometimes take up my paper, like a perfect fool, with no idea of what to say or of how to begin. I fully realize how important it is for you that I should explain certain interior matters to the best of my ability; for we continually hear what a good thing prayer is, and our Constitutions oblige us to engage in it for so many hours daily, yet they tell us nothing beyond what we ourselves have to do and say very little about the work done by the Lord in the soul—I mean, supernatural work. As I describe the things He does, and give various explanations of them, it will be very helpful for us to think of this celestial building that is within us and is so little understood by mortals, although many of them frequent it. And although the Lord has thrown some light upon many matters of which I have written, I do not think I have understood some of them, especially the most difficult, as well as I do now. The trouble, as I have said, is that, before I can get to them, I shall have to explain many things that are well known—it is bound to be so when a person is as stupid as I.

Let us now turn to our castle with its many mansions. You must not imagine these mansions as arranged in a row, one behind another, but fix your attention on the center, the room or palace occupied by the King. Think of a palmetto,[5] which has many outer rinds surrounding the savory part within, all of which must be taken away before the center can be eaten. Just so around this central room are many more, as there also are above it. In speaking of the soul we must always think of it as spacious, ample and lofty; and this can be done without the least exaggeration, for the soul's capacity is much greater than we can realize, and this Sun, Which is in the palace, reaches every part of it. It is very important that no soul that practices prayer, whether little or much, should be subjected to undue constraint or limitation. Since God has given it such dignity, it must be allowed to roam through these mansions—through those above, those below and those on either side. It must not be compelled to remain for a long time in one single room—not, at least, unless it is in the room of self-knowledge.[6] How necessary that is (and be sure you understand me here) even to those whom the Lord keeps in the same mansion in which He Himself is! However high a state the soul may have attained, self-knowledge is incumbent upon it, and this it will never be able to neglect even should it so desire. Humility must always be doing its work like a bee making its honey in the hive: without humility all will be lost. Still, we should remember that the bee is constantly flying about from flower to flower, and in the same way, believe me, the soul must sometimes emerge from self-knowledge and soar aloft in meditation upon the greatness and the majesty of its God. Doing this will help it to realize its own baseness better than thinking of its own nature, and it will be freer from the reptiles that enter the first rooms—that is, the rooms of self-knowledge. For although, as I say, it is through the abundant mercy of God that the soul studies to know itself, yet one can have too much of a good thing, as the saying goes,[7] and believe me, we shall reach much greater heights of virtue by thinking upon the virtue of God than if we stay in our own little plot of ground and tie ourselves down to it completely.

I do not know if I have explained this clearly: self-knowledge is so important that, even if you were raised right up to the heavens, I should like you never to relax your cultivation of it; so long as we are on this earth, nothing matters more to us than humility. And so I repeat that it is a very good thing—excellent, indeed—to begin by entering the room where humility is acquired rather than by flying off to the other rooms. For that is the way to make progress, and, if we have a safe, level road to walk along, why should we desire wings to fly? Let us rather try to get the greatest possible profit out of walking. As I see it, we shall never succeed in knowing ourselves unless we seek to know God: let us think of His greatness and then come back to our own baseness; by looking at His purity we shall see our foulness; by meditating upon His humility, we shall see how far we are from being humble.

There are two advantages in this. First, it is clear that anything white looks very much whiter against something black, just as the black looks blacker against the white. Secondly, if we turn from self toward God, our understanding and our will become nobler and readier to embrace all that is good: if we never rise above the slough of our own miseries we do ourselves a great disservice. We were saying just now how black and noisome are the streams that flow from souls in mortal sin. Similarly, although this is not the same thing—God forbid! It is only a comparison—so long as we are buried in the wretchedness of our earthly nature these streams of ours will never disengage themselves from the slough of cowardice, pusillanimity and fear. We shall always be glancing around and saying: "Are people looking at me or not?" "If I take a certain path shall I come to any harm?" "Dare I begin such and such a task?" "Is it pride that is impelling me to do so?" "Can anyone as wretched as I engage in so lofty an exercise as prayer?" "Will people think better of me if I refrain from following the crowd?" "For extremes are not good," they say, "even in virtue; and I am such a sinner that if I were to fail I should only have farther to fall; perhaps I shall make no progress and in that case I shall only be doing good people harm; anyway, a person like myself has no need to make herself singular."

Oh, God help my daughters, how many souls the devil must have ruined in this way! They think that all these misgivings, and many more that I could describe, arise from humility, whereas they really come from our lack of self-knowledge. We get a distorted idea of our own nature, and, if we never stop thinking about ourselves, I am not surprised if we experience these fears and others that are still worse. It is for this reason, daughters, that I say we must set our eyes upon Christ our Good, from Whom we shall learn true humility, and also upon His saints. Our understanding, as I have said, will then be ennobled, and self-knowledge will not make us timorous[8] and fearful; for, although this is only the first Mansion, it contains riches of great price, and any who can elude the reptiles that are to be found in it will not fail to go farther. Terrible are the crafts and wiles that the devil uses to prevent souls from learning to know themselves and understanding his ways.

With regard to these first Mansions I can give some very useful information out of my own experience. I must tell you, for example, to think of them as comprising not just a few rooms, but a very large number.[9] There are many ways in which souls enter them, always with good intentions; but as the devil's intentions are always very bad, he has many legions of evil spirits in each room to prevent souls from passing from one to another, and as we, poor souls, fail to realize this, we are tricked by all kinds of deceptions. The devil is less successful with those who are nearer the King's dwelling-place; but at this early stage, as the soul is still absorbed in worldly affairs, engulfed in worldly pleasure and puffed up with worldly honors and ambitions, its vassals, which are the senses and the faculties given to it by God as part of its nature, have not the same power, and such a soul is easily vanquished, although it may desire not to offend God and may perform good works. Those who find themselves in this state need to take every opportunity of repairing to His Majesty, and to make His blessed Mother their intercessor, and also His saints, so that these may do battle for them, since their own servants have little strength for defending themselves. In reality it is necessary in every state of life for our help to come from God. May His Majesty grant us this through His mercy. Amen.

How miserable is this life that we live! As I have said a great deal elsewhere, daughters, about the harm that comes to us through our not properly understanding this matter of humility and self-knowledge, I am not saying more to you here, though it is a matter of the greatest importance to us. May the Lord grant that something I have said will be of use to you.

You must note that the light which comes from the palace occupied by the King hardly reaches these first Mansions at all; for, although they are not dark and black, as when the soul is in a state of sin, they are to some extent darkened, so that they cannot be seen (I mean by anyone who is in them); and this not because of anything that is wrong with the room, but rather (I hardly know how to explain myself) because there are so many bad things—snakes and vipers and poisonous creatures—that have come in with the soul that they prevent it from seeing the light. It is as if one were to enter a place flooded by sunlight with his eyes so full of dust[10] that he could hardly open them. The room itself is light enough, but he cannot enjoy the light because he is prevented from doing so by these wild beasts and animals, which force him to close his eyes to everything but themselves. This seems to me to be the condition of a soul which, though not in a bad state, is so completely absorbed in things of the world and so deeply immersed, as I have said, in possessions or honors or business, that, although as a matter of fact it would like to gaze at the castle and enjoy its beauty, it is prevented from doing so, and seems quite unable to free itself from all these impediments. Everyone, however, who wishes to enter the second Mansions, will be well advised, as far as his state of life permits, to try to put aside all unnecessary affairs and business. For those who hope to reach the principal Mansion, this is so important that unless they begin in this way I do not believe they will ever be able to get there. Nor, indeed, even though it has entered the castle, is the soul free from great peril in the Mansion that it actually inhabits; for, being among such poisonous things, it cannot, at some time or another, escape being bitten by them.

What would happen, then, daughters, if those who, like ourselves, are free from these obstacles, and have already entered much farther into other secret mansions of the castle, should, through their own fault, go out again into this hurly-burly? Our sins must have led many people whom God has granted favors to relapse through their faults into this wretched state. We here, so far as outward things are concerned, are free; may it please the Lord to make us free as regards inward things as well and to deliver us from evil. Beware, my daughters, of cares that have nothing to do with you. Remember that in few of the mansions of this castle are we free from struggles with devils. It is true that in some of them, the wardens, who, as I think I said, are the faculties, have strength for the fight; but it is most important that we should not cease to be watchful against the devil's wiles, lest he deceive us in the guise of an angel of light. For there are a multitude of ways in which he can deceive us, and gradually make his way into the castle, and until he is actually there we do not realize it.

As I told you before, he works like a noiseless file, and we must be on the look-out for him from the beginning. In order to explain this better I want to give you several illustrations. He inspires a sister with yearnings to do penance, so that she seems to have no peace save when she is torturing herself. This, in itself, is good; but, if the prioress has ordered that no penance is to be done without leave, and yet the sister thinks that she can venture to persist in so beneficial a practice, and secretly orders her life in such a way that in the end she ruins her health and is unable to do what her Rule demands, you see what this apparently good thing has led to. Another sister is inspired with zeal for the greatest possible perfection. This, again, is a very good thing; but the result of it might be that she would think any little fault on the part of the sisters a serious failure, and would always be looking out for such things and running to the prioress about them; sometimes she might even be so zealous about religious observances as to be unable to see her own faults; and this the others, observing only her zeal about their misdeeds and not understanding the excellence of her intentions, might well take none too kindly.

The devil's aim here must not be made light of, for he is trying to bring about a cooling of charity and love among the sisters, and if he could do this he would be working a great deal of harm. Let us realize, my daughters, that true perfection consists in the love of God and of our neighbor, and the more nearly perfect is our observance of these two commandments, the nearer to perfection we shall be. Our entire Rule and Constitutions are nothing but means that enable us to do this the more perfectly. Let us refrain from indiscreet zeal, which may do us great harm: let each one of you look to herself. As I have said a great deal to you about this elsewhere[11] I will not enlarge on it further.

This mutual love is so important for us that I should like you never to forget it; for if the soul goes about looking for trifling faults in others (which sometimes may not be imperfections at all, though perhaps our ignorance may lead us to make the worst of them) it may lose its own peace of mind and perhaps disturb that of others. See, then, how dearly perfection can be bought. The devil might also use this temptation in the case of a prioress, and then it would be more dangerous still. Much discretion is necessary here; for, if it were a question of her contravening the Rule and Constitutions, it would not always do to take a lenient view of the matter—she would have to be spoken to about it; and, if she did not then amend, the prelate would have to be told: to do this would be a charity. This would also apply to the sisters, where the fault was a grave one: to say nothing through fear that taking the matter up would be yielding to temptation would itself be to yield to temptation. However, to prevent deception by the devil, it should be strongly stressed that no sister must discuss such things with any other, for from this practice the devil can pluck great advantage and start habits of slander; these matters must be discussed, as I have said, only with the person whose concern they are. Here, glory be to God, we keep almost continuous silence, so that the opportunity does not arise; none the less, it is well that we should be on our guard.

Exploring the Interior Castle

- What is your understanding of mortal sin? Does it coincide with Teresa's understanding of it? Are you aware of the three conditions necessary for it: a very serious breach of divine law, full knowledge, and full consent? Do you believe that such deadly sins are common or uncommon occurrences? What do you think Teresa believed? Do you agree with her? What must one do to be forgiven such a grave act of alienation from God?

- Do you believe that self-knowledge and humility are important for growth in the spiritual life? If so, how do you deepen your knowledge of yourself and how do you know when you are being humble? What is the difference between true and false humility? Do you agree with Teresa that true self-knowledge comes through one's search for God?

- Why does Teresa insist that the soul must never be forced to remain in a single mansion for a great length of time? Are such efforts counterproductive for growth in the spiritual life? Does she want to avoid imposing a set of rules or guidelines on growth in the mystical life? Does she believe that there are many paths one might walk in the interior castle that will ultimately lead one to God?

- Why does Teresa use so many images to explain her spiritual doctrine? The soul is an interior castle; God is like the Sun; the soul is like a tree planted near a clear spring and like a bee constantly flying from flower to flower; the faculties are the governors and butlers of the senses; the devil is like a noiseless file. How do these and other images affect the way her teaching is perceived? Does using them make her teaching easier to comprehend? Do you like the images she employs? Are they meaningful and relevant today? Are there any you would do away with today? Are there any you would add?

Second Mansions

✥

Introduction

Teresa devotes but a single chapter to her treatment of the second mansions. She does so not because this stage of the soul's spiritual journey is less important than the others, but because she has treated it at length elsewhere and does not wish to repeat herself. For this reason, those wishing to get a fuller picture of Teresa's spiritual doctrine need to supplement this part of her *Interior Castle* with relevant sections from her other earlier works, most notably from her *Life* and *The Way of Perfection* (see notes 2, 6, and 11).

That said, Teresa still offers many valuable insights into the beginning stages of the practice of prayer, if under a slightly different format. Teresa's presentation of the various stages of prayer does not follow exactly the same pattern in all of her writings. She changed her presentation of the material as she herself matured in the spiritual life. She also felt free to use different images and metaphors to express her thinking on the subject.

Because the *Interior Castle* represents Teresa's most mature presentation of the spiritual life, even the little she says about the life in this second stage of spiritual progress should be readily welcomed and studied with great care. Carefully trying not to repeat herself, she offers her readers the central features of her teaching on this stage of the spiritual life in a creative and innovative presentation.

Of particular note in this section is her distinction between those in the first and second mansions, her presentation on how the Lord speaks to those in the latter, as well as her emphasis on perseverance in carrying one's cross. Throughout this section of her work, Teresa encourages her readers not to lose heart. Their focus, she maintains, should not be on receiving rich spiritual experiences and consolations, but on discerning and doing the Lord's will.

Chapter One[1]

✛

Introduction

Teresa opens this chapter on the second mansions expressly stating her intention to limit her treatment of what she has written on elsewhere at great length. She also admits that she will probably be repeating herself a bit, although she is going to try to arrange the material differently.

Her focus in this chapter is on those who have already entered the first mansions and understand the importance of moving on, but are not yet committed enough to the spiritual life to do so. These souls, she claims, are in a very dangerous position, although less so than those not wishing to go further on their inward spiritual journey. Those wishing to move into the second mansions understand their state and hope to make their way further into the castle. The others, by way of contrast, are virtually deaf and dumb when it comes to their spiritual lives.

Teresa goes on to describe how the Lord speaks to those wishing to make their way from the first to second mansions. His words come to them through conversations with virtuous people, preaching, spiritual reading, illness, difficult times, and while engaged in prayer. She also emphasizes the Lord's patience and says that he highly values a person's feeble attempts to pray. The Lord, she says, is willing to wait a long time to reap his desired results.

Even though the Lord speaks to these people, Teresa points out that the evil one works very hard to confuse them with all kinds of temptations and compromising thoughts. For this reason, these people need to be all the more diligent and persevering in their prayers. They should not turn back to the prior rooms they inhabited or, worse yet, decide to leave the interior castle altogether. Instead they should listen to their God-given faculties for discerning the proper course of action. Reason, for example, points out errors in thinking; faith teaches what must be done to make up for these errors; memory reveals the transient nature of all things; the will inclines the soul to love; the understanding helps one realize that Jesus is the best friend one could ever have. It is these kinds of thoughts that help people overcome temptations and the vices they seek to instill.

Teresa points out that people making their way into the second mansions will be sure to suffer great trials. The evil one will use everything in his repertoire of malice and hate to prevent a person from making progress in the spiritual life. For this reason, Teresa advises such people to steer clear of harmful relationships and to seek out saintly companions. She also emphasizes the importance for those at these beginning stages of prayer not to look for spiritual consolations, but to embrace the hardship of the cross and do all in their power to discern and implement the will of God. Progress in the spiritual life is measured by one's capacity to carry out God's will.

Teresa encourages her readers not to get discouraged if they give in to temptation. The Lord, she says, often demonstrates his power by bringing good out of evil. What is more, those who fall discover the scope of their human weakness and understand better than before how much they must rely on the Lord's help to persevere in their journey to God. Those in the second mansions begin to recognize the importance of the inward journey. They begin to see that they cannot promote peace with others if they are divided within themselves. To calm their inner passions and the war waging in their inner faculties, they must persevere in prayer and entrust themselves entirely to the God of mercy. People, however, should not try to force prayer, especially as they seek to have extended periods of recollection. Such growth in prayer must come gently. What is more, it is very important that people at this stage of their spiritual journey consult with wise and experienced counselors. Otherwise, they run the risk of harming themselves. At all costs, they are not to give up the practice of prayer which, as Teresa stated in an earlier chapter and finds worth repeating, is the door into the castle and the key to one's faith-filled knowledge of self in God. Such knowledge, Teresa, concludes, must lead loving actions, for faith without works has no value in the eyes of the Lord.

Brief though it is, Teresa's treatment of the second mansions is by no means superficial. She covers ground that she believes her readers already know very well. Despite this impression, she takes great pains to identify key areas and trouble spots that those entering into the second mansions must seek to avoid. She offers sound advice for all of her readers to keep in mind and implement as they continue their spiritual journey.

✣

Text

Treats of the great importance of perseverance if we are to reach the final Mansions and of the fierce war that the devil wages against us. Tells how essential it is, if we are to attain our goal, not to miss our way at the beginning. Gives a method that has proved very efficacious.

L et us now come to consider who the souls are that enter the second Mansions and what they do there. I want to say very little to you about this, because elsewhere I have written of it at length,[2] and it will be impossible for me to avoid repeating a great deal of this, because I cannot remember anything of what I said. If it could be arranged[3] in a different form, I am quite sure you would not mind, as we are never tired of books that treat of this, numerous though they are.

This chapter has to do with those who have already begun to practice prayer and who realize the importance of not remaining in the first Mansions, but who often are not yet resolute enough to leave those Mansions, and will not avoid occasions of sin, which is a very perilous condition. But it is a very great mercy that they should contrive to escape from the snakes and other poisonous creatures, if only for short periods and should realize that it is good to flee from them. In some ways, these souls have a much harder time than those in the first Mansions; but they are in less peril, for they seem now to understand their position and there is great hope that they will get farther into the castle still. I say they have a harder time because the souls in the first Mansions are, as it were, not only dumb, but can hear nothing, and so it is not such a trial to them to be unable to speak; the others, who can hear and not speak, would find the trial much harder to bear. But that is no reason for envying those who do not hear, for after all it is a great thing to be able to understand what is said to one.

These souls, then, can understand the Lord when He calls them; for, as they gradually get nearer to the place where His Majesty dwells, He becomes a very good Neighbor to them. And such are His mercy and goodness that, even when we are engaged in our worldly pastimes and businesses and pleasures and hagglings, when we are falling into sins and rising from them again (because these creatures are at once so venomous and so active and it is so dangerous for us to be among them that it will be a miracle if we escape stumbling over them and falling)—in spite of all that, this Lord of ours is so anxious that we should desire Him and strive after His companionship that He calls us ceaselessly, time after time, to approach Him; and this voice of His is so sweet that the poor soul is consumed with grief at being unable to do His bidding immediately, and thus, as I say, it suffers more than if it could not hear Him.

I do not mean by this that He speaks to us and calls us in the precise way that I shall describe later; His appeals come through the conversations of good people, or from sermons, or through the reading of good books; and there are many other ways, of which you have heard, in which God calls us. Or they come through sicknesses and trials, or by means of truths that God teaches us at times when we are engaged in prayer; however feeble such prayers may be God values them highly. You must not despise this first favor, sisters, nor be disconsolate, even though you have not responded immediately to the Lord's call; for His Majesty is quite prepared to wait for many days, and even years, especially when He sees we are persevering and have good desires. This is the most necessary thing here; if we have this we cannot fail to gain greatly. Nevertheless, the assault that the devils now make upon the soul, in all kinds of ways, is terrible; and the soul suffers more than in the preceding Mansions; for there it was deaf and dumb, or at least it could hear very little, and so it offered less resistance, like one who to a great extent has lost hope of gaining the victory. Here the understanding is keener and the faculties are more alert, while the clash of arms and the noise of cannon are so loud that the soul cannot help hearing them. For here the devils once more show the soul these vipers—that is, the things of the world—and they pretend that earthly pleasures are almost eternal: they remind the soul of the esteem in which it is held in the world, of its friends and relatives, of the way in which its health will be endangered by penances (which the soul always wants to do when it first enters this Mansion) and of impediments of a thousand other kinds.

Oh, Jesus! What confusion the devils bring about in the poor soul, and how distressed it is, not knowing if it ought to proceed farther or return to the room where it was before! On the other hand, reason tells the soul how mistaken it is in thinking that all these earthly things are of the slightest value by comparison with what it is seeking, faith instructs it in what it must do to find satisfaction; memory shows it how all these things come to an end, and reminds it that those who have derived so much enjoyment from the things which it has seen have died. Sometimes they have died suddenly and been quickly forgotten by all: people whom we once knew to be very prosperous are now beneath the ground, and we trample upon their graves, and often, as we pass them, we reflect that their bodies are seething with worms—of these and many other things the soul is reminded by memory. The will inclines to love One in Whom it has seen so many acts and signs of love, some of which it would like to return. In particular, the will shows the soul how this true Lover never leaves it, but goes with it everywhere and gives it life and being. Then the understanding comes forward and makes the soul realize that, for however many years it may live, it can never hope to have a better friend, for the world is full of falsehood and these pleasures that the devil pictures to it are accompanied by trials and cares and annoyances; and tells it to be certain that outside this castle it will find neither security nor peace: let it refrain from visiting one house after another when its own house is full of good things, if it will only enjoy them. How fortunate it is to be able to find all that it needs, as it were, at home, especially when it has a Host Who will put all good things into its possession, unless, like the Prodigal Son, it desires to go astray and eat the food of the swine.[4]

It is reflections of this kind which vanquish devils. But, oh, my God and Lord, how everything is ruined by the vain habits we fall into and the way everyone else follows them! So dead is our faith that we desire what we see more than what faith tells us about—though what we actually see is that people who pursue these visible things meet with nothing but ill fortune. All this is the work of these poisonous creatures that we have been describing. For, if a man is bitten by a viper, his whole body is poisoned and swells up; and so it is in this case, and yet we take no care of ourselves. Obviously a great deal of attention will be necessary if we are to be cured and only the great mercy of God will preserve us from death. The soul will certainly suffer great trials at this time, especially if the devil sees that its character and habits are such that it is ready to make further progress: all the powers of hell will combine to drive it back again.

Ah, my Lord! It is here that we have need of Thine aid, without which we can do nothing. Of Thy mercy, allow not this soul to be deluded and led astray when its journey is but begun. Give it light so that it may see how all its welfare consists in this and may flee from evil companionship. It is a very great thing for a person to associate with others who are walking in the right way: to mix, not only with those whom he sees in the rooms where he himself is, but with those whom he knows to have entered the rooms nearer the center, for they will be of great help to him and he can get into such close touch with them that they will take him with them. Let him have a fixed determination not to allow himself to be beaten, for, if the devil sees that he has firmly resolved to lose his life and his peace and everything that he can offer him rather than to return to the first room, he will very soon cease troubling him. Let him play the man and not be like those who went down on their knees in order to drink when they went to battle—I forget with whom[5]—but let him be resolute, for he is going forth to fight with all the devils and there are no better weapons than the Cross.

There is one thing so important that, although I have said it on other occasions,[6] I will repeat it once more here: it is that at the beginning one must not think of such things as spiritual favors, for that is a very poor way of starting to build such a large and beautiful edifice. If it is begun upon sand, it will all collapse:[7] souls which build like that will never be free from annoyances and temptations. For it is not in these Mansions, but in those which are farther on, that it rains manna; once there, the soul has all that it desires, because it desires only what is the will of God. It is a curious thing: here we are, meeting with hindrances and suffering from imperfections by the thousand, with our virtues so young that they have not yet learned how to walk—in fact, they have only just been born: God grant that they have even been born at all!—and yet we are not ashamed to be wanting consolations in prayer and to be complaining about periods of aridity. This must not be true of you, sisters: embrace the Cross which your Spouse bore upon His shoulders and realize that this Cross is yours to carry too: let her who is capable of the greatest suffering suffer most for Him and she will have the most perfect freedom. All other things are of quite secondary importance: if the Lord should grant them to you, give Him heartfelt thanks.

You may think that you will be full of determination to resist outward trials if God will only grant you inward favors. His Majesty knows best what is suitable for us; it is not for us to advise Him what to give us, for He can rightly reply that we know not what we ask.[8] All that the beginner in prayer has to do—and you must not forget this, for it is very important—is to labor and be resolute and prepare himself with all possible diligence to bring his will into conformity with the will of God. As I shall say later, you may be quite sure that this comprises the very greatest perfection that can be attained on the spiritual road. The more perfectly a person practices it, the more he will receive of the Lord and the greater the progress he will make on this road; do not think we have to use strange jargon or dabble in things of which we have no knowledge or understanding; our entire welfare is to be found in what I have described. If we go astray at the very beginning and want the Lord to do our will and to lead us just as our fancy dictates, how can this building possibly have a firm foundation? Let us see that we do as much as in us lies and avoid these venomous reptiles, for often it is the Lord's will that we should be persecuted and afflicted by evil thoughts, which we cannot cast out, and also by aridities; and sometimes He even allows these reptiles to bite us, so that we may learn better how to be on our guard in the future and see if we are really grieved at having offended Him.

If, then, you sometimes fail, do not lose heart, or cease striving to make progress, for even out of your fall God will bring good, just as a man selling an antidote will drink poison before he takes it in order to prove its power. If nothing else could show us what wretched creatures we are and what harm we do to ourselves by dissipating our desires, this war that goes on within us would be sufficient to do so and to lead us back to recollection. Can any evil be greater than the evil that we find in our own house? What hope can we have of being able to rest in other people's homes[9] if we cannot rest in our own? For none of our friends and relatives are as near to us as our faculties, with which we have always to live, whether we like it or not, and yet our faculties seem to be making war upon us, as if they were resentful of the war made upon them by our vices. "Peace, peace," said the Lord, my sisters, and many a time He spoke words of peace to His Apostles.[10] Believe me, unless we have peace, and strive for peace in our own home, we shall not find it in the homes of others. Let this war now cease. By the blood that Christ shed for us, I beg this of those who have not begun to enter within themselves; and those who have begun to do so must not allow such warfare to turn them back. They must realize that to fall a second time is worse than to fall once. They can see that it will lead them to ruin: let them place their trust, not in themselves, but in the mercy of God, and they will see how His Majesty can lead them on from one group of Mansions to another and set them on safe ground where these beasts cannot harass or hurt them, for He will place the beasts in their power and laugh them to scorn; and then they themselves—even in this life, I mean—will enjoy many more good things than they could ever desire.

As I said first of all, I have already written to you about how you ought to behave when you have to suffer these disturbances with which the devil torments you;[11] and about how recollection cannot be begun by making strenuous efforts, but must come gently, after which you will be able to practice it for longer periods at a time. So I will say no more about this now, except that it is very important for you to consult people of experience; for otherwise you will imagine that you are doing yourselves great harm by pursuing your necessary occupations. But, provided we do not abandon our prayer, the Lord will turn everything we do to our profit, even though we may find no one to teach us. There is no remedy for this evil of which we have been speaking except to start again at the beginning; otherwise the soul will keep on losing a little more every day—please God that it may come to realize this.

Some of you might suppose that, if it is such a bad thing to turn back, it would have been better never to have begun, but to have remained outside the castle. I told you, however, at the outset, and the Lord Himself says this, that he who goes into danger shall perish in it,[12] and that the door by which we can enter this castle is prayer. It is absurd to think that we can enter Heaven without first entering our own souls—without getting to know ourselves, and reflecting upon the wretchedness of our nature and what we owe to God, and continually imploring His mercy. The Lord Himself says: "No one will ascend to My Father, but by Me"[13] (I am not sure if those are the exact words, but I think they are)[14] and "He that sees Me sees My Father."[15] Well, if we never look at Him or think of what we owe Him, and of the death that He suffered for our sakes, I do not see how we can get to know Him or do good works in His service. For what can be the value of faith without works, or of works which are not united with the merits of our Lord Jesus Christ? And what but such thoughts can arouse us to love this Lord? May it please His Majesty to grant us to understand how much we cost Him, that the servant is not greater than his Lord,[16] that we must needs work if we would enjoy His glory, and that for that reason we must perforce pray, lest we enter continually into temptation.[17]

Exploring the Interior Castle

- Does Teresa's description of the second mansions make sense to you? Does it resonate with your experience? Do you feel you have already entered the second mansions? If so, would you add anything to Teresa's description of it? Would you take anything away?

- Do you believe that God speaks to you through conversations with others? Through preaching? Through spiritual reading? Through your illnesses and difficulties? Through prayer? Has Teresa exhausted the list? How else does God speak to you? How do you know it is God?

- Teresa speaks of the great trials that people in the second mansions will undergo. How do you deal with temptations and spiritual trials? Do you find that you easily waver and give in to them? Do you try to handle them yourself or do you seek help from others? Do you share them with the Lord in prayer? Do you seek sound advice from reputable counselors on how to deal with them? What have you found helpful in dealing with such difficulties?

- Teresa emphasizes the importance of perseverance (particularly in prayer) for the spiritual life. Do you agree with her assessment of its importance? Is perseverance of value to you? If so, what have you found helpful in your efforts to persevere? In your opinion, what are the qualities of a persevering person? Is prayerfulness one of them? Can you think of any qualities that Teresa may have overlooked?

Third Mansions

✛

Introduction

Teresa devotes two chapters to her treatment of the third mansions. In them, she examines what it means to fear the Lord and what lies beyond it. Those who have entered the third mansions deeply desire not to offend him. They seek to do good and avoid even the slightest of affronts to God. They discipline themselves through penance and spend extended amounts of time in prayer. They devote themselves to charitable works and are careful about their speech and deportment.

Despite all of these good and virtuous qualities, however, still more is required if a person is to give himself or herself totally over to God. Unlike the rich young man of the gospel story (Mt 19:16–22), people in the third mansions must be ready to leave everything for the sake of Christ. They should be ready to face long periods of aridity in prayer and consider themselves fortunate to be humble servants of the Lord. Humility and the resolute desire to follow God's will are what enable those in the third mansions to make progress in their spiritual lives.

For Teresa, the journey to perfection involves a deepening consciousness of one's limitations and weaknesses and a growing recognition of one's need to rely totally on God's love and mercy. People in the third mansions must be ready to make a complete surrender of their wills to the Lord. They must not hesitate in their actions, but be ready to do the Lord's will at all times. They must be conscious of their own shortcomings rather than those of others and come to understand that not everyone travels to God by the same designated path.

Chapter One

✢

Introduction

In this chapter, Teresa speaks of those who have overcome the struggles depicted in the first and second mansions and made their way into the third. These people have gained a certain steadiness of conscience as a result of their struggles and, knowing that nothing in life is absolutely secure, live in a healthy fear of offending God by their thoughts, words, and actions.

Teresa points out, however, that the spiritual life is not meant to be one of misery, but of happiness. God does not wish his subjects to be living in constant fear of giving in to the temptations of the evil one. If such were the case, people would be constantly begging God to take their life lest they lose it through their own carelessness. God created human beings to live in the happiness of divine friendship, and one's only pleasure should consist in pleasing God. The happiness people should pray for, she adds, is not that which comes from worldly honors or material goods, but from the desire to please God by carrying out his will. The happiness of the saints comes from their ability to focus on this one important desire.

Teresa reveals a great deal about herself in this chapter. She speaks of herself as "a bird with a broken wing" and strongly emphasizes her stupidity, sinfulness, and misspent life. She asks her readers not to be depressed by her revealing this to them. People may think her holy, but she knows how she truly is before God: a poor, miserable sinner. Teresa is not putting on a show of false humility here: she writes these words of daunting self-criticism with complete and utter sincerity. It seems true that the closer one gets to God, the more one is aware of one's own creaturely limitations and smallness before God. Such a person also becomes conscious of and deeply sorry for even the slightest offense given to God and neighbor. The only recourse is to rely on God's merciful love and the powerful intercession of his loving mother.

Teresa reveals all this about herself because she doesn't want her readers to be too sure of themselves before God. Even if some of the saints fell into serious sin and eventually repented for their sins, no one should presume that God will extend his hand in a similar way to help someone repent and do penance for his or her sins. For this reason, those in the third mansions should bear constantly in mind that those who fear the Lord are truly blessed. At the same time, they should also come to understand that more is required of them than living a virtuous life.

God wants people to live not out of fear of offending him, but out of a loving desire to discern and carry out his will. It is one thing to avoid sin, do penance, and act charitably towards one's neighbor and quite another to allow the Lord to take over one's life completely. This is the goal of the spiritual life and Teresa points out that those in the third mansions must look upon themselves in all humility as the Lord's poor, unprofitable servants. She tells her readers that all the good they do by way of detaching themselves from worldly goals and aspirations does not obligate the Lord to bless them with spiritual favors. On the contrary, it is Jesus' obedience to the Father and death on the cross that puts all human beings in debt to him. What God desires most from them is not good works, but the union of their wills with his in love. Tests and trials come in life to challenge the soul and help it give of itself in the fullest measure.

✢

Text

Treats of the insecurity from which we cannot escape in this life of exile, however lofty a state we may reach, and of how good it is for us to walk in fear. This chapter contains several good points.

To those who by the mercy of God have overcome in these combats, and by dint of perseverance have entered the third Mansions, what shall we say but "Blessed is the man that feareth the Lord"?[1] As I am so stupid in these matters, it has been no small thing that His Majesty should have enabled me to understand the meaning of this verse in the vernacular. We shall certainly be right in calling such a man blessed, for, unless he turns back, he is, so far as we can tell, on the straight road to salvation. Here, sisters, you will see the importance of having overcome in your past battles; for I am convinced that the Lord never fails to give a person who does this security of conscience, which is no small blessing. I say "security," but that is the wrong word, for there is no security in this life, so, whenever I use it, you must understand the words "unless he strays from the path on which he has set out."

It is really a perfect misery to be alive when we have always to be going about like men with enemies at their gates, who cannot lay aside their arms even when sleeping or eating, and are always afraid of being surprised by a breaching of their fortress in some weak spot. Oh, my Lord and my God! How canst Thou wish us to desire such a miserable life as that? It would be impossible to refrain from wishing and begging Thee to take us from it, were it not for our hope that we may lose it for Thy sake, or spend it wholly in Thy service—and, above all, for the realization that it is Thy will for us. If that is indeed so, my God, let us die with Thee, as Saint Thomas said,[2] for life without Thee is nothing but death many times over and constant dread at the possibility of losing Thee forever. So I think, daughters, that the happiness we should pray for is to enjoy the complete security of the blessed;[3] for what pleasure can anyone have when beset by these fears if his only pleasure consists in pleasing God? Remember that all this, and much more, could be said of some of the saints, and yet they fell[4] into grave sins, and we cannot be certain that God will give us His hand and help us to renounce them[5] and do penance for them. (This refers to particular help.)[6]

Truly, my daughters, I am so fearful as I write this that, when it comes to my mind, as is very often the case, I hardly know how to get the words down, or how to go on living. Beseech His Majesty, my daughters, always to live within me, for otherwise what security can there be in a life as misspent as mine? And do not let it depress you to realize that I am like that—I have sometimes seen you depressed when I have told you so. The reason it affects you in that way is that you would like to think I had been very holy. That is quite right of you: I should like to think so myself. But what can I do about it when I have lost so much through my own fault? I shall not complain that God ceased giving me all the help I needed if your wishes were to be fulfilled: I cannot say this without tears and great confusion when I realize that I am writing for those who are themselves capable of teaching me. Rigorous has been the task that obedience has laid upon me![7] May it please the Lord that, as it is being done for His sake, you may gain some profit from it and may ask Him to pardon this wretched and foolhardy woman. But His Majesty well knows that I can count only upon His Mercy, and, as I cannot help having been what I have, there is nothing for me to do but approach God and trust in the merits of His Son, and of the Virgin, His Mother, whose habit both you and I unworthily wear. Praise Him, my daughters, for you are really the daughters of Our Lady, and when you have as good a Mother as that there is no reason for you to be scandalized at my unworthiness. Imitate Our Lady and consider how great she must be and what a good thing it is that we have her for our Patroness; even my sins and my being what I am have not been sufficient to bring any kind of tarnish upon this sacred Order.

But of one thing I must warn you: although you are in this Order, and have such a Mother, do not be too sure of yourselves; for David was a very holy man, yet you know what Solomon[8] became. Nor must you set store by the fact that you are cloistered and lead lives of penitence. Nor must you become confident because you are always talking about God, continually engaging in prayer, withdrawing yourselves completely from the things of this world and (to the best of your belief) abhorring them. All that is good, but, as I have said, it is not enough to justify us in laying aside our fears. So you must repeat this verse and often bear it in mind: *Beatus vir, qui timet Dominum.*[9]

And now I forget what I was saying—I have been indulging in a long digression. Whenever I think of myself I feel like a bird with a broken wing and I can say nothing of any value. So I will leave all this for now and return to what I had begun to explain concerning the souls that have entered the third Mansions. In enabling these souls to overcome their initial difficulties, the Lord has granted them no small favor, but a very great one. I believe that, through His goodness, there are many such souls in the world: they are most desirous not to offend His Majesty; they avoid committing even venial sins;[10] they love doing penance, they spend hours in recollection; they use their time well; they practice works of charity toward their neighbors; and they are very careful in their speech and dress and in the government of their household if they have one. This is certainly a desirable state and there seems no reason why they should be denied entrance to the very last of the Mansions; nor will the Lord deny them this if they desire it, for their disposition is such that He will grant them any favor.

Oh, Jesus! How could anyone ever say that he has no desire for such a wonderful thing, especially when he has got over the most troublesome stages leading to it? Surely no one could do so. We all say we desire it; but if the Lord is to take complete possession of the soul more than that is necessary. Words are not enough, any more than they were for the young man when the Lord told him what to do if he wished to be perfect.[11] Ever since I began to speak of these Mansions I have had that young man in mind, for we are exactly like him; and this as a rule is the origin of our long periods of aridity in prayer, although these have other sources as well. I am saying nothing here of interior trials, which vex many good souls to an intolerable degree, and through no fault of their own, but from which the Lord always rescues them, to their great profit, as He does also those who suffer from melancholy and other infirmities. In all things we must leave out of account the judgments of God.

Personally, I think that what I have said is the most usual thing. These souls know that nothing would induce them to commit a sin— many of them would not intentionally commit even a venial sin—and they make good use of their lives and their possessions. So they cannot be patient when the door is closed to them and they are unable to enter the presence of the King, Whose vassals they consider themselves, and in fact are. Yet even on earth a king may have many vassals and they do not all get so far as to enter his chamber. Enter, then, enter within yourselves, my daughters; and get right away from your own trifling good works, for these you are bound, as Christians, to perform, and, indeed, many more. It will be enough for you that you are vassals of God; do not try to get so much that you achieve nothing. Look at the saints who have entered the King's chamber and you will see the difference between them and ourselves. Do not ask for what you have not deserved. For we have offended God, and, however faithfully we serve Him, it should never enter our heads that we can deserve anything.

Oh, humility, humility! I do not know why I have this temptation, but whenever I hear people making so much of their times of aridity, I cannot help thinking that they are somewhat lacking in it. I am not, of course, referring to the great interior trials of which I have spoken, for they amount to much more than a lack of devotion. Let us test ourselves, my sisters, or allow the Lord to test us; for He knows well how to do it, although often we refuse to understand Him. And now let us return to these carefully-ordered souls and consider what they do for God, and we shall then see how wrong we are to complain of His Majesty. For, if, when He tells us what we must do in order to be perfect, we turn our backs upon Him and go away sorrowfully, like the young man in the Gospel,[12] what do you expect His Majesty to do, for the reward which He is to give us must of necessity be proportionate with the love that we bear Him? And this love, daughters, must not be wrought in our imagination but must be proved by works. Yet do not suppose God has any need of our works; what He needs is the resoluteness of our will.

It may seem to us that we have done everything—we who wear the religious habit, having taken it of our own will and left all the things of the world and all that we had for His sake (for although, like Saint Peter, we may have left only our nets, yet He esteems a person who gives all that he has as one who gives in fullest measure).[13] This is a very good beginning; and, if we persevere in it, instead of going back, even if only in desire, to consort with the reptiles in the first rooms, there is no doubt that, by persevering in this detachment and abandonment of everything, we shall attain our object. But it must be on this condition—and note that I am warning you of this—that we consider ourselves unprofitable servants, as we are told, either by Saint Paul or by Christ,[14] and realize that we have in no way obliged Our Lord to grant us such favors; but rather that, the more we have received of Him, the more deeply do we remain in His debt. What can we do for so generous a God, Who died for us and created us and gives us being, without counting ourselves fortunate in being able to repay Him something of what we owe Him for the way He has served us[15] (I write this word reluctantly, but it is the truth,[16] for all the time He lived in the world He did nothing but serve) without asking Him once more for gifts and favors?

Consider carefully, daughters, these few things that have been set down here, though they are in rather a jumbled state, for I cannot explain them better; the Lord will make them clear to you, so that these periods of aridity may teach you to be humble, and not make you restless, which is the aim of the devil. Be sure that, where there is true humility, even if God never grants the soul favors, He will give it peace and resignation to His will, with which it may be more content than others are with favors. For often, as you have read, it is to the weakest that His Divine Majesty gives favors, which I believe they would not exchange for all the fortitude given to those who go forward in aridity. We are fonder of spiritual sweetness than of crosses. Test us, O Lord, Thou Who knowest all truth, that we may know ourselves.

Exploring the Interior Castle

- What do you understand by fear of the Lord? Is it a good thing or something to outgrow or do away with? In what way is it related to a deep reverence for and awe of God? Can one fear the Lord too little? Too much? Do you agree with Teresa's assessment of it? Is it possible to fear God and love him at the same time? What does the gospel writer mean when he writes: "There is no fear in love, but perfect love casts out fear" (1 Jn 4:18)?

- Teresa describes herself as "a bird with a broken wing." What is the relationship between holiness and self-knowledge? Do you believe that the closer one gets to God, the deeper awareness one has of one's weaknesses and limitations? Do you see a relationship between self-knowledge and getting closer to God in your own life?

- Teresa again emphasizes the importance of humility for growth in the spiritual life and wonders if those who complain of aridity or dryness in their lives of prayer are somewhat lacking in it. Do you agree with such an assessment? Do you consider yourself a humble person? Do you ever reveal things about yourself in order to get people to think more highly of you?

- Teresa measures growth in the spiritual life by one's capacity to do God's will. Do you agree with this understanding of growth in holiness? Why is doing God's will so important? Are there any other important elements needed for growth in holiness?

Chapter Two

✣

Introduction

In this chapter, Teresa speaks about some of the people she has met who have reached the third mansions. Their main difficulty, she claims, is that they have lived virtuous lives for a long time, but become anxious and troubled when trials come their way. Because of their good example, they believe they are qualified to teach others about the path to perfection when, in truth, they do not see the role their own imperfections play in bringing them to their present circumstances. She points out that God sometimes withholds his aid for a while from those he loves in order to test them and to give them a deeper understanding of their drawbacks and limitations. With this increase in self-knowledge, they are able to draw closer to God and move forward in their spiritual journey.

By way of contrast, those in the third mansions who do not understand the nature of their trials are too focused on themselves and concerned about what others think of them. To drive her point home, she gives her readers some examples of people who exhibited these traits in their lives. In all cases, she points out that these people cannot control their emotions and are not sufficiently detached from worldly desires. She implores her readers to test themselves in times of even small trials to see if they themselves have mastered their passions and are totally detached from the things they said they have abandoned and left behind. The key to growth in the spiritual life is to conform one's will completely to God and to order one's life to what God commands.

According to Teresa, people at this stage of the spiritual life tend not to grow because of their lack of humility. They think more highly of themselves than they should and often believe they have progressed much further along the road of holiness than they actually have. Such people have extremely well-ordered lives and are very careful about the penances they perform for fear of damaging their health. Teresa claims that such people often use too much discretion in their approach to the spiritual life. As a result they move along at a snail's pace when they really should be much further along in their journey.

Such people, Teresa maintains, proceed with too much caution and are afraid of nearly everything. They see obstacles everywhere and do not make any real effort to draw closer to God. Teresa points out that there are already enough real dangers on the road to God for people to spend their time imagining others. She tells her readers that progress in the spiritual life requires the disciplined effort of leaving one's fears and rational concerns in God's hands. She also tells her readers to let their superiors worry about their bodily concerns. They should be concerned only with making swift and sound progress in their spiritual journey. This journey, she adds, requires a great deal of humility and a concerted effort not to seek the acclaim of others.

For Teresa, living in the state of the third mansions demands a total renunciation of self. Failure to do so makes being there very trying and burdensome. This is so because, unlike the later mansions, while sojourning there, one must still carry the full weight of one's human weaknesses. Unless one has embraced the cross of self-denial, the effect on one's soul can be trying and wearisome. At this point, Teresa introduces a distinction between spiritual sweetness and spiritual consolations, but postpones explaining it until the fourth mansions. She does say, however, that once a person understands the nature of each, it will be easier for him or her to seek spiritual consolations, which bring solace to the humble heart and shame to those who think they have it all.

As she winds up her thoughts on the third mansions, Teresa reminds her readers that perfection depends not on consolation, but on the increase in a person's capacity to love. She encourages those in this state to have someone they could go to, preferably a saintly person and someone who knows them well, in order to help them discern the Lord's will for them. Trying to do so alone is not only difficult, but can also cause great harm. She also encourages her readers not to seek spiritual favors and consolation from the Lord, but to trust in his love and believe that he always does what is best for them. What is more, she urges them not to look at the faults and weaknesses of others, but to stay focused on what they themselves must do to draw closer to the Lord. Those in this state must remember that they are still so close to the earlier mansions that, if care is not taken, they could easily relapse and go back to them.

✤

Text

Continues the same subject and treats of aridities in prayer and of what the author thinks may result from them; and of how we must test ourselves; and of how the Lord proves those who are in these Mansions.

I have known a few souls who have reached this state—I think I might even say a great many—and who, as far as we can see, have for many years lived an upright and carefully ordered life, both in soul and in body and then, after all these years, when it has seemed as if they must have gained the mastery over the world, or at least must be completely detached from it, His Majesty has sent them tests that have been by no means exacting, and they have become so restless and depressed in spirit that they have exasperated me,[1] and have even made me thoroughly afraid for them. It is of no use offering them advice, for they have been practicing virtue for so long that they think they are capable of teaching others and have ample justification for feeling as they do.

Well, I cannot find, and have never found, any way of comforting such people, except to express great sorrow at their trouble, which, when I see them so miserable, I really do feel. It is useless to argue with them, for they brood over their woes and make up their minds that they are suffering for God's sake, and thus never really understand that it is all due to their own imperfection. And in persons who have made so much progress this is a further mistake; one cannot be surprised if they suffer, though I think this kind of suffering ought to pass quickly. For often it is God's will that His elect should be conscious of their misery and so He withdraws His help from them a little—and no more than that is needed to make us recognize our limitations very quickly. They then realize that this is a way of testing them, for they gain a clear perception of their shortcomings, and sometimes they derive more pain from finding that, in spite of themselves, they are still grieving about earthly things, and not very important things either, than from the matter that is troubling them. This, I think, is a great mercy on the part of God, and even though they are at fault they gain a great deal in humility.

With those other persons of whom I am speaking it is different: they consider they have acted in a highly virtuous way, as I have said, and they wish others to think so too. I will tell you about some of them so that we may learn to understand and test ourselves before we are tested by the Lord—and it would be a very great advantage if we were prepared and had learned to know ourselves first

A rich man, who is childless and has no one to leave his money to, loses part of his wealth; but not so much that he has not enough for himself and his household—he still has enough and to spare. If he begins to get restless and worried, as though he had not a crust of bread left to eat, how can Our Lord ask him to leave all for His sake? It may be, of course, that he is suffering because he wants to give the money to the poor. But I think God would rather I were resigned to what His Majesty does, and kept my tranquility of soul, than that I should do such acts of charity as these. If this man cannot resign himself, because the Lord has not led him thus far, well and good; but he ought to realize that he lacks this freedom of spirit and in that case he will pray for it and prepare himself for the Lord to give it to him.

Another person, who has means enough to support himself, and indeed an excess of means, sees an opportunity of acquiring more property. Let him take such an opportunity, certainly, if it comes to him; but if he strives after it, and, on obtaining it, strives after more and more, however good his intention may be (and good it must be, because, as I have said, these are all virtuous people and given to prayer), he need not be afraid that he will ever ascend[2] to the Mansions that are nearest the King.

It is much the same thing if such people are despised in any way or lose some of their reputation. God often grants them grace to bear this well, for He loves to help people to be virtuous in the presence of others, so that the virtue itself that they possess may not be thought less of, or perhaps He will help them because they have served Him, for this our God is good indeed. And yet they become restless, for they cannot do as they would like to and control their feelings all at once.

Yet oh, dear me! Are not these the same persons who some time ago were meditating upon how the Lord suffered, and upon what a good thing it is to suffer, and who were even desiring to suffer? They would like every one else to live as well-ordered a life as they do themselves; all we can hope is that they will not begin to imagine that the trouble they have is somebody else's fault and represent it to themselves as meritorious.

You will think, sisters, that I am wandering from the point, and am no longer addressing myself to you, and that these things have nothing to do with us, as we own no property and neither desire it nor strive after it and nobody ever slights us. It is true that these examples are not exactly applicable to us, but many others that are can be deduced from them, though it is unnecessary, and would be unseemly, for me to detail them. From these you will find out if you are really detached from the things you have abandoned, for trifling incidents arise, though not precisely of this kind, which give you the opportunity to test yourselves and discover if you have obtained the mastery over your passions. And believe me, what matters is not whether or not we wear a religious habit; it is whether we try to practice the virtues, and make a complete surrender of our wills to God and order our lives as His Majesty ordains: let us desire that not our wills, but His will, be done.[3] If we have not progressed as far as this, then, as I have said, let us practice humility, which is the ointment for our wounds; if we are truly humble, God, the Physician,[4] will come in due course, even though He tarry, to heal us.

The penances done by these persons are as carefully ordered as their lives. They have a great desire for penance, so that by means of it they may serve Our Lord—and there is nothing wrong in that—and for this reason they observe great discretion in their penances, lest they should injure their health. You need never fear that they will kill themselves: they are eminently reasonable folk! Their love is not yet ardent enough to overwhelm their reason. How I wish ours would make us dissatisfied with this habit of always serving God at a snail's pace! As long as we do that we shall never get to the end of the road. And as we seem to be walking along and getting fatigued all the time—for, believe me, it is an exhausting road—we shall be very lucky if we escape getting lost. Do you think, daughters, if we could get from one country to another in a week, it would be advisable, with all the winds and snow and floods and bad roads, to take a year over it? Would it not be better to get the journey over and done with? For there are all these obstacles for us to meet and there is also the danger of serpents. Oh, what a lot I could tell you about that! Please God I have got farther than this myself—though I often fear I have not!

When we proceed with all this caution, we find stumbling-blocks everywhere; for we are afraid of everything, and so dare not go farther, as if we could arrive at these Mansions by letting others make the journey for us! That is not possible, my sisters; so, for the love of the Lord, let us make a real effort: let us leave our reason and our fears in His hands and let us forget the weakness of our nature which is apt to cause us so much worry. Let our superiors see to the care of our bodies; that must be their concern: our own task is only to journey with good speed so that we may see the Lord. Although we get few or no comforts here, we shall be making a great mistake if we worry over our health, especially as it will not be improved by our anxiety about it—that I well know. I know, too, that our progress has nothing to do with the body, which is the thing that matters least What the journey that I am referring to demands is great humility, and it is the lack of this, I think, if you see what I mean, that prevents us from making progress. We may think we have advanced only a few steps, and we should believe that this is so and that our sisters' progress is much more rapid; and further we should not only want them to consider us worse than anyone else, but we should contrive to make them do so.

If we act thus, this state is a most excellent one, but otherwise we shall spend our whole lives in it and suffer a thousand troubles and miseries. Without complete self-renunciation, the state is very arduous and oppressive, because, as we go along, we are laboring under the burden of our miserable nature, which is like a great load of earth and has not to be borne by those who reach the later Mansions. In these present Mansions the Lord does not fail to recompense us with just measure, and even generously, for He always gives us much more than we deserve by granting us a spiritual sweetness much greater than we can obtain from the pleasures and distractions of this life. But I do not think that He gives many consolations, except when He occasionally invites us to see what is happening in the remaining Mansions, so that we may prepare to enter them.

You will think that spiritual sweetness and consolations are one and the same thing: why, then, this difference of name? To me it seems that they differ a very great deal, though I may be wrong. I will tell you what I think about this when I write about the fourth Mansions, which will follow these, because, as I shall then have to say something about the consolations which the Lord gives in those Mansions, it will come more appropriately. The subject will seem an unprofitable one, yet none the less it may be of some use, for, once you understand the nature of each, you can strive to pursue the one that is better. This latter is a great solace to souls whom God has brought so far, while it will make those who think they have everything feel ashamed; and if they are humble they will be moved to give thanks. Should they fail to experience it, they will feel an inward discouragement—quite unnecessarily, however, for perfection consists not in consolations, but in the increase of love; on this, too, will depend our reward, as well as on the righteousness and truth that are in our actions.

If this is true—and it is—you will wonder what is the use of my discussing these interior favors, and explaining what they are. I do not know: you must ask the person who commanded me to write, for I am under an obligation not to dispute with my superiors, but to obey them, and it would not be right for me to dispute with them. What I can tell you truly is that, when I had had none of these favors, and knew nothing of them by experience, and indeed never expected to know about them all my life long (and rightly so, though it would have been the greatest joy for me to know, or even to conjecture, that I was in any way pleasing to God), none the less, when I read in books of these favors and consolations that the Lord grants to souls that serve Him, it would give me the greatest pleasure and lead my soul to offer fervent praises to God. Now if I, who am so worthless a person, did that, surely those who are good and humble will praise Him much more. If it only enables a single person to praise Him once, I think it is a good thing that all this should be said, and that we should realize what pleasure and what delights we lose through our own fault. All the more so because, if they come from God, they come laden with love and fortitude, by the help of which a soul can progress with less labor and grow continually in good works and virtues. Do not suppose that it matters little whether or not we do what we can to obtain them. But if the fault is not yours, the Lord is just, and what His Majesty denies you in this way He will give you in other ways—His Majesty knows how. His secrets are hidden deep; but all that He does will be best for us, without the slightest doubt.

What I think would be of the greatest profit to those of us who, by the goodness of the Lord, are in this state—and, as I have said, He shows them no little mercy in bringing them to it, for, when here, they are on the point of rising still higher—is that they should be most studious to render ready obedience. Even though they be not in a religious Order, it would be a great thing for them to have someone to whom they could go, as many people do, so that they might not be following their own will in anything, for it is in this way that we usually do ourselves harm. They should not look for anyone (as the saying has it) cast in the same mold as themselves[5] who always proceeds with great circumspection; they should select a man who is completely disillusioned with the things of the world. It is a great advantage for us to be able to consult someone who knows us, so that we may learn to know ourselves. And it is a great encouragement to see that things that we thought impossible are possible to others, and how easily these others do them. It makes us feel that we may emulate their flights and venture to fly ourselves, as the young birds do when their parents teach them; they are not yet ready for great flights but they gradually learn to imitate their parents. This is a great advantage, as I know. However determined such persons may be not to offend the Lord, they will do well not to run any risk of offending Him; for they are so near the first Mansions that they might easily return to them, since their fortitude is not built upon solid ground like that of souls who are already practiced in suffering. These last are familiar with the storms of the world, and realize how little need there is to fear them or to desire worldly pleasures. If those of whom I am speaking, however, had to suffer great persecutions, they might well return to such pleasures and the devil well knows how to contrive such persecutions in order to do us harm; they might be pressing onward with great zeal, and trying to preserve others from sin, and yet be unable to resist any temptations that came to them.

Let us look at our own shortcomings and leave other people's alone; for those who live carefully ordered lives are apt to be shocked at everything and we might well learn very important lessons from the persons who shock us. Our outward comportment and behavior may be better than theirs, but this, though good, is not the most important thing: there is no reason why we should expect everyone else to travel by our own road, and we should not attempt to point them to the spiritual path when perhaps we do not know what it is. Even with these desires that God gives us to help others, sisters, we may make many mistakes, and thus it is better to attempt to do what our Rule tells us—to try to live ever in silence and in hope, and the Lord will take care of His own. If, when we beseech this of His Majesty, we do not become negligent ourselves, we shall be able, with His help, to be of great profit to them. May He be forever blessed.

Exploring the Interior Castle

- What, in your opinion, distinguishes the third mansions from the earlier two? Are the differences pronounced or more nuanced and difficult to grasp? Is it possible to be in more than one mansion at the same time? Is it possible to alternate between one or the other room, moving back and forth from one to the other without making much progress?

- Do you understand what Teresa means by spiritual aridity? Have you ever experienced dryness in your life? In your prayer? If so, how did you deal with it? Does Teresa's advice make sense to you? Does anything she says sound misconstrued or out of date?

- Teresa says that, if care is not taken, people in the third mansions can be too cautious and progress on their journey at a snail's pace. How does one determine when one is being too cautious and using too much discretion? How does one deal with the tendency to find obstacles almost anywhere and in anything? Does such a tendency indicate a lack of trust in oneself? In others? In God?

- Teresa says that living in the third mansions is very burdensome without a complete renunciation of self. Yet the gospels require people to love others as they love themselves. What is the relationship between self-love and self-denial? Are they mutually exclusive? One and the same? Is it possible to love and deny oneself at the same time? Is it possible to love oneself too much? To deny oneself too much?

Fourth Mansions

✜

Introduction

Teresa devotes three chapters to her treatment of the fourth mansions. This state marks the beginning of mystical prayer. In the previous mansions, the person praying was the principal actor, and the Holy Spirit provided the ancillary help of divine grace. Now the Holy Spirit takes on a more prominent role. In addition to grace, he now takes possession of the soul and becomes the primary agent of prayer. This does not mean, however, that the person praying becomes completely passive before God. On the contrary, through the power of the Spirit, he or she is gradually becoming more and more himself or herself. While the power of the divine predominates, it does not overwhelm or cancel out the unique contribution of the human.

Teresa commends herself to the Holy Spirit, asking him to help her capture with words something of the nature of this supernatural prayer. She says that venomous creatures seldom find entry into these mansions and, if they do, are actually beneficial to the soul. She also explains the distinction she first introduced in the third mansions between spiritual sweetness and spiritual consolations. While the former come through human effort, the latter are entirely a gift from the Lord. Love rather than thought, she adds, is most important for progress in the spiritual life.

Teresa describes two closely related types of mystical prayer that a person experiences in these mansions: the prayer of quiet (chapter two) and the prayer of infused recollection (chapter three). Although she treats the prayer of quiet first, possibly because it is the deeper and more sublime of the two, it normally comes after the prayer of infused recollection. The difference between these two forms of mystical prayer is primarily one of intensity and the powers of the soul most affected. In the prayer of infused recollection, one's understanding is flooded with a divine light and the person praying has an intense awareness of God's nearness to it. In the prayer of quiet, that light penetrates the soul even more deeply and takes possession of the person's will. In keeping with her simple and pragmatic style, Teresa uses a variety of images to explain the difference between natural and supernatural prayer, as well as between infused recollection and the prayer of quiet.

Chapter One

✠

Introduction

Teresa begins by asking the Holy Spirit to show her what to say about the next mansions, for she is about to touch on the nature of supernatural prayer. She knows that she cannot explain this difficult subject without divine assistance. The Lord helped her when she wrote on the subject some fourteen years ago, and even though she thinks she has a slightly better understanding of it now, she still needs help to explain it.

Teresa says that the mansions of mystical prayer are very beautiful and very difficult to describe to those who have not experienced them for themselves. She also says that one usually must dwell in the earlier mansions a long time before finding one's way into them, although the Lord can dispense his gifts at any time and to whomever he pleases. She makes the interesting remark that temptations are rare in these mansions and that those that do arise actually benefit the soul by giving it the opportunity to cooperate with God's grace. Besides, without temptations the evil one might lead a soul astray in the consolations given it by the Lord. She does not think it safe (or even possible) in this life for a person to be continuously absorbed in the throes of mystical prayer. For this reason, temptations that do make their way into these mansions keep the person awake, aware of surrounding dangers, and dutifully occupied with daily concerns.

Teresa's main purpose in this first chapter is to draw some distinctions. In the first place, she explains the difference between sweetness in prayer and spiritual consolations. The first, she says, flows naturally from a person's virtuous actions. It is a natural satisfaction arising from a work well done. It is very similar to the delight one feels when something good happens in one's life. In this case, it comes not because one has acquired a piece of property at a good price or has met a good friend, but because one has performed a good action. The soul is happy because it has done something for God's sake. This feeling of delight or sweetness is purely natural and should be understood and enjoyed for what it is. Spiritual consolations, by way of contrast, are gifts that come entirely from God. Their source is divine, not human, and their purpose is to draw the soul into deeper and more intimate union with God. Teresa offers some examples from her own experience of the difference between sweetness in prayer and spiritual consolations and again reminds her readers that the most important thing in the spiritual life is to love much.

Teresa's second distinction is between thought and understanding. She says it took her a long time to understand the difference between the two and that she verified her distinction with a man of learning, who said it was valid. Understanding, she says, is a faculty of the soul, while thoughts (or imagination, if you will) run wildly and are difficult to control. She says she found it difficult to understand how, on one level, the soul could be recollected in God and on another so distracted by unwieldy thoughts and images. Eventually she came to understand that the soul could be immersed in its interior world and wholly united with God, while at the same time under siege by a thousand or more ruinous distractions. Such thoughts, she claims, are due to a lack of self-understanding. She concludes that it does not do any good to be disturbed by distracting thoughts during prayer or to worry about them in any way. Nor should one blame oneself for the result of a weak imagination, the limitations of human nature, or the forces of evil.

✢

Text

Treats of the difference between sweetness or tenderness in prayer and con-solations, and tells of the happiness that the author gained from learning how different thought is from understanding. This chapter is very profitable for those who suffer greatly from distractions during prayer.

B efore I begin to speak of the fourth Mansions, it is most neces-sary that I should do what I have already done—namely, com-mend myself to the Holy Spirit, and beg Him from this point onward to speak for me, so that you may understand what I shall say about the Mansions still to be treated. For we now begin to touch the super-natural[1] and this is most difficult to explain unless His Majesty takes it in hand, as He did when I described as much as I understood of the subject, about fourteen years ago.[2] Although I think I have now a little more light upon these favors which the Lord grants to some souls, it is a different thing to know how to explain them. May His Majesty undertake this if there is any advantage to be gained from its being done, but not otherwise.

As these Mansions are now getting near to the place where the King dwells, they are of great beauty and there are such exquisite things to be seen and appreciated in them that the understanding is incapable of describing them in any way accurately without being completely obscure to those devoid of experience. But any experienced person will understand quite well, especially if his experience has been consider-able. It seems that, in order to reach these Mansions, one must have lived for a long time in the others; as a rule one must have been in those which we have just described, but there is no infallible rule about it, as you must often have heard, for the Lord gives when He wills and as He wills and to whom He wills, and, as the gifts are His own, this is doing no injustice to anyone.

Into these Mansions poisonous creatures seldom enter, and, if they do, they prove quite harmless—in fact they do the soul good. I think in this state of prayer it is much better for them to enter and make war upon the soul, for, if it had no temptations, the devil might mislead it with regard to the consolations which God gives, and do much more harm than he can when it is being tempted. The soul, too, would not gain so much, for it would be deprived of all occasions of merit and be living in a state of permanent absorption. When a soul is continuously in a condition of this kind I do not consider it at all safe, nor do I think it possible for the Spirit of the Lord to remain in a soul continuously in this way during our life of exile.

Returning to what I was saying, I would describe here—namely, the difference between sweetness in prayer and spiritual consolations—it seems to me that we may describe as sweetness what we get from our meditations and from petitions made to Our Lord. This proceeds from our own nature, though, of course, God plays a part in the process (and in everything I say you must understand this, for we can do nothing without Him). This spiritual sweetness arises from the actual virtuous work that we perform, and we think we have acquired it by our labors. We are quite right to feel satisfaction[3] at having worked in such a way. But, when we come to think of it, the same satisfaction[4] can be derived from numerous things that may happen to us here on earth. When, for example, a person suddenly acquires some valuable property; or equally suddenly meets a person whom he dearly loves; or brings some important piece of business or some other weighty matter to a successful conclusion, so that everyone speaks well of him; or when a woman has been told that her husband or brother or son is dead and he comes back to her alive. I have seen people shed tears over some great joy;[5] sometimes, in fact, I have done so myself.

It seems to me that the feelings[6] that come to us from Divine things are as purely natural as these, except that their source is nobler, although these worldly joys are in no way bad. To put it briefly, worldly joys have their source in our own nature and end in God, whereas spiritual consolations have their source in God, but we experience them in a natural way and enjoy them as much as we enjoy those I have already mentioned, and indeed much more. Oh, Jesus! How I wish I could make myself clear about this! For I think I can see a very marked difference between these two things and yet I am not clever enough to make my meaning plain: may the Lord explain it for me!

I have just remembered a verse which we say at the end of the last psalm at Prime. The last words of the verse are *Cum dilatasti cor meum.*[7] To anyone who has much experience, this will suffice to explain the difference between the two; though, to anyone who has not, further explanation is necessary. The spiritual sweetness that has been described does not enlarge the heart; as a rule, it seems to oppress it somewhat. The soul experiences a great happiness[8] when it realizes what it is doing for God's sake; but it sheds a few bitter tears that seem in some way to be the result of passion.[9] I know little about these passions of the soul; if I knew more, perhaps I could make the thing clear, and explain what proceeds from sensuality and what from our own nature. But I am very stupid; I could explain this state if only I could understand my own experience of it. Knowledge and learning are a great help in everything.

My own experience of this state—I mean of these favors and this sweetness in meditation—was that, if I began to weep over the Passion, I could not stop until I had a splitting headache; and the same thing happened when I wept for my sins. This was a great grace granted me by Our Lord, and I will not for the moment examine each of these favors and decide which is the better of the two; I wish, however, that I could explain the difference between them. In the state I am now describing, the tears and longings sometimes arise partly from our nature and from the state of preparedness we are in;[10] but nevertheless, as I have said, they eventually lead one to God. And this is an experience to be greatly prized, provided the soul be humble, and can understand that it does not make it any the more virtuous; for it is impossible to be sure that these feelings are effects of love, and, even so, they are a gift of God. Most of the souls which dwell in the Mansions already described are familiar with these feelings of devotion, for they labor with the understanding almost continuously, and make use of it in their meditations. They are right to do this, because nothing more has been given them; they would do well, however, to spend short periods in making various acts, and in praising God and rejoicing in His goodness and in His being Who He is, and in desiring His honor and glory. They should do this as well as they can, for it goes a long way toward awakening the will. But, when the Lord gives them this other grace, let them be very careful not to reject it for the sake of finishing their customary meditation.

As I have written about this at great length elsewhere,[11] I will not repeat it here. I only want you to be warned that, if you would progress a long way on this road and ascend to the Mansions of your desire, the important thing is not to think much, but to love much; do, then, whatever most arouses you to love. Perhaps we do not know what love is: it would not surprise me a great deal to learn this, for love consists, not in the extent of our happiness, but in the firmness of our determination to try to please God in everything, and to endeavor, in all possible ways, not to offend Him, and to pray Him ever to advance the honor and glory of His Son and the growth of the Catholic Church. Those are the signs of love; do not imagine that the important thing is never to be thinking of anything else and that if your mind becomes slightly distracted all is lost.

I have sometimes been terribly oppressed by this turmoil of thoughts and it is only just over four years ago that I came to understand by experience that thought (or, to put it more clearly, imagination)[12] is not the same thing as understanding. I asked a learned man about this and he said I was right, which gave me no small satisfaction. For, as the understanding is one of the faculties of the soul, I found it very hard to see why it was sometimes so timid;[13] whereas thoughts, as a rule, fly so fast that only God can restrain them; which He does by uniting us in such a way that we seem in some sense to be loosed from this body.[14] It exasperated me[15] to see the faculties of the soul, as I thought, occupied with God and recollected in Him, and the thought, on the other hand, confused and excited.

O Lord, do Thou remember how much we have to suffer on this road through lack of knowledge! The worst of it is that, as we do not realize we need to know more when we think about Thee, we cannot ask those who know; indeed we have not even any idea what there is for us to ask them. So we suffer terrible trials because we do not understand ourselves; and we worry over what is not bad at all, but good, and think it very wrong. Hence proceed the afflictions of many people who practice prayer, and their complaints of interior trials—especially if they are unlearned people—so that they become melancholy, and their health declines, and they even abandon prayer altogether, because they fail to realize that there is an interior world close at hand. Just as we cannot stop the movement of the heavens, revolving as they do with such speed, so we cannot restrain our thought. And then we send all the faculties of the soul after it, thinking we are lost, and have misused the time that we are spending in the presence of God. Yet the soul may perhaps be wholly united with Him in the Mansions very near His presence, while thought remains in the outskirts of the castle, suffering the assaults of a thousand wild and venomous creatures and from this suffering winning merit. So this must not upset us, and we must not abandon the struggle, as the devil tries to make us do. Most of these trials and times of unrest come from the fact that we do not understand ourselves.

As I write this, the noises in my head are so loud that I am begin-ning to wonder what is going on in it.[16] As I said at the outset, they have been making it almost impossible for me to obey those who commanded me to write. My head sounds just as if it were full of brim-ming rivers, and then as if all the water in those rivers came suddenly rushing downward; and a host of little birds seem to be whistling, not in the ears, but in the upper part of the head, where the higher part of the soul is said to be; I have held this view for a long time, for the spirit seems to move upward with great velocity. Please God I may remember to explain the cause of this when I am writing of the later Mansions: here it does not fit in well. I should not be surprised to know that the Lord has been pleased to send me this trouble in my head so that I may understand it better, for all this physical turmoil is no hindrance either to my prayer or to what I am saying now, but the tranquility and love in my soul are quite unaffected, and so are its desires and clear-ness of mind.

But if the higher part of the soul is in the upper part of the head, how is it that it experiences no disturbance? That I do not know, but I do know that what I say is true. I suffer when my prayer is not accompanied by suspension of the faculties, but, when the faculties are suspended, I feel no pain until the suspension is over; it would be a terrible thing if this obstacle forced me to give up praying altogether. It is not good for us to be disturbed by our thoughts or to worry about them in the slightest; for if we do not worry and if the devil is respon-sible for them they will cease, and if they proceed, as they do, from the weakness that we inherit from the sin of Adam, and from many other weaknesses, let us have patience and bear everything for the love of God. Similarly we are obliged to eat and sleep, and we cannot escape from these obligations, though they are a great burden to us.

Let us recognize our weakness in these respects and desire to go where nobody will despise us. I sometimes recall words I have heard, spoken by the Bride in the Canticles,[17] and really I believe there is no point in our lives at which they can more properly be used, for I do not think that all the scorn and all the trials which we may have to suffer in this life can equal these interior battles. Any unrest and any strife can be borne, as I have already said, if we find peace where we live; but if we would have rest from the thousand trials that afflict us in the world and the Lord is pleased to prepare such rest for us, and yet the cause of the trouble is in ourselves, the result cannot but be very painful, indeed almost unbearable. For these causes, Lord, do Thou take us to a place where these weaknesses, which sometimes seem to be making sport of the soul, do not cause us to be despised. Even in this life the Lord will free the soul from this, when it has reached the last Mansion, as, if it please God, we shall explain.

These weaknesses will not give everyone so much trouble, or assail everyone as violently, as for many years they troubled and assailed me. For I was a wicked person and it seemed as though I were trying to take vengeance on myself. As it has been such a troublesome thing for me, it may perhaps be so for you as well, so I am just going to describe it, first in one way and then in another, hoping that I may succeed in making you realize how necessary it is, so that you may not grow restless and distressed. The clacking old mill must keep on going round and we must grind our own flour: neither the will nor the understanding must cease working.

This trouble will sometimes be worse, and sometimes better, according to our health and according to the times and seasons. The poor soul may not be to blame for this, but it must suffer none the less, for, as we shall commit other faults, it is only right that we should have patience. And as we are so ignorant that what we read and are advised—namely, that we should take no account of these thoughts—is not sufficient to teach us, it does not seem to me a waste of time if I go into it further and offer you some consolation about it; though this will be of little help to you until the Lord is pleased to give us light. But it is necessary (and His Majesty's will) that we should take proper measures and learn to understand ourselves, and not blame our souls for what is the work of our weak imagination and our nature and the devil.

Exploring the Interior Castle

- Do you understand the difference between natural and supernatural prayer? If so, how would you best describe the difference? Is some kind of help from God needed whenever a person prays? Do you believe mystical prayer is for everyone or only for a select few? Have you ever had anything at all like a mystical experience? If so, what was it like? How could you tell if it was real or imaginary?

- Do you understand the difference between spiritual sweetness and spiritual consolations? What is the main difference between them? Have you ever experienced delight from prayer or from performing a virtuous action? Have you ever experienced a spiritual consolation?

- Do you understand the difference between thought and understanding? How are they different? How are they related? Which is more important? Do you agree with Teresa that it is possible to be at one with God on one level and harrowed by unwieldy thoughts on another? Have you ever felt this way?

- Have you ever been distracted by wild and unruly thoughts during your prayer time? At other times during the day? If so, how do you deal with them? Do you agree with Teresa that one should not be anxious or worry about them? Have you found any other approach helpful?

Chapter Two

✣

Introduction

In this chapter, Teresa develops the distinction between sweetness in prayer and spiritual consolations a bit further. She tells her readers that spiritual consolations can also be referred to as the prayer of quiet, a term that has become one of the most recognizable terms of Teresa's doctrine of prayer and has found a secure place in the classical presentation of the degrees of mystical prayer. She also tells her readers that she had to postpone her writing for some time due to administrative concerns and poor health. She apologizes to them for her poor memory and apparent confusion as she attempts to pick up where she left off.

To explain the difference between spiritual sweetness and the prayer of quiet, Teresa asks her readers to imagine two fountains with basins that can be filled with water. The water comes to the first through a series of manmade ducts and conduits, but to the second through a flowing spring, the source of which rises up quietly at the very base of the fountain. She likens the first fountain to spiritual sweetness, which comes mainly through the practice of meditation—that is, discursive prayer involving thoughtful reflection on the mysteries of the faith and sharing one's affections with God. The second fountain, by way of contrast, relates to the prayer of quiet—a mystical, supernatural prayer that comes directly from God and is accompanied by a deep sense of peace, quiet, and inner contentment. She also points out that, once this basin is filled, the water flows out into the other mansions of the soul and eventually even reaches the body. According to Teresa, this deep sense of happiness arises not from the heart, but from the deepest recesses of the soul, where the interior springs run very deep and ultimately find their source in the divine.

Teresa admits having difficulty in describing the nature of such mystical experiences to others. She speaks of God's greatness and majesty and says that her meager attempts to learn about him amount to nothing. She has a deep sense of her own inadequacy as an author and spiritual guide and of the limitations of human language to convey a sense of the infinite. Even the images she uses to explain the nature of the prayer of quiet conceal as much as they reveal, perhaps even more. Still, she affirms her conviction that mystical prayer is a gift from God and cannot be manufactured or induced in any way. She also admits the possibility that what she is writing about mystical prayer may contradict what she has already said elsewhere and attributes this to a deepening of her insights over time into the meaning of her experiences.

Teresa understands that her readers will want to experience such prayer and even strive for it. She says that they are right in wanting to experience it, but underscores her belief that such prayer is entirely a gift of God. The only way to dispose oneself to the possibility of receiving such favors is to practice humility: one should not consider oneself deserving of such favors in any way and not actively strive after them. She gives five reasons for not striving after such experiences: (1) one's motivation in prayer should be love of God and not self-interest; (2) to think that God will convey a favor in return for service reveals a lack of humility; (3) one should strive to embrace the cross rather than looking for such consolations; (4) the Lord is not obliged to grant such mystical favors as he is bound to save someone who keeps the commandments; and (5) human effort alone will not produce fruit, for the water comes from a bubbling spring rather than through manmade conduits. Her point is that no amount of meditation, ascetical practice, or devotion can make the water flow in this way. The prayer of quiet is a complete and utter gift that the Lord gives to whomever he wishes, where and whenever he so desires. The only way to receive such a blessing is to follow the way of humility and true detachment.

✠

Text

Continues the same subject and explains by a comparison what is meant by consolations and how we must obtain them without striving to do so.

God help me in this task which I have embarked upon.[1] I had quite forgotten what I was writing about, for business matters and ill-health forced me to postpone continuing it until a more suitable time, and, as I have a poor memory, it will all be very much confused, for I cannot read it through again. It may even be that everything I say is confused; that, at least, is what I am afraid of. I think I was talking about spiritual consolations and explaining how they are sometimes bound up with our passions. They often cause fits of sobbing; I have heard, indeed, that some persons find they produce constrictions of the chest and even exterior movements, which cannot be controlled, and which are violent enough to make blood gush from the nose and produce similar disconcerting symptoms. About this I can say nothing, for I have not experienced it, but there must be some cause for comfort in it, for, as I say, it all leads to a desire to please God and to have fruition of His Majesty.

What I call consolations from God, and elsewhere have termed the Prayer of Quiet, is something of a very different kind, as those of you will know, who by the mercy of God have experienced it. To understand it better, let us suppose that we are looking at two fountains, the basins of which can be filled with water. There are certain spiritual things that I can find no way of explaining more aptly than by this element of water; for, as I am very ignorant, and my wits give me no help, and I am so fond of this element, I have observed it more attentively than anything else. In all the things that have been created by so great and wise a God there must be many secrets by which we can profit, and those who understand them do profit by them, although I believe that in every little thing created by God there is more than we realize, even in so small a thing as a tiny ant.

These two large basins can be filled with water in different ways: the water in the one comes from a long distance, by means of numerous conduits and through human skill; but the other has been constructed at the very source of the water and fills without making any noise. If the flow of water is abundant, as in the case we are speaking of, a great stream still runs from it after it has been filled; no skill is necessary here, and no conduits have to be made, for the water is flowing all the time. The difference between this and the carrying of the water by means of conduits is, I think, as follows. The latter corresponds to the spiritual sweetness that, as I say, is produced by meditation. It reaches us by way of the thoughts; we meditate upon created things and fatigue the understanding; and when at last, by means of our own efforts, it comes, the satisfaction that it brings to the soul fills the basin, but in doing so makes a noise, as I have said.

To the other fountain the water comes direct from its source, which is God, and, when it is His Majesty's will and He is pleased to grant us some supernatural favor, its coming is accompanied by the greatest peace and quietness and sweetness within ourselves—I cannot say where it arises or how. And that content and delight are not felt, as earthly delights are felt, in the heart—I mean not at the outset, for later the basin becomes completely filled, and then this water begins to overflow all the Mansions and faculties, until it reaches the body. It is for that reason that I said it has its source in God and ends in ourselves—for it is certain, and anyone will know this who has experienced it, that the whole of the outer man enjoys this consolation and sweetness.

I was thinking just now, as I wrote this, that a verse that I have already quoted, *Dilatasti cor meum*,[2] speaks of the heart's being enlarged. I do not think that this happiness has its source in the heart at all. It arises in a much more interior part, like something of which the springs are very deep; I think this must be the center of the soul, as I have since realized and as I will explain hereafter. I certainly find secret things in ourselves that often amaze me—and how many more there must be! O my Lord and my God! How wondrous is Thy greatness! And we creatures go about like silly little shepherd boys, thinking we are learning to know something of Thee when the very most we can know amounts to nothing at all, for even in ourselves there are deep secrets that we cannot fathom. When I say "amounts to nothing at all" I mean because Thou art so surpassingly great, not because the signs of greatness that we see in Thy works are not very wonderful, even considering how very little we can learn to know of them.

Returning to this verse, what it says about the enlargement of the heart may, I think, be of some help to us. For apparently, as this heavenly water begins to flow from this source of which I am speaking—that is, from our very depths—it proceeds to spread within us and cause an interior dilation and produce ineffable blessings, so that the soul itself cannot understand all that it receives there. The fragrance it experiences, we might say, is as if in those interior depths there were a brazier on which were cast sweet perfumes; the light cannot be seen, nor the place where it dwells, but the fragrant smoke and the heat penetrate the entire soul, and very often, as I have said, the effects extend even to the body. Observe—and understand me here—that no heat is felt, nor is any fragrance perceived: it is a more delicate thing than that; I only put it in that way so that you may understand it. People who have not experienced it must realize that it does in very truth happen; its occurrence is capable of being perceived, and the soul becomes aware of it more clearly than these words of mine can express it. For it is not a thing that we can fancy, nor, however hard we strive, can we acquire it, and from that very fact it is clear that it is a thing made, not of human metal, but of the purest gold of Divine wisdom. In this state the faculties are not, I think, in union, but they become absorbed and are amazed as they consider what is happening to them.

It may be that in writing of these interior things I am contradicting what I have myself said elsewhere. This is not surprising, for almost fifteen years have passed since then,[3] and perhaps the Lord has now given me a clearer realization of these matters than I had at first Both then and now, of course, I may be mistaken in all this, but I cannot lie about it: by the mercy of God I would rather die a thousand deaths: I am speaking of it just as I understand it.

The will certainly seems to me to be united in some way with the will of God; but it is by the effects of this prayer and the actions that follow it that the genuineness of the experience must be tested and there is no better crucible for doing so than this. If the person who receives such a grace recognizes it for what it is, Our Lord is granting him a surpassingly great favor, and another very great one if he does not turn back. You will desire, then, my daughters, to strive to attain this way of prayer, and you will be right to do so, for, as I have said, the soul cannot fully understand the favors that the Lord grants it there or the love that draws it ever nearer to Himself, it is certainly desirable that we should know how to obtain this favor. I will tell you what I have found out about it.

We may leave out of account occasions when the Lord is pleased to grant these favors for no other reason than because His Majesty so wills. He knows why He does it and it is not for us to interfere. As well as acting, then, as do those who have dwelt in the Mansions already described, have humility and again humility! It is by humility that the Lord allows Himself to be conquered so that He will do all we ask of Him, and the first way in which you will see if you have humility is that if you have it you will not think you merit these favors and consolations of the Lord or are likely to get them for as long as you live. "But how," you will ask, "are we to gain them if we do not strive after them?" I reply that there is no better way than this one that I have described. There are several reasons why they should not be striven for. The first is because the most essential thing is that we should love God without any motive of self-interest. The second is because there is some lack of humility in our thinking that in return for our miserable services we can obtain anything so great. The third is because the true preparation for receiving these gifts is a desire to suffer and to imitate the Lord, not to receive consolations; for, after all, we have often offended Him. The fourth reason is because His Majesty is not obliged to grant them to us, as He is obliged to grant us glory if we keep His commandments, without doing which we could not be saved, and He knows better than we what is good for us and which of us truly love Him. That is certain truth, as I know; and I also know people who walk along the road of love, solely, as they should, in order to serve Christ crucified, and not only do they neither ask for consolations nor desire them, but they beg Him not to give them to them in this life. The fifth reason is that we should be laboring in vain; for this water does not flow through conduits, as the other does, and so we gain nothing by fatiguing ourselves if it cannot be had at the source. I mean that, however much we may practice meditation, however much we do violence to ourselves,[4] and however many tears we shed, we cannot produce this water in those ways; it is given only to whom God wills to give it and often when the soul is not thinking of it at all.

We are His, sisters; may He do with us as He will and lead us along whatever way He pleases. I am sure that if any of us achieve true humility and detachment (I say "true" because it must not be in thought alone, for thoughts often deceive us; it must be total detachment) the Lord will not fail to grant us this favor, and many others that we shall not even know how to desire. May He be forever praised and blessed. Amen.

Exploring the Interior Castle

- Like Teresa, have you ever had to interrupt an important project due to administrative concerns or poor health? If so, how long of an interruption did you have? Was it easy to pick up where you left off? What did you do to ensure continuity? Some say that it took Teresa nearly three months to resume her writing. Do you notice any disjunction in this chapter with the previous chapters?

- Do you understand Teresa's use of the metaphor of the two fountains to describe the distinction between ascetical and mystical prayer? Do you see any weaknesses in this analogy? Can you think of any other metaphors that can be used to describe the distinction?

- Teresa has a deep sense of the inability of words to capture fully the various nuances of mystical prayer. In your opinion, how big a gap is there between the words she uses and the experiences she is trying to describe? Is the gap finite or infinite? Does Teresa's language conceal the truth as much as reveal it?

- Once again, Teresa places humility and love of God at the center of the spiritual journey. Do you agree with her? Is there anything else you would place at the center? Why does Teresa believe it is useless to strive after spiritual consolations? What does it mean to strive for something by not striving for it?

Chapter Three

✛

Introduction

In this chapter, Teresa discusses the prayer of recollection, a state of mystical prayer that normally precedes the prayer of quiet. The inverted order in her treatment of these two forms of prayer may well be a consequence of her having to stop her writing for a time because of her business and poor health. It sometimes happens that, when a writer resumes working after an extended interruption, it is difficult to recapture the flow of one's thoughts and to maintain continuity with what went before. Teresa herself admits that she has a poor memory, is afraid of confusing her readers, and does not have the time to reread her previous chapters.

For Teresa, the prayer of recollection is a form of infused prayer in which the divine light completely absorbs a person's understanding, thus giving him or her a deep sense and knowledge of God's presence within. This experience comes without human effort and is used by God to draw those who have wandered outside the soul's interior castle back to the inner chambers. Although she does not have great confidence in her ability to convey the essence of this experience in a manner intelligible to others and claims not to have the skill to describe this experience in the manner of other authors, she still likens God's role in it to that of a good shepherd who gently calls his wandering sheep back to himself. Having taught them to recognize his voice and to follow his lead, he speaks so powerfully to them that they cannot help but return to him.

For Teresa, the prayer of recollection is a supernatural gift. One cannot arrive at this level of infused understanding by simply thinking about God or by exercising the imagination to envision his presence within the soul. It is not the sort of prayer that one can learn and practice for oneself. On the contrary, those who arrive at this stage of mystical prayer are given an immediate, infused understanding of God before they even begin to think. They hear God's call and withdraw into themselves to have an entire world opened up before their eyes.

One should respond to such an experience by giving praise and thanksgiving to God for the favors received. Doing so will prepare a person for even greater gifts. Teresa points out that there is still much that needs to be accomplished in a soul once God has stilled the understanding. Although the capacity to love has already been awakened in the soul, this stage of prayer will deepen that capacity even more and enable it to love under the direct guidance of the Spirit.

For Teresa, those in this stage of mystical prayer must leave themselves in God's hands and allow him to influence the movement of their thoughts. They can try to discontinue discursive thinking, but they should not try to force it. Nor should they seek to stop exercising their faculty of understanding. Teresa is not a quietist, someone who remains totally passive before God both in prayer and in living out one's life. In her mind, one remains completely free under the influence of God's penetrating light. She recognizes, however, that because of this light, one is now able to see oneself as one truly is before God. One begins to see how small one is before God and to recognize that the spiritual consolations of mystical prayer far exceed the attractions of the world. As a result, the soul becomes more and more detached from earthly things and more and more attached to the love of God.

Teresa concludes this chapter with some warnings to her Carmelite sisters about the dangers of false mysticism. She tells them to be careful of mistaking true mystical experiences from the consequences of the weak and languid bodily disposition arising from poor health and a life of strict ascetical practices. If the experience truly comes from God, there will be no languor in the soul, but only the joy of finding itself near God. They should be completely honest to their superiors about such matters and follow their prescriptions closely.

✛

Text

Describes what is meant by the Prayer of Recollection, which the Lord gener-
ally grants before that already mentioned. Speaks of its effects and of the remain-
ing effects of the former kind of prayer, which had to do with the consolations
given by the Lord.

The effects of this kind of prayer are numerous; some of them I shall explain. First of all, I will say something (though not much, as I have dealt with it elsewhere)[1] about another kind of prayer, which almost invariably begins before this one. It is a form of recollection that also seems to me supernatural for it does not involve remaining in the dark, or closing the eyes, nor is it dependent upon anything exterior. A person involuntarily closes his eyes and desires solitude; and, without the display of any human skill there seems gradually to be built for him a temple in which he can make the prayer already described; the senses and all external things seem gradually to lose their hold on him, while the soul, on the other hand, regains its lost control.

It is sometimes said that the soul enters within itself and sometimes that it rises above itself;[2] but I cannot explain things in that kind of language, for I have no skill in it. However, I believe you will understand what I am able to tell you, though I may perhaps be intelligible only to myself. Let us suppose that these senses and faculties (the inhabitants, as I have said, of this castle, which is the figure that I have taken to explain my meaning) have gone out of the castle, and, for days and years, have been consorting with strangers, to whom all the good things in the castle are abhorrent. Then, realizing how much they have lost, they come back to it, though they do not actually re-enter it, because the habits they have formed are hard to conquer. But they are no longer traitors and they now walk about in the vicinity of the castle. The great King, Who dwells in the Mansion within this castle, perceives their good will, and in His great mercy desires to bring them back to Him. So, like a good Shepherd, with a call so gentle that even they can hardly recognize it, He teaches them to know His voice and not to go away and get lost but to return to their Mansion; and so powerful is this Shepherd's call that they give up the things outside the castle that had led them astray, and once again enter it.

I do not think I have ever explained this before as clearly as here. When we are seeking God within ourselves (where He is found more effectively and more profitably than in the creatures, to quote Saint Augustine, who, after having sought Him in many places, found Him within),[3] it is a great help if God grants us this favor. Do not suppose that the understanding can attain to Him, merely by trying to think of Him as within the soul, or the imagination, by picturing Him as there. This is a good habit and an excellent kind of meditation, for it is founded upon a truth—namely, that God is within us. But it is not the kind of prayer that I have in mind, for anyone (with the help of the Lord, you understand) can practice it for himself. What I am describing is quite different. These people are sometimes in the castle before they have begun to think about God at all. I cannot say where they entered it or how they heard their Shepherd's call: it was certainly not with their ears, for outwardly such a call is not audible. They become markedly conscious that they are gradually retiring[4] within themselves; anyone who experiences this will discover what I mean: I cannot explain it better. I think I have read that they are like a hedgehog or a tortoise withdrawing into itself;[5] and whoever wrote that must have understood it well. These creatures, however, enter within themselves whenever they like; whereas with us it is not a question of our will—it happens only when God is pleased to grant us this favor. For my own part, I believe that, when His Majesty grants it, He does so to people who are already leaving the things of the world. I do not mean that people who are married must actually leave the world—they can do so only in desire: His call to them is a special one and aims at making them intent upon interior things. I believe, however, that if we wish to give His Majesty free course, He will grant more than this to those whom He is beginning to call still higher.

Anyone who is conscious that this is happening within himself should give God great praise, for he will be very right to recognize what a favor it is; and the thanksgiving that he makes for it will prepare him for greater favors. One preparation for listening to Him, as certain books tell us, is that we should contrive, not to use our reasoning powers, but to be intent upon discovering what the Lord is working in the soul; for, if His Majesty has not begun to grant us absorption, I cannot understand how we can cease thinking in any way that will not bring us more harm than profit, although this has been a matter of continual discussion among spiritual persons. For my own part, I confess my lack of humility, but their arguments have never seemed to me good enough to lead me to accept what they say. One person told me of a certain book by the saintly Fray Peter of Alcántara (for a saint I believe he is), which would certainly have convinced me, for I know how much he knew about such things; but we read it together, and found that he says exactly what I say, although not in the same words; it is quite clear from what he says that love must already be awake.[6] It is possible that I am mistaken, but I base my position on the following reasons.

First, in such spiritual activity as this, the person who does most is he who thinks least and desires to do least:[7] what we have to do is to beg like poor and needy persons coming before a great and rich Emperor and then cast down our eyes in humble expectation. When from the secret signs He gives us we seem to realize that He is hearing us, it is well for us to keep silence, since He has permitted us to be near Him and there will be no harm in our striving not to labor with the understanding—provided, I mean, that we are able to do so. But if we are not quite sure that the King has heard us, or sees us, we must not stay where we are like ninnies, for there still remains a great deal for the soul to do when it has stilled the understanding; if it did nothing more it would experience much greater aridity and the imagination would grow more restless because of the effort caused it by cessation from thought. The Lord wishes us rather to make requests of Him and to remember that we are in His presence, for He knows what is fitting for us. I cannot believe in the efficacy of human activity in matters where His Majesty appears to have set a limit to it and to have been pleased to reserve action to Himself. There are many other things in which He has not so reserved it, such as penances, works of charity, and prayers; these, with His aid, we can practice for ourselves, as far as our miserable nature is capable of them.

The second reason is that all these interior activities are gentle and peaceful, and to do anything painful brings us harm rather than help. By "anything painful" I mean anything that we try to force ourselves to do; it would be painful, for example, to hold our breath. The soul must just leave itself in the hands of God, and do what He wills it to do, completely disregarding its own advantage and resigning itself as much as it possibly can to the will of God. The third reason is that the very effort that the soul makes in order to cease from thought will perhaps awaken thought and cause it to think a great deal. The fourth reason is that the most important and pleasing thing in God's eyes is our remembering His honor and glory and forgetting ourselves and our own profit and ease and pleasure. And how can a person be forgetful of himself when he is taking such great care about his actions that he dare not even stir, or allow his understanding and desires to stir, even for the purpose of desiring the greater glory of God or of rejoicing in the glory which is His? When His Majesty wishes the working of the understanding to cease, He employs it in another manner, and illumines the soul's knowledge to so much higher a degree than any we can ourselves attain that He leads it into a state of absorption, in which, without knowing how, it is much better instructed than it could ever be as a result of its own efforts, which would only spoil everything. God gave us our faculties to work with, and everything will have its due reward; there is no reason, then, for trying to cast a spell over them—they must be allowed to perform their office until God gives them a better one.

As I understand it, the soul whom the Lord has been pleased to lead into this Mansion will do best to act as I have said. Let it try, without forcing itself or causing any turmoil, to put a stop to all discursive reasoning, yet not to suspend the understanding, nor to cease from all thought, though it is well for it to remember that it is in God's presence and Who this God is. If feeling this should lead it into a state of absorption, well and good; but it should not try to understand what this state is, because that is a gift bestowed upon the will. The will, then, should be left to enjoy it, and should not labor except for uttering a few loving words, for although in such a case one may not be striving to cease from thought, such cessation often comes, though for a very short time.

I have explained elsewhere[8] the reason why this occurs in this kind of prayer (I am referring to the kind that I began to explain in this Mansion). With it I have included this Prayer of Recollection that ought to have been described first, for it comes far below the consolations of God already mentioned, and is indeed the first step toward attaining them. For in the Prayer of Recollection, it is unnecessary to abandon meditation and the activities of the understanding. When, instead of coming through conduits, the water springs directly from its source, the understanding checks its activity, or rather the activity is checked for it when it finds it cannot understand what it desires, and thus it roams about all over the place, like a demented creature, and can settle down to nothing. The will is fixed so firmly upon its God that this disturbed condition of the understanding causes it great distress; but it must not take any notice of this, for if it does so it will lose a great part of what it is enjoying; it must forget about it, and abandon itself into the arms of love, and His Majesty will teach it what to do next; almost its whole work is to realize its unworthiness to receive such great good and to occupy itself in thanksgiving.

In order to discuss[9] the Prayer of Recollection, I passed over the effects or signs to be observed in souls to whom this prayer is granted by God Our Lord. It is clear that a dilation or enlargement of the soul takes place, as if the water proceeding from the spring had no means of running away, but the fountain had a device ensuring that, the more freely the water flowed, the larger became the basin. So it is in this kind of prayer, and God works many more wonders in the soul, thus fitting and gradually disposing it to retain all that He gives it. So this gentle movement and this interior dilation cause the soul to be less constrained in matters relating to the service of God than it was before and give it much more freedom. It is not oppressed, for example, by the fear of hell, for, though it desires more than ever not to offend God (of Whom, however, it has lost all servile fear), it has firm confidence that it is destined to have fruition of Him. A person who used to be afraid of doing penance lest he should ruin his health now believes that in God he can do everything, and has more desire to do such things than he had previously. The fear of trials that he was wont to have is now largely assuaged, because he has a more lively faith, and realizes that, if he endures these trials for God's sake, His Majesty will give him grace to bear them patiently, and sometimes even to desire them, because he also cherishes a great desire to do something for God. The better he gets to know the greatness of God, the better he comes to realize the misery of his own condition; having now tasted the consolations of God, he sees that earthly things are mere refuse; so, little by little, he withdraws from them and in this way becomes more and more his own master. In short, he finds himself strengthened in all the virtues and will infallibly continue to increase in them unless he turns back and commits offenses against God—when that happens, everything is lost, however far a man may have climbed toward the crest of the mountain. It must not be understood, however, that all these things take place because once or twice God has granted a soul this favor; it must continue receiving them, for it is from their continuance that all our good proceeds.

There is one earnest warning that I must give those who find themselves in this state: namely, that they exert the very greatest care to keep themselves from occasions of offending God. For as yet the soul is not even weaned but is like a child beginning to suck the breast If it be taken from its mother, what can it be expected to do but die? That, I am very much afraid, will be the lot of anyone to whom God has granted this favor if he gives up prayer; unless he does so for some very exceptional reason, or unless he returns to it quickly, he will go from bad to worse. I am aware how much ground there is for fear about this, and I have been very much grieved by certain people I know, in whom I have seen what I am describing; they have left Him Who in His great love was yearning to give Himself to them as a Friend, and to prove His friendship by His works. I earnestly warn such people not to enter upon occasions of sin, because the devil sets much more store by one soul in this state than by a great number of souls to whom the Lord does not grant these favors. For those in this state attract others, and so they can do the devil great harm and may well bring great advantage to the Church of God. He may see nothing else in them except that His Majesty is showing them especial love, but this is quite sufficient to make him do his utmost to bring about their perdition. The conflict, then, is sterner for such souls than for others, and if they are lost their fate is less remediable. You, sisters, so far as we know, are free from these perils. May God free you from pride and vainglory and grant that the devil may not counterfeit these favors. Such counterfeits, however, will be recognizable because they will not produce these effects, but quite contrary ones.

There is one peril of which I want to warn you, though I have spoken of it elsewhere; I have seen persons given to prayer fall into it, and especially women, for, as we are weaker than men, we run more risk of what I am going to describe. It is this: some women, because of prayers, vigils and severe penances, and also for other reasons, have poor health. When they experience any spiritual consolation, therefore, their physical nature is too much for them; and as soon as they feel any interior joy there comes over them a physical weakness and languor, and they fall into a sleep, which they call "spiritual," and which is a little more marked than the condition that has been described. Thinking the one state to be the same as the other, they abandon themselves to this absorption; and the more they relax, the more complete becomes this absorption, because their physical nature continues to grow weaker. So they get it into their heads that it is *arrobamiento*, or rapture. But I call it *abobamiento*, foolishness;[10] for they are doing nothing but wasting their time at it and ruining their health.

One person was in this state for eight hours; she was not unconscious, nor was she conscious of anything concerning God. She was cured by being told to take more food and sleep and to do less penance; for, though she had misled both her confessor and other people and, quite involuntarily, deceived herself, there was one person who understood her. I believe the devil would go to any pains to gain such people as that, and he was beginning to make good progress with this one.

It must be understood that although, when this state is something that really comes from God, there may be languor, both interior and exterior, there will be none in the soul, which, when it finds itself near God, is moved with great joy. The experience does not last long, but only for a little while. Although the soul may become absorbed again, yet this kind of prayer, as I have said, except in cases of physical weakness, does not go so far as to overcome the body or to produce in it any exterior sensation. Be advised, then, and, if you experience anything of this kind, tell your superior, and relax as much as you can. The superior should give such persons fewer hours of prayer—very few, indeed—and should see that they sleep and eat well, until their physical strength, if it has become exhausted, comes back again. If their constitution is so weak that this does not suffice, they can be certain that God is not calling them to anything beyond the active life. There is room in convents for people of all kinds; let anyone of this type, then, be kept busy with duties, and let care be taken that she is not left alone very much, or her health will be completely ruined. This sort of life will be a great mortification to her, but it is here that the Lord wishes to test her love for Him by seeing how she bears His absence, and after a while He may well be pleased to restore her strength; if He is not, her vocal prayer and her obedience will bring her as much benefit and merit as she would have obtained in other ways, and perhaps more.

There may also be some that are so weak in intellect and imagination—I have known such—that they believe they actually see all they imagine. This is highly dangerous and perhaps we shall treat of it later, but no more shall be said here; for I have written at great length of this

Mansion, as it is the one that the greatest number of souls enter. As the natural is united with the supernatural in it, it is here that the devil can do most harm; for in the Mansions of which I have not yet spoken the Lord gives him fewer opportunities. May He be forever praised. Amen.

Exploring the Interior Castle

- Why does Teresa treat the prayer of recollection after the prayer of quiet when she readily admits that it normally occurs before it? Do you think it has anything to do with the interruptions in her writing schedule she faced at the time? Could it be because she considers the prayer of quiet more central to the fourth mansions and wished to give it more prominence in her presentation? Can you think of any other reason for why she might have written the work in this way?

- Elsewhere in her writings, Teresa draws the distinction between acquired and infused recollection. The first is a simple resting in God's presence and is often a naturally acquired outcome of meditative prayer. The second is a supernatural gift from God that precedes thought and penetrates the understanding. Which type of recollection is she referring to in this chapter? Why does she not make the distinction more explicit in this work? Does it arise out of fear of unnecessarily repeating herself? Could it be, once again, on account of the interruption in her writing schedule? Can you think of any other reason why this very beneficial distinction is not emphasized in her presentation?

- Why does the prayer of infused (supernatural) recollection normally come before the prayer of quiet? Why, in other words, does the divine light penetrate the understanding before the will? Does it have anything to do with the relationship between reason and the will? Does it really matter which is illumined or quieted first?

- In the fourth mansions, Teresa describes the beginning stages of mystical prayer. Do you understand the distinction between infused (supernatural) recollection and the prayer of quiet? Does her description of these stages of prayer correspond in any way to your lived experience? Do you think anyone today has been gifted by God in this way? Do you think her description has universal value for Christian mysticism?

Fifth Mansions

✛

Introduction

Teresa devotes four chapters to her treatment of the fifth mansions. In them, she explains the next state of mystical prayer, known as the prayer of union. In these mansions, God enters the inner sanctum of the soul so deeply that when it returns to itself, it has no doubt whatsoever that it has shared with God an experience of mutual indwelling: "God has been in it, and it in God." It is important to remember that Teresa is addressing the nuns of her Carmelite reform. She states that there are very few of them who will not reach this state, although some go further in than others. She uses the image of a silkworm to describe the great change that comes over a soul as a result of this experience. The silkworm feeds on mulberry leaves until it reaches maturity. Then it spins and buries itself in a tightly wound cocoon and eventually is transformed into a beautiful butterfly. Through the power of the Holy Spirit, the soul goes through a similar metamorphosis.

Teresa points out that, as a result of its transformation, the soul feels no longer tied to bonds of kinship, friendship, and property. It understands that it can find no true rest in this world and is wearied by such associations. She also points out that, although the effects are different, the experiences of this mansion and those that follow are almost identical. Once the soul experiences this intense degree of union with the divine, it has no desire whatsoever to be attached to the things of the world. The movement of detachment from worldly cares and desires is near complete.

The experience of union with God gives it a deep sense of peace, which inspires it as it continues its earthly sojourn.

To describe the prayer of union more fully, Teresa likens it to the process of betrothal and matrimony. On a spiritual level, those in the prayer of union are like two people who have fallen deeply in love with one another and are about to be betrothed. This state is different from the actual betrothal itself and the marriage that flows from it, although all are involved in a single process of falling in love and making a mutual commitment to that love. Teresa admits that her description of the prayer of union is a little obscure. She nonetheless emphasizes all that can be gained by entering this state of mystical prayer by simply submitting one's will entirely to God.

Chapter One

✛

Introduction

In this chapter, Teresa begins with some comments on the great spiritual delights to be found in the fifth mansions. She wonders if she should even attempt to describe them, since there is nothing in human experience with which to compare them. She asks the Lord for help in explaining these dwelling places to her readers, for she believes that most of them will experience this spiritual state at some point in their lives. Having said this, she readily admits that some will get only to the door, while others will penetrate these rooms further and go deeper and deeper into a state of intimate union with God. Since reaching this spiritual state depends so much on the soul turning itself entirely over to God, Teresa advises her readers to pray for the necessary strength of soul that will make this happen. The soul must keep nothing back from the Lord if it wishes to enter into an intimate friendship with him. It can do so, however, only with the help of God and an attitude of complete trust in his love and mercy.

Once the soul has entered these mansions, it is blessed with a deep certainty of God's presence deep within it. Unlike the previous mansions, there is no suspicion or doubt about what it is experiencing. Nor can one be deceived by the evil one into thinking that it is experiencing a dream or an illusion instead of the quiet indwelling of God. The evil one has no access to the rooms of the fifth mansions. Evil thoughts and temptations cannot penetrate them because the memory and the imagination are completely permeated by the divine light. For this reason, the evil one has no idea of the secrets that God reveals to the souls inhabiting them. Nothing can compare with the peace and joy experienced by the soul in this advanced spiritual state, except perhaps that which comes afterward.

Even though one has complete certainty in these mansions regarding God's abiding presence within oneself, Teresa tells her readers that it is still worthwhile to verify their experience by seeking out the counsel of learned men. Even if they have not experienced it for themselves, such men have a certain instinct for discerning the truth. In deference to their position of authority, Teresa tells her readers, to say "I think" (rather than "I know") in order to be ready to admit being mistaken and accept correction from them. At the same time, she warns her readers to be careful with the advice given by those of lesser learning. Those who are truly wise are never surprised at God's greatness and his desire to work great wonders in the life of a soul.

Finally, Teresa emphasizes the need to trust God in everything. In the state of union, the soul has such deep certainty about the way God has visited it that, even after extended periods of dryness, it still knows when to question dubious advice and to seek out the opinion of more experienced counselors to verify her claims. She also states that the whole soul is united with God in this state, not just one or two of its faculties. It is God, moreover, who accomplishes this union, not the soul. People cannot enter these mansions on their own efforts. Only God can lead them into the center of their souls and reveal himself to them in this endearing and intimate way. What is more, he does not need the doors of the senses and faculties of the soul to do so. The Risen Lord was not impeded by doors when he appeared to the disciples, and he has the power to reveal himself immediately to the soul at its very center.

✦

Text

Begins to explain how in prayer the soul is united with God. Describes how we may know that we are not mistaken about this.

Oh, sisters! How shall I ever be able to tell you of the riches and the treasures and the delights that are to be found in the fifth Mansions? I think it would be better if I were to say nothing of the Mansions I have not yet treated, for no one can describe them: the understanding is unable to comprehend them and no comparisons will avail to explain them, for earthly things are quite insufficient for this purpose. Send me light from Heaven, my Lord, that I may enlighten these Thy servants, to some of whom Thou art often pleased to grant fruition of these joys, lest, when the devil transfigures himself into an angel of light, he should deceive them, for all their desires are occupied in desiring to please Thee.

Although I said "to some," there are really very few who do not enter these Mansions that I am about to describe. Some get farther than others; but, as I say, the majority manage to get inside. Some of the things that are in this room, and which I will mention here, are, I am sure, attained by very few;[1] but, if they do no more than reach the door, God is showing them great mercy by granting them this; for, though many are called, few are chosen.[2] So I must say here that, though all of us who wear this sacred habit of Carmel are[3] called to prayer and contemplation—because that was the first principle of our Order and because we are descendent upon the line of those holy Fathers of ours from Mount Carmel who sought this treasure, this precious pearl of which we speak, in such great solitude and with such contempt for the world—few of us[4] prepare ourselves for the Lord to reveal it to us. As far as externals are concerned, we are on the right road to attaining the essential virtues; but we shall need to do a very great deal before we can attain to this higher state, and we must on no account be careless. So let us pause here, my sisters, and beg the Lord that, since to some extent it is possible for us to enjoy Heaven upon earth, He will grant us His help so that it will not be our fault if we miss anything. May He also show us the road and give strength to our souls so that we may dig until we find this hidden treasure, since it is quite true that we have it within ourselves. This I should like to explain if the Lord is pleased to give me the knowledge.

I said "strength to our souls," because you must understand that we do not need bodily strength if God our Lord does not give it us; there is no one for whom He makes it impossible to buy His riches; provided each gives what he has, He is content. Blessed be so great a God! But observe, daughters, that, if you are to gain this, He would have you keep back nothing; whether it be little or much, He will have it all for Himself, and according to what you know yourself to have given, the favors He will grant you will be small or great. There is no better test than this of whether or not our prayer attains to union. Do not think it is a state, like the last, in which we dream; I say "dream" because the soul seems to be, as it were, drowsy, so that it neither seems asleep nor feels awake. Here we are all asleep, and fast asleep, to the things of the world, and to ourselves (in fact, for the short time that the condition lasts, the soul is without consciousness and has no power to think, even though it may desire to do so). There is no need now for it to devise any method of suspending the thought. Even in loving, if it is able to love, it cannot understand how or what it is that it loves, nor what it would desire; in fact, it has completely died to the world so that it may live more fully in God. This is a delectable death, a snatching of the soul from all the activities that it can perform while it is in the body; a death full of delight, for, in order to come closer to God, the soul appears to have withdrawn so far from the body that I do not know if it has still life enough to be able to breathe.[5] I have just been thinking about this and I believe it has not; or at least, if it still breathes, it does so without realizing it. The mind would like to occupy itself wholly in understanding something of what it feels, and, as it has not the strength to do this, it becomes so dumbfounded that, even if any consciousness remains to it, neither hands nor feet can move; as we commonly say of a person who has fallen into a swoon, it might be taken for dead. Oh, the secrets of God! I should never weary of trying to describe them to you, if I thought I could do so successfully. I do not mind if I write any amount of nonsense, provided that just once in a way I can write sense, so that we may give great praise to the Lord.

I said that there was no question here of dreaming, whereas in the Mansion that I have just described, the soul is doubtful as to what has really happened until it has had a good deal of experience of it. It wonders if the whole thing was imagination, if it has been asleep, if the favor was a gift of God, or if the devil was transfigured into an angel of light. It retains a thousand suspicions, and it is well that it should, for, as I said, we can sometimes be deceived in this respect, even by our own nature. For, although there is less opportunity for the poisonous creatures to enter, a few little lizards, being very agile, can hide themselves all over the place; and, although they do no harm—especially, as I said, if we take no notice of them—they correspond to the little thoughts that proceed from the imagination, and from what has been said, it will be seen that they are often very troublesome. Agile though they are, however, the lizards cannot enter this Mansion, for neither imagination nor memory nor understanding can be an obstacle to the blessings that are bestowed in it. And I shall venture to affirm that, if this is indeed union with God,[6] the devil cannot enter or do any harm; for His Majesty is in such close contact and union with the essence of the soul[7] that he will not dare to approach, nor can he even understand this secret thing. That much is evident: for it is said that he does not understand our thoughts;[8] still less, therefore, will he understand a thing so secret that God will not even entrust our thoughts with it.[9] Oh, what a great blessing is this state in which that accursed one can do us no harm! Great are the gains that come to the soul with God working in it and neither we ourselves nor anyone else hindering Him. What will He not give Who so much loves giving and can give all that He will?

I fear I may be leaving you confused by saying "if this is indeed union with God" and suggesting that there are other kinds of union. But of course there are! If we are really very fond of vanities, the devil will send us into transports over them; but these are not like the transports of God, nor is there the same delight and satisfaction for the soul or the same peace and joy. That joy is greater than all the joys of earth, and greater than all its delights, and all its satisfactions, so that there is no evidence that these satisfactions and those of the earth have a common origin; and they are apprehended, too, very differently, as you will have learned by experience. I said once[10] that it is as if the one kind had to do with the grosser part of the body, and the other kind penetrated to the very marrow of the bones; that puts it well, and I know no better way of expressing it.

But I fancy that even now you will not be satisfied, for you will think that you may be mistaken, and that these interior matters are difficult to investigate. In reality, what has been said will be sufficient for anyone who has experienced this blessing, for there is a great difference between the false and the true. But I will give you a clear indication that will make it impossible for you to go wrong or to doubt if some favor has come from God; His Majesty has put it into my mind only today, and I think it is quite decisive. In difficult matters, even if I believe I understand what I am saying and am speaking the truth, I use this phrase "I think," because, if I am mistaken, I am very ready to give credence to those who have great learning. For even if they have not themselves experienced these things, men of great learning have a certain instinct[11] to prompt them. As God uses them to give light to

His Church, He reveals to them anything that is true so that it shall be accepted; and if they do not squander their talents, but are true servants of God, they will never be surprised at His greatness, for they know quite well that He is capable of working more and still more. In any case, where matters are in question for which there is no explanation, there must be others about which they can read, and they can deduce from their reading that it is possible for these first-named to have happened.

Of this I have the fullest experience; and I have also experience of timid, half-learned men whose shortcomings have cost me very dear. At any rate, my own opinion is that anyone who does not believe that God can do much more than this, and that He has been pleased, and is sometimes still pleased, to grant His creatures such favors, has closed the door fast against receiving them. Therefore, sisters, let this never be true of you, but trust God more and more, and do not consider whether those to whom He communicates His favors are bad or good. His Majesty knows all about this, as I have said; intervention on our part is quite unnecessary; rather must we serve His Majesty with humility and simplicity of heart, and praise Him for His works and wonders.

Turning now to the indication that I have described as[12] a decisive one: here is this soul that God has made, as it were, completely foolish in order the better to impress upon it true wisdom. For as long as such a soul is in this state, it can neither see nor hear nor understand: the period is always short and seems to the soul even shorter than it really is. God implants Himself in the interior of that soul in such a way that, when it returns to itself, it cannot[13] possibly doubt that God has been in it and it has been in God; so firmly does this truth remain within it that, although for years God may never grant it that favor again, it can neither forget it nor doubt that it has received it (and this quite apart from the effects that remain within it, and of which I will speak later). This certainty of the soul is very material.

But now you will say to me: How did the soul see it and understand it if it can neither see nor understand? I am not saying that it saw it at the time,[14] but that it sees it clearly afterward, and not because it is a vision, but because of a certainty which remains in the soul, which can be put there only by God. I know of a person who had not learned that God was in all things by presence and power and essence; God granted her a favor of this kind, which convinced her of this so firmly[15] that, although one of those half-learned men whom I have been talking about, and whom she asked in what way God was in us (until God granted him an understanding of it, he knew as little of it as she), told her that He was in us only by grace, she had the truth so firmly implanted within her that she did not believe him, and asked others, who told her the truth, which was a great consolation to her.[16]

Do not make the mistake of thinking that this certainty has anything to do with bodily form—with the presence of Our Lord Jesus Christ, for example, unseen by us, in the Most Holy Sacrament. It has nothing to do with this—only with His Divinity. How, you will ask, can we become so convinced of what we have not seen? That I do not know; it is the work of God. But I know I am speaking the truth; and if anyone has not that certainty, I should say that what he has experienced is not union of the whole soul with God but only union of one of the faculties or some one of the many other kinds of favor which God grants the soul. In all these matters we must stop looking for reasons why they happened; if our understanding cannot grasp them, why should we try to perplex it? It suffices us to know that He Who brings this to pass is all-powerful,[17] and as it is God Who does it and we, however hard we work, are quite incapable of achieving it, let us not try to become capable of understanding it either.

With regard to what I have just said about our incapability, I recall that, as you have heard, the Bride in the *Songs* says: "The King brought me" (or "put me," I think the words are) "into the cellar of wine."[18] It does not say that she went. It also says that she was wandering about in all directions seeking her Beloved.[19] This, as I understand it, is the cellar where the Lord is pleased to put us, when He wills and as He wills. But we cannot enter by any efforts of our own; His Majesty must put us right into the center[20] of our soul, and must enter there Himself; and, in order that He may the better show us His wonders, it is His pleasure that our will, which has entirely surrendered itself to Him, should have no part in this. Nor does He desire the door of the faculties and senses, which are all asleep, to be opened to Him; He will come into the center of the soul without using a door, as He did when He came in to His disciples, and said *Pax vobis*,[21] and when He left the sepulcher without removing the stone. Later on you will see how it is His Majesty's will that the soul should have fruition of Him in its very center, but you will be able to realize that in the last Mansion much better than here.

Oh, daughters, what a lot we shall see if we desire to see no more than our own baseness and wretchedness and to understand that we are not worthy to be the handmaidens of so great a Lord, since we cannot comprehend His marvels. May He be forever praised. Amen.

Exploring the Interior Castle

- How would you best describe the difference between someone in the fifth mansions as opposed to someone in the immediately preceding ones? What does it mean for the whole soul to be in union with God as opposed to only one or two faculties of it, such as the reason and will? Are there different intensities of being in union with God? Have you ever experienced one of these different intensities? Have you ever felt a particular faculty being in union with God?

- Why is it so difficult for the evil one to penetrate the fifth mansions with temptations and evil thoughts? Do you believe it possible for the divine light to penetrate the memory and imagination and purify them so fully that even the slightest hint of a temptation to sin would be unthinkable? If so, would the person still be free? In what sense?

- Teresa says that someone in the fifth mansions possesses a certainty of having been visited by God. Where does this certainty come from? Does it need to be verified? Have you ever felt this way? What is the relationship between certainty and doubt? Is certainty always a good thing? Is doubt always a bad thing? How can you tell the difference?

- In the fifth mansions, Jesus enters the center of the soul without using the doors of the senses and faculties. Do you believe this is possible? Do you believe that this can actually happen to someone? If God enters the very heart of the soul from within rather than from without, what does this say about the relationship between God and the human person? What does it say about the relationship between body and soul? What does it say about the nature of Christian mysticism?

Chapter Two

✛

Introduction

In this chapter, Teresa uses the metaphor of a silkworm to continue her discussion of the prayer of union. She uses this image as a way of making her teaching more accessible to her readers so that they will understand it better and be encouraged to do all they can to prepare for it. The metaphor is a simple one that deftly describes the process involved in the soul's metamorphosis. Silkworms are fed on mulberry leaves until they become fully-grown. Then they spin a cocoon out of silk and die soon afterwards. From this death, there arises in time a small white butterfly. (As might be expected, some of her science isn't quite right here: the silkworm does not "die" while undergoing metamorphosis. Instead it enters a catatonic state, and technically, it turns into a moth, not a butterfly. I simply use her terminology for the sake of simplicity.) She asks her readers to imagine who would believe such a story, if it had not been such a commonplace earthly occurrence. To be sure, few arguments could be found that would convince a suspicious audience.

In Teresa's mind, the same holds true for what happens to the soul in the prayer of union. The developing silkworm represents the soul in the early stages of spiritual growth, which feeds itself on the sacraments, spiritual reading, and the preached word of God. Once it has matured, it is ready to spin a cocoon that will eventually become both its home and sepulcher. Christ is the mansion within which the soul seeks to enclose itself. Hidden in that mansion, the soul dies and eventually becomes totally transformed by Christ. Teresa certainly does not wish to give the impression that this transformation is caused by the soul. On the contrary, the mansion built by the soul is as insignificant as the cocoon spun by the silkworm. God, however, takes this small accomplishment and causes the metamorphosis to take place. She is also careful to point out that the soul cannot add or take anything away from God. The soul builds its mansion by adding and detracting from itself. It does so by detaching itself increasingly from the things of the world and by seeking to do God's will in all things. The soul in no way merits the new creation that it has become. Its transformation is a work of God that comes through the heights of mystical prayer.

For Teresa, to enter the fifth mansions means that the soul has spun its cocoon and has completely died to the world. This dying, however, is only a prelude to its later rising. God, she maintains, changes the soul so thoroughly that it can no longer recognize itself. In this state of mystical prayer, which she says will last for only a short period of time (a half an hour or less), the soul becomes totally one with God. It praises God in all circumstances, wishes to lay down its life for him, and seeks out a life of penance and solitude. It considers itself a stranger to earthly things and is dissatisfied with all else except doing the will of God. In a veiled reference to her own experience of these spiritual mansions, Teresa tells her readers how she herself suffered from seeing God offended so often in the world around her and asks them to imagine how Jesus himself must have felt when he walked the earth. Like Jesus, the only joy for a soul in this state is doing the will of God. At this stage of spiritual growth, the soul embraces the cross with joy and finds great delight in doing God's will.

✛

Text

Continues the same subject. Explains the Prayer of Union by a delicate comparison. Describes the effects that it produces in the soul. Should be studied with great care.

You will suppose that all there is to be seen in this Mansion has been described already, but there is much more yet to come, for, as I said, some receive more and some less. With regard to the nature of union, I do not think I can say anything further; but when the soul to which God grants these favors prepares itself for them, there are many things to be said concerning what the Lord works in it. Some of these I shall say now, and I shall describe that soul's state. In order the better to explain this, I will make use of a comparison that is suitable for the purpose; and that will also show us how, although this work is performed by the Lord, and we can do nothing to make His Majesty grant us this favor, we can do a great deal to prepare ourselves for it.

You will have heard of the wonderful way in which silk is made—a way which no one could invent but God—and how it comes from a kind of seed that looks like tiny peppercorns[1] (I have never seen this, but only heard of it, so if it is incorrect in any way, the Fault is not mine). When the warm weather comes, and the mulberry trees begin to show leaf, this seed starts to take life; until it has this sustenance, on which it feeds, it is as dead. The silkworms feed on the mulberry leaves until they are full-grown, when people put down twigs, upon which, with their tiny mouths, they start spinning silk, making themselves very tight little cocoons, in which they bury themselves. Then, finally, the worm, which was large and ugly, comes right out of the cocoon a beautiful white butterfly.

Now if no one had ever seen this, and we were only told about it as a story of past ages, who would believe it? And what arguments could we find to support the belief that a thing as devoid of reason as a worm or a bee could be diligent enough to work so industriously for our advantage, and that in such an enterprise the poor little worm would lose its life? This alone, sisters, even if I tell you no more, is sufficient for a brief meditation, for it will enable you to reflect upon the wonders and the wisdom of our God. What, then, would it be if we knew the properties of everything? It will be a great help to us if we occupy ourselves in thinking of these wonderful things and rejoice in being the brides of so wise and powerful a King.

But to return to what I was saying. The silkworm is like the soul, which takes life when, through the heat that comes from the Holy Spirit, it begins to utilize the general help that God gives to us all, and to make use of the remedies that He left in His Church—such as frequent confessions, good books, and sermons, for these are the remedies for a soul dead in negligences and sins and frequently plunged into temptation. The soul begins to live and nourishes itself on this food, and on good meditations, until it is full-grown—and this is what concerns me now: the rest is of little importance.

When it is full-grown, then, as I wrote at the beginning, it starts to spin its silk and to build the house in which it is to die. This house may be understood here to mean Christ I think I read or heard somewhere that our life is hid in Christ, or in God (for that is the same thing), or that our life is Christ.[2] (The exact form of this[3] is little to my purpose.)

Here, then, daughters, you see what we can do, with God's favor. May His Majesty Himself be our Mansion as He is in this Prayer of Union, which, as it were, we ourselves spin. When I say He will be our Mansion, and we can construct it for ourselves and hide ourselves in it, I seem to be suggesting that we can subtract from God, or add to Him. But of course we cannot possibly do that! We can neither subtract from, nor add to, God, but we can subtract from, and add to, ourselves, just as these little silkworms do. And, before we have finished doing all that we can in that respect, God will take this tiny achievement of ours, which is nothing at all, unite it with His greatness, and give it such worth that its reward will be the Lord Himself. And as it is He Whom it has cost the most, so His Majesty will unite our small trials with the great trials that He suffered, and make both of them into one.

On, then, my daughters! Let us hasten to perform this task and spin this cocoon. Let us renounce our self-love and self-will, and our attachment to earthly things. Let us practice penance, prayer, mortification, obedience, and all the other good works that you know of. Let us do what we have been taught; and we have been instructed about what our duty is. Let the silkworm die—let it die, as in fact it does when it has completed the work that it was created to do. Then we shall see God and shall ourselves be as completely hidden in His greatness as is this little worm in its cocoon. Note that, when I speak of seeing God, I am referring to the way in which, as I have said, He allows Himself to be apprehended in this kind of union.

And now let us see what becomes of this silkworm, for all that I have been saying about it is leading up to this. When it is in this state of prayer, and quite dead to the world, it comes out a little white butterfly. Oh, greatness of God, that a soul should come out like this after being hidden in the greatness of God, and closely united with Him, for so short a time—never, I think, for as long as half an hour! I tell you truly, the very soul does not know itself. For think of the difference between an ugly worm and a white butterfly; it is just the same here. The soul cannot think how it can have merited such a blessing—whence such a blessing could have come to it, I meant to say, for it knows quite well that it has not merited it at all.[4] It finds itself so anxious to praise the Lord that it would gladly be consumed and die a thousand deaths for His sake. Then it finds itself longing to suffer great trials and unable to do otherwise. It has the most vehement desires for penance, for solitude, and for all to know God. And hence, when it sees God being offended, it becomes greatly distressed. In the following Mansion we shall treat of these things further and in detail, for, although the experiences of this Mansion and of the next are almost identical, their effects come to have much greater power; for, as I have said, if after God comes to a soul here on earth it strives to progress still more, it will experience great things.

To see, then, the restlessness of this little butterfly—though it has never been quieter or more at rest in its life! here is something to praise God for—namely, that it knows not where to settle and make its abode. By comparison with the abode it has had, everything it sees on earth leaves it dissatisfied, especially when God has again and again given it this wine that almost every time has brought it some new blessing. It sets no store by the things it did when it was a worm—that is, by its gradual weaving of the cocoon. It has wings now: how can it be content to crawl along slowly when it is able to fly? All that it can do for God seems to it slight by comparison with its desires. It even attaches little importance to what the saints endured, knowing by experience how the Lord helps and transforms a soul, so that it seems no longer to be itself, or even its own likeness. For the weakness that it used to think it had when it came to doing penance is now turned into strength. It is no longer bound by ties of relationship, friendship or property.

Previously all its acts of will and resolutions and desires were powerless to loosen these and seemed only to bind them the more firmly; now it is grieved at having even to fulfill its obligations in these respects lest these should cause it to sin against God. Everything wearies it, because it has proved that it can find no true rest in the creatures.

I seem to be enlarging on this subject and there is much more that I could say: anyone to whom God has granted this favor will realize that I have said very little. It is not surprising, then, that, as this little butterfly feels a stranger to things of the earth, it should be seeking a new resting-place. But where will the poor little creature go? It cannot return to the place it came from, for, as has been said, however hard we try, it is not in our power to do that until God is pleased once again to grant us this favor. Ah, Lord! What trials begin afresh for this soul! Who would think such a thing possible after it had received so signal a favor? But, after all,[5] we must bear crosses in one way or another for as long as we live. And if anyone told me that, after reaching this state, he had enjoyed continual rest and joy, I should say that he had not reached it at all, but that if he had got as far as the previous Mansion, he might possibly have experienced some kind of consolation, the effect of which was enhanced by physical weakness, and perhaps even by the devil, who gives peace to the soul in order later to wage a far severer war upon it.

I do not mean that those who attain to this state have no peace: they do have it, and to a very high degree, for even their trials are of such sublimity and come from so noble a source that, severe though they are, they bring peace and contentment. The very discontent caused by the things of the world arouses a desire to leave it, so grievous that any alleviation it finds can only be in the thought that its life in this exile is God's will. And even this is insufficient to comfort it, for, despite all it has gained, the soul is not wholly resigned to the will of God, as we shall see later. It does not fail to act in conformity with God's will, but it does so with many tears and with great sorrow at being unable to do more because it has been given no more capacity. Whenever it engages in prayer, this is a grief to it. To some extent, perhaps, it is a result of the great grief caused by seeing how often God is offended, and how little esteemed, in this world, and by considering how many souls are lost, both of heretics and of Moors; although its greatest grief is over the loss of Christian souls, many of whom, it fears, are condemned, though so great is God's mercy that, however evil their lives have been, they can amend them and be saved.

Oh, the greatness of God! Only a few years since—perhaps only a few days—this soul was thinking of nothing but itself. Who has plunged it into such grievous anxieties? Even if we tried to meditate for years on end, we could not feel this as keenly as the soul does now. God help me! If I were able to spend many days and years in trying to realize how great a sin it is to offend God, and in reflecting that those who are damned are His children, and my brothers and sisters, and in meditating upon the dangers in which we live, and in thinking how good it would be for us to depart from this miserable life, would all that suffice? No, daughters; the grief I am referring to is not like that caused by these kinds of meditation. That grief we could easily achieve, with the Lord's help, by thinking a great deal about those things; but it does not reach to the depths of our being, as does this grief, which, without any effort on the soul's part, and sometimes against its will, seems to tear it to pieces and grind it to powder. What, then, is this grief? Whence does it come? I will tell you.

Have you not heard concerning the Bride (I said this a little while back,[6] though not with reference to the same matter) that God put her in the cellar of wine and ordained charity in her? Well, that is the position here. That soul has now delivered itself into His hands, and His great love has so completely subdued it that it neither knows nor desires anything save that God shall do with it what He wills. Never, I think, will God grant this favor save to the soul that He takes for His very own. His will is that, without understanding how, the soul shall go thence sealed with His seal. In reality, the soul in that state does no more than the wax when a seal is impressed upon it—the wax does not impress itself; it is only prepared for the impress: that is, it is soft—and it does not even soften itself so as to be prepared; it merely remains quiet and consenting. Oh, goodness of God, that all this should be done at Thy cost! Thou dost require only our wills and dost ask that Thy wax may offer no impediment.

Here, then, sisters, you see what our God does to the soul in this state so that it may know itself to be His. He gives it something of His own, which is what His Son had in this life: He can grant us no favor greater than that. Who could have wanted to depart from this life more than His Son did? As, indeed, His Majesty said at the Last Supper: "With desire have I desired."[7] "Did not the painful death that

Thou were to die present itself to Thee, O Lord, as something grievous and terrible?" "No, because My great love and My desire that souls
shall be saved transcend these pains beyond all comparison and the
very terrible things that I have suffered since I lived in the world, and
still suffer, are such that by comparison with them these are nothing."

I have often thought about this: I know that the torment that a
certain person of my acquaintance[8] has suffered, and suffers still, at
seeing the Lord offended, is so intolerable that she would far sooner
die than suffer it. And, I reflected, if a soul that has so very little charity
by comparison with Christ's that it might be said to be almost nothing
beside His felt this torment to be so intolerable, what must the feelings
of Our Lord Jesus Christ have been, and what a life must He have lived,
if He saw everything and was continually witnessing the great offenses
that were being committed against His Father? I think this must certainly have caused Him much greater grief than the pains of His most
sacred Passion; for there He could see the end of His trials; and that
sight, together with the satisfaction of seeing our redemption achieved
through His death, and of proving what love He had for His Father by
suffering so much for Him, would alleviate His pains, just as, when
those who have great strength of love perform great penances, they
hardly feel them, and would like to do more and more, and everything
that they do seems very small to them. What, then, would His Majesty
feel when He found Himself able to prove so amply to His Father how
completely He was fulfilling the obligation of obedience to Him and
showing His love for His neighbor? Oh, the great delight of suffering
in doing the will of God! But the constant sight of so many offences
committed against His Majesty and so many souls going to hell must,
I think, have been so painful to Him that, had He not been more than
man, one day of that grief would have sufficed to put an end to any
number of lives that He might have had, let alone to one.

Exploring the Interior Castle

- Do you like Teresa's metaphor of the silkworm, cocoon, and butterfly? Do you think it helps the reader understand the fifth mansions better? What impresses you most about it? Can you detect any weaknesses in it? Can you think of any other metaphors for one's experience of prayer of union?

- Where do you see yourself on the path of spiritual maturity? Do you consider yourself a beginner in the spiritual life or more advanced in it? Where do you find spiritual nourishment? How do you know that it is what you need at this particular stage of your life? Do those further along the way necessarily leave their beginning practices behind?

- Only a full-grown silkworm is able to spin its cocoon. Do you consider yourself spiritually mature? If so, at what stage are you in the spinning of your cocoon? What is your cocoon made of? What does it look like? Does the metaphor of the silkworm resonate at all with your experience of God at prayer? Does it offer you a glimpse of things still to come?

- After its death, the silkworm is transformed into a small white butterfly. Have you ever experienced death in your interior life? If so, what was it like? Can you point to something specific? Did the experience end in death or did something rise up out of the ashes? Do all experiences of personal transformation require a prior dying to self? Can you think of any that would not?

Chapter Three

✛

Introduction

In this chapter, Teresa continues her discussion of the prayer of union by focusing on the importance of uniting one's will with God's. To be one with God requires a union of wills. One knows one is following God's will if one follows his commandments. Even if their actions benefit others in some way, those who stray from this path will not inherit eternal life. In another veiled reference to herself, Teresa tells her readers that she knows of a person who was granted the favor of union with God and then lost it through her own carelessness. There is a difference between teaching others about progress in the spiritual life and one's own personal growth in virtue and holiness. She tells her readers that to live in the fifth mansions presupposes that a person will always wish to grow in self-knowledge and service to God.

Teresa says there are many examples of people who were called to serve the Lord and enjoy fellowship with him and then became lost through their own carelessness. She insists that the only way to keep this from happening is through unfailing obedience to God's law. It is one thing to say and even think that one desires to follow God's will and quite another to actually carry it out. Teresa wishes to be clear: it is impossible to attain the heights of which she has spoken if one has not submitted one's will entirely to God. Once this has happened, a person will live in peace both now and in the life to come. Nothing will disturb this person, for whatever trials come will touch only the senses and faculties but will fail to penetrate the depths of the soul.

Teresa wants her readers to know that the union of their will with God is both possible and within reach. They achieve this union not through their own efforts, but by pleading with God to make it happen. God's will consists of two things: love of God and love of neighbor. It is impossible to carry out his will without God's help since a person's weakness will always prevent him or her from doing so. With God, however, all things are possible. Teresa points out that the love of God and neighbor are closely related and that the best way of knowing if one is keeping these commandments is to be very diligent in one's love of neighbor. The perfect love of neighbor is rooted in the love of God.

Teresa emphasizes the importance of self-knowledge and of knowing one's weaknesses when it comes to loving one's neighbor. She encourages her readers to strive to be faithful even in the smallest matters. She says that it is so easy to have a mistaken notion of one's own spiritual state and that the evil one will go out of his way to stir one's imagination and convince a person that he or she is virtuous and in the state of grace. She gives examples of people who think of themselves one way and act in another. Growth in the spiritual life is not about having deep experiences of prayer, but of uniting one's will to God's. One manifests this union by keeping the commandments, the greatest of which are love of God and neighbor. For this reason, it is much more important to help a person in need and to rejoice in the good fortunes of others than remaining absorbed in one's prayerful devotions. One does not grow in holiness by seeking spiritual experiences but by growing in the virtue of love of God and neighbor. Since it is difficult to know if one truly loves God, she tells her readers to ask God to develop in them a perfect love of neighbor. She asks them to look to how the Lord laid down his life for them and encourages them do so for others, even in the smallest matters.

✤

Text

Continues the same matter. Describes another kind of union that, with the help of God, the soul can attain, and the important part played in it by the love of our neighbor. This chapter is of great profit.

L et us now return to our little dove, and see something of what God gives her in this state. It must always be understood that she will try to advance in the service of Our Lord and in self-knowledge. If she does no more than receive this favor, and, as though she enjoyed complete security, begins to lead a careless life and stray from the road to Heaven—that is, from the Commandments—there will happen to her what happens to the creature that comes out of the silkworm, which leaves seed for the production of more silkworms and then dies forever. I say it leaves seed because for my own part I believe it is God's will that so great a favor should not be given in vain, and that if the soul that receives it does not profit by it others will do so. For, as the soul possesses these aforementioned desires and virtues, it will always profit other souls so long as it leads a good life, and from its own heat new heat will be transmitted to them. Even after losing this, it may still desire others to profit, and take pleasure in describing the favors given by God to those that love and serve Him.

I knew a person to whom this happened,[1] and who, though having herself gone far astray, was glad that others should profit by the favors God had shown her, she would describe the way of prayer to those who did not understand it, and she brought them very, very great profit.[2] Later, the Lord gave her new light. It is true that she had not yet experienced the effects that have been mentioned. But how many are called by the Lord to apostleship, as Judas was, and enjoy communion with Him, or are called to be made kings, as Saul was, and afterward, through their own fault, are lost! From this, sisters, we may deduce that, if we are to acquire increasing merit, and not, like Saul and Judas, to be lost, our only possible safety consists in obedience and in never swerving from the law of God; I am referring to those to whom He grants these favors, and in fact to all.

Despite all I have said, this Mansion seems to me a little obscure. There is a great deal to be gained by entering it, and those from whom the Lord withholds such supernatural gifts will do well to feel that they are not without hope; for true union can quite well be achieved, with the favor of Our Lord, if we endeavor to attain it by not following our own will but submitting it to whatever is the will of God. Oh, how many of us there are who say we do this and think we want nothing else, and would die for this truth, as I believe I have said! For I tell you, and I shall often repeat this, that when you have obtained this favor from the Lord, you need not strive for that other delectable union that has been described, for the most valuable thing about it is that it proceeds from this union that I am now describing; and we cannot attain to the heights I have spoken of if we are not sure that we have the union in which we resign our wills to the will of God.

Oh, how much to be desired is this union! Happy the soul that has attained to it, for it will live peacefully both in this life and in the next as well. Nothing that happens on earth will afflict it unless it finds itself in peril of losing God, or sees that He is offended—neither sickness nor poverty nor death, except when someone dies who was needed by the Church of God. For this soul sees clearly that He knows what He does better than it knows itself what it desires.

You must observe that there are many kinds of grief. Some of them come upon us suddenly, in natural ways, just as pleasures do; they may even arise from charity, which makes us pity our neighbors, as Our Lord did when He raised Lazarus;[3] and these do not prevent union with the will of God, nor do they cause a restless, unquiet passion which disturbs the soul and lasts for a long time. They are griefs that pass quickly; for, as I said of joys in prayer, they seem not to penetrate to the depth of the soul but only reach these senses and faculties. They characterize all the Mansions so far described but do not enter that which will be dealt with last of all, from which the suspension of the faculties already referred to is inseparable. The Lord can enrich souls in many ways and bring them to these Mansions by many other paths than the shortcut that has been described.

But note very carefully, daughters, that the silkworm has of necessity to die; and it is this that will cost you most; for death comes more easily[4] when one can see oneself living a new life, whereas our duty now is to continue living this present life, and yet to die of our own free will.[5] I confess to you that we shall find this much harder, but it is of the greatest value, and the reward will be greater, too, if you gain the victory. But you must not doubt the possibility of this true union with the will of God. This is the union that I have desired all my life;

it is for this that I continually beseech Our Lord; it is this that is the most genuine and the safest.

But alas that so few of us are destined to attain it! A person who takes care not to offend the Lord and has entered the religious life may think he has done everything. But oh, there are always a few little worms that do not reveal themselves until, like the worm that gnawed through Jonah's ivy,[6] they have gnawed through our virtues. Such are self-love, self-esteem, censoriousness (even if only in small things) concerning our neighbors, lack of charity toward them, and failure to love them as we love ourselves. For, although late in the day we may fulfill our obligations and so commit no sin, we are far from attaining a point necessary to complete union with the will of God.

What do you suppose His will is, daughters? That we should be altogether perfect, and be one with Him and with the Father,[7] as in His Majesty's prayer. Consider what a long way we are from attaining this. I assure you that it causes me real distress to write in this way because I know how far I am from it myself, and entirely through my own fault. For we do not require great favors from the Lord before we can achieve this; He has given us all we need in giving us His Son to show us the way. Do not think that if, for example, my father or my brother dies, I ought to be in such close conformity with the will of God that I shall not grieve at his loss, or that, if I have trials or illnesses, I must enjoy bearing them. It is good if we can do this, and sometimes it is a matter of common sense: being unable to help ourselves, we make a virtue of necessity. How often philosophers used to act thus in matters of this kind, or in similar matters—and they were very wise men! But here the Lord asks only two things of us: love for His Majesty and love for our neighbor. It is for these two virtues that we must strive, and if we attain them perfectly we are doing His will and so shall be united with Him. But, as I have said, how far we are from doing these two things in the way we ought for a God Who is so great! May His Majesty be pleased to give us grace so that we may deserve to reach this state, as it is in our power to do if we wish.

The surest sign that we are keeping these two commandments is, I think, that we should really be loving our neighbor; for we cannot be sure if we are loving God, although we may have good reasons for believing that we are, but we can know quite well if we are loving our neighbor. And be certain that, the farther advanced you find you are in this, the greater the love you will have for God; for so dearly does

His Majesty love us that He will reward our love for our neighbor by increasing the love that we bear to Himself, and that in a thousand ways: this I cannot doubt.

It is most important that we should proceed in this matter very carefully, for, if we have attained great perfection here, we have done everything. Our nature being so evil, I do not believe we could ever attain perfect love for our neighbor unless it had its roots in the love of God. Since this is so important, sisters, let us strive to get to know ourselves better and better, even in the very smallest matters, and take no notice of all the fine plans that come crowding into our minds when we are at prayer, and that we think we will put into practice and carry out for the good of our neighbors in the hope of saving just one soul. If our later actions are not in harmony with those plans, we can have no reason for believing that we should ever have put them into practice. I say the same of humility and of all the virtues; the wiles of the devil are terrible: he will run a thousand times round hell if by so doing he can make us believe that we have a single virtue that we have not. And he is right, for such ideas are very harmful, and such imaginary virtues, when they come from this source, are never unaccompanied by vainglory; just as those that God gives are free both from this and from pride.

I like the way in which some souls, when they are at prayer, think that, for God's sake, they would be glad if they could be humbled and put to open shame—and then try to conceal quite a slight failure. Oh, and if they should be accused of anything that they have not done—! God save us from having to listen to them then! Let anyone who cannot bear trials like that be very careful to pay no heed to the resolutions he may have made when he was alone. For they could not in fact have been resolutions made by the will (a genuine act of the will is quite another matter); they must have been due to some freak of the imagination. The devil makes good use of the imagination in practicing his surprises and deceptions, and there are many such that he can practice on women, or on unlettered persons, because we do not understand the difference between the faculties and the imagination, and thousands of other things belonging to the interior life. Oh, sisters, how clearly it can be seen what love of your neighbor really means to some of you, and what an imperfect stage it has reached in others! If you understood the importance of this virtue to us all, you would strive after nothing but gaining it.

When I see people very diligently trying to discover what kind of prayer they are experiencing and so completely wrapped up[8] in their prayers that they seem afraid to stir, or to indulge in a moment's thought, lest they should lose the slightest degree of the tenderness and devotion that they have been feeling, I realize how little they understand of the road to the attainment of union. They think that the whole thing consists in this. But no, sisters, no; what the Lord desires is works. If you see a sick woman to whom you can give some help, never be affected by the fear that your devotion will suffer, but take pity on her: if she is in pain, you should feel pain too; if necessary, fast so that she may have your food, not so much for her sake as because you know it to be your Lord's will. That is true union with His will. Again, if you hear someone being highly praised, be much more pleased than if they were praising you; this is really easy if you have humility, for in that case you will be sorry to hear yourself praised. To be glad when your sisters' virtues are praised is a great thing, and, when we see a fault in someone, we should be as sorry about it as if it were our own and try to conceal it from others.

I have said a great deal about this elsewhere,[9] sisters, because I know that, if we were to fail here, we should be lost May the Lord grant us never to fail, and, if that is to be so, I tell you that you must not cease to beg His Majesty for the union that I have described. It may be that you have experienced devotion and consolations, so that you think you have reached this stage, and even enjoyed some brief period of suspension in the Prayer of Quiet, which some people always take to mean that everything is accomplished. But, believe me, if you find you are lacking in this virtue, you have not yet attained union. So ask Our Lord to grant you this perfect love for your neighbor, and allow His Majesty to work, and, if you use your best endeavors and strive after this in every way that you can, He will give you more even than you can desire. You must do violence to your own will, so that your sister's will is done in everything, even though this may cause you to forgo your own rights and forget your own good in your concern for theirs, and however much your physical powers may rebel. If the opportunity presents itself, too, try to shoulder some trial in order to relieve your neighbor of it. Do not suppose that it will cost you nothing or that you will find it all done for you. Think what the love that our Spouse had for us cost Him, when, in order to redeem us from death, He died such a grievous death as the death of the Cross.

Exploring the Interior Castle

- Holiness, for Teresa, is a matter of uniting one's will with God's. Do you agree with her? If so, why is the will so important for growth in the spiritual life? If not, can you think of another way of gauging a person's growth in holiness?

- Have you ever found yourself thinking and saying one thing and then acting in an entirely different way? Have you found yourself acting like this rarely or often? Do you want to narrow this gap in any way? What practical measures can help you to do so?

- What does it mean to die to oneself? Is it possible to die to oneself and still love oneself? What is the relationship between dying to oneself and submitting one's will to God? Is true love of self rooted in a firm willingness and desire to discern and carry out God's will?

- Teresa sees a close relationship between love of God and love of neighbor. How do you see these two important virtues relating? Which is more important? How would you distinguish them? Is one a manifestation of another? Is it possible to have one without the other?

Chapter Four

✤

Introduction

In this chapter, Teresa brings her discussion of the prayer of union to a close. She says that it has been five months since she began writing the book at the request of her confessor and apologizes to her readers if she repeats herself. She knows that her readers are eager to learn how high the soul can fly and tells them that she will not be able to fully please them until she reaches the final mansion.

As she takes up her subject again, Teresa offers her readers yet another metaphor for understanding the prayer of union, this time from the sacrament of marriage. She admits that she is drawing a very rough analogy and takes great pains to highlight the differences between the two: the prayer of union is a purely spiritual relationship, while matrimony has to do with carnal relations between man and woman. Despite this fundamental disparity, she believes that the metaphor will help her readers gain a better understanding of the prayer of union and how it differs from the later mansions.

To understand how this metaphor works, it is important to understand that, in Teresa's day, marriage was preceded by an act of betrothal made through a formal contract between the parties involved. This act was itself preceded by a brief meeting between the two individuals to see if they were compatible with each other. If they believed they were, the betrothal contract would be drawn up and the courtship begun. Since many marriages in Teresa's day were prearranged, the meeting before the official act of betrothal was important for the two persons involved. It was not unusual that the couple would meet for the first time at this brief encounter. Much would happen during this meeting, and on many levels, since the decision made would affect these individuals for the rest of their lives.

Teresa states that the prayer of union is something like the brief meeting the couple has before their betrothal. In her judgment, spiritual betrothal has not yet taken place between the soul and God. The two have encountered one another—be it ever so briefly—and affirmed not only their compatibility, but also their love for each other. In this meeting, a union of hearts takes place, which allows them to share a deep intimacy. Spiritual betrothal and marriage flow from this all-important union. Without it, the betrothal is nothing but a business contract and the marriage likely to be empty of love.

Teresa spends much of this final chapter of the fifth mansions imploring her readers not to be negligent in nurturing their relationship with God. She tells them to ask the Lord for the strength to avoid anything that might lead them away from God. The prayer of union, she states, is a brief but intense union of the soul and God. This brief encounter can lead to even higher mystical states, but the soul must take care not to allow the evil one to lead it astray. Even though a person in these mansions has united his or her will to God's, Teresa says that the evil one can use his wiles in many ways to darken one's mind and compromise one's will. The evil one can strike even in the most carefully guarded places. One must never presume to be beyond his influence. She gives the example of Judas, who, even though he walked with God and shared fellowship with the apostles, allowed the evil one to lead him astray.

Teresa advises her readers to pray to God constantly for help, to remember that they are nothing without him, and that they have no reason to be confident in their own abilities. She also tells them to take special care that they are making progress in the virtues and going forward in the spiritual life. She reminds them that, having brought the soul to this level of intimacy, the Lord is not going to let it go so easily. Because of the many inner warnings the Lord gives to the soul in danger, the evil one can lead it astray only with great effort.

Teresa concludes this chapter by giving her readers a brief glimpse of the favors of the next mansions. She knows that she will need the Lord's guidance as she sets out to describe these great delights. She hopes that what she has written thus far has been of benefit to her readers. Through it all, her sole desire has been to praise the name of the Lord and humbly serve him.

✢

Text

Continues the same subject and gives a further explanation of this kind of prayer. Describes the great importance of proceeding carefully, since the devil is most careful to do all he can to turn souls back from the road they have begun to tread.

I think you will be anxious now to learn what this little dove is doing, and where it is going to settle, for of course it cannot rest in spiritual consolations or in earthly pleasures. It is destined to fly higher than this, and I cannot fully satisfy your anxiety until we come to the last Mansion. God grant I may remember it then and find an opportunity to write about it, for almost five months have passed since I began this book, and, as my head is not in a fit state for me to read it through again, it must all be very confused and I may possibly say a few things twice over. As it is for my sisters, however, that matters little.

I want to explain to you still further what I think this Prayer of Union is; and I will make a comparison as well as my wit will allow. Afterwards we will say more about this little butterfly, which never rests—though it is always fruitful in doing good to itself and to other souls—because it has not yet found true repose.[1] You will often have heard that God betroths Himself to souls spiritually. Blessed be His mercy, which is pleased so to humble itself! I am only making a rough comparison, but I can find no other which will better explain what I am trying to say than the Sacrament of Matrimony. The two things work differently, for in this matter that we are treating there is nothing that is not spiritual: corporeal union is quite another thing, and the spiritual joys and consolations given by the Lord are a thousand leagues removed from those experienced in marriage. It is all a union of love with love, and its operations are entirely pure, and so delicate and gentle that there is no way of describing them; but the Lord can make the soul very deeply conscious of them.

It seems to me that this union has not yet reached the point of spiritual betrothal, but is rather like what happens in our earthly life when two people are about to be betrothed. There is a discussion as to whether or not they are suited to each other and are both in love; and then they meet again so that they may learn to appreciate each other better. So it is here. The contract is already drawn up and the soul has

been clearly given to understand the happiness of her lot and is determined to do all the will of her Spouse in every way in which she sees
that she can give Him pleasure. His Majesty, Who will know quite well
if this is the case, is pleased with the soul, so He grants her this mercy,
desiring that she shall get to know Him better, and that, as we may say,
they shall meet together,[2] and He shall unite her with Himself. We can
compare this kind of union to a short meeting of that nature because
it is over in the very shortest time. All giving and taking have now
come to an end, and in a secret way the soul sees Who this Spouse is
that she is to take.[3] By means of the senses and faculties, she could not
understand in a thousand years what she understands in this way in
the briefest space of time. But the Spouse, being Who He is, leaves her,
after that one visit, worthier to join hands (as people say) with Him;
and the soul becomes so fired with love that for her part she does her
utmost not to thwart this Divine betrothal. If she is neglectful, however, and sets her affection on anything other than Himself, she loses
everything, and that is a loss every bit as great as are the favors He has
been granting her, which are far greater than it is possible to convey.

So, Christian souls, whom the Lord has brought to this point on
your journey, I beseech you, for His sake, not to be negligent, but to
withdraw from occasions of sin—for even in this state the soul is not
strong enough to be able to run into them safely, as it is after the
betrothal has been made—that is to say, in the Mansion that we shall
describe after this one. For this communication has been no more
than (as we might say) one single, short meeting,[4] and the devil will
take great pains about combating it and will try to hinder the betrothal. Afterwards, when he sees that the soul is completely surrendered to
the Spouse, he dare not do this, for he is afraid of such a soul as that,
and he knows by experience that if he attempts anything of the kind
he will come out very much the loser and the soul will achieve a corresponding gain.

I tell you, daughters, I have known people of a very high degree of
spirituality who have reached this state, and whom, notwithstanding,
the devil, with great subtlety and craft, has won back to himself. For
this purpose he will marshal all the powers of hell, for, as I have often
said, if he wins a single soul in this way he will win a whole multitude.
The devil has much experience in this matter. If we consider what a
large number of people God can draw to Himself through the agency
of a single soul, the thought of the thousands converted by the

martyrs gives us great cause for praising God. Think of a maiden like Saint Ursula. And of the souls whom the devil must have lost through Saint Dominic and Saint Francis and other founders of Orders, and is losing now through Father Ignatius, who founded the Company[5]—all of whom, of course, as we read, received such favors from God! What did they do but endeavor that this Divine betrothal should not be frustrated through their fault? Oh, my daughters, how ready this Lord still is to grant us favors, just as He was then! In some ways it is even more necessary that we should wish to receive them, for there are fewer than there used to be who think of the Lord's honor! We are so very fond of ourselves and so very careful not to lose any of our rights! Oh, what a great mistake we make! May the Lord in His mercy give us light lest we fall into such darkness.

There are two things about which you may ask me, or be in doubt. The first is this: If the soul is so completely at one with the will of God, as has been said, how can it be deceived, since it never desires to follow its own will? The second: By what avenues can the devil enter and lead you into such peril that your soul may be lost, when you are so completely withdrawn from the world and so often approach the Sacraments? For you are enjoying the companionship, as we might say, of angels, since, by the goodness of the Lord, you have none of you any other desires than to serve and please Him in everything. It would not be surprising, you might add, if this should happen to those who are immersed in the cares of the world. I agree that you are justified in asking this—God has been abundantly merciful to us. But when I read, as I have said, that Judas enjoyed the companionship of the Apostles, had continual intercourse with God Himself, and could listen to His own words, I realize that even this does not guarantee our safety.

To the first question, my reply would be that, if this soul invariably followed the will of God, it is clear that it would not be lost But the devil comes with his artful wiles, and, under color of doing good, sets about undermining it in trivial ways, and involving it in practices that, so he gives it to understand, are not wrong; little by little he darkens its understanding, and weakens its will, and causes its self-love to increase, until in one way and another he begins to withdraw it from the love of God and to persuade it to indulge its own wishes. And this is also an answer to the second question, for there is no enclosure so strictly guarded that he cannot enter it, and no desert so solitary that he cannot visit it. And I would make one further remark—namely, that the reason the Lord permits this may possibly be so that He may observe the behavior of the soul that He wishes to set up as a light to others; for, if it is going to be a failure, it is better that it should be so at the outset than when it can do many souls harm.

What we should be most diligent about, I think, is this. First, we must continually ask God in our prayers to keep us in His hand, and bear constantly in mind that, if He leaves us, we shall at once be down in the depths, as indeed we shall. So we must never have any confidence in ourselves—that would simply be folly. But most of all we must walk with special care and attention, and watch what progress we make in the virtues, and discover if, in any way, we are either improving or going back, especially in our love for each other and in our desire to be thought least of, and in ordinary things; for if we look to this, and beg the Lord to give us light, we shall at once discern whether we have gained or lost. Do not suppose, then, that when God brings a soul to such a point He lets it go so quickly out of His hand that the devil can recapture it without much labor. His Majesty is so anxious for it not to be lost that He gives it a thousand interior warnings of many kinds, and thus it cannot fail to perceive the danger.

Let the conclusion of the whole matter be this. We must strive all the time to advance, and, if we are not advancing, we must cherish serious misgivings, as the devil is undoubtedly anxious to exercise his wiles upon us. For it is unthinkable that a soul that has arrived so far should cease to grow: love is never idle, so failure to advance would be a very bad sign. A soul that has once set out to be the bride of God Himself, and has already had converse with His Majesty and reached the point that has been described, must not lie down and go to sleep again. And so that you may see, daughters, how Our Lord treats those whom He makes His brides, let us begin to discuss the sixth Mansions, and you will see how slight is all the service we can render Him, all the suffering we can undergo for Him, and all the preparation we can make for such great favors. It may have been by Our Lord's ordinance that I was commanded to write this so that we shall forget our trivial earthly pleasures when we fix our eyes on the reward and see how boundless is the mercy that makes Him pleased to communicate and reveal Himself in this way to us worms. So, fired by love of Him, we shall run our race, with our eyes fixed upon His greatness.

May He be pleased to enable me to explain something of these difficult things, which I know will be impossible unless His Majesty and the Holy Spirit[6] guide my pen. Were it not to be for your profit I should beseech Him to prevent me from explaining any of it, for His Majesty knows that, so far as I myself can judge, my sole desire is that His name should be praised, and that we should make every effort to serve a Lord Who gives us such a reward here below, and thus conveys to us some idea of what He will give us in Heaven, without the delays and trials and perils incident to this sea of tempests. For, were it not that we might lose Him and offend Him, it would be a comfort if our life did not end until the end of the world, so that we could work for so great a God and Lord and Spouse. May it please His Majesty that we be worthy to do Him some service, unmarred by the many faults that we always commit, even in doing our good works! Amen.

Exploring the Interior Castle

- Why does Teresa warn her readers so often of the dangers of being negligent in the quest for holiness? Are these dangers real? Does she overemphasize them? Is she speaking from her own experience? What do you think is the greatest danger to making progress in the spiritual life?

- Do you like Teresa's use of the betrothal/marriage metaphor? Does it reveal anything new to you? Does it obscure anything? How does it differ from the metaphor of the silkworm? Do these metaphors conflict in any way? Do they complement each other? Which do you prefer?

- Is the notion of a pre-betrothal meeting too foreign to be helpful for you? Does Teresa's extended use of the betrothal/ marriage metaphor to explain the relationship between the prayer of union, spiritual betrothal, and spiritual marriage make sense for you? Does it resonate with you? Can you think of another metaphor that might do a better job for modern readers?

- Is Teresa consistent throughout her presentation of the prayer of union? Is there anything in it that you have failed to grasp? Have you found any apparent contradictions? Is there anything on which you would have liked more clarity? If you had to describe the prayer of union in a few brief paragraphs, what would you say?

Sixth Mansions

✛

Introduction

T eresa devotes eleven chapters to the sixth mansions, by far the longest and most developed section in the entire treatise. In them, she examines the prayer of spiritual betrothal, the mystical state that flows directly from the prayer of union. This stage of the soul's inner journey has a lot to do with rarefied mystical experiences such as locutions, visions (both intellectual and imaginative), and raptures.

To understand the role of these experiences in Teresa's overall teaching, we must remember how she sets out to explain the various stages of prayer associated with the seven mansions of the interior castle. In the first three mansions, she deals with the beginning stages of prayer and the ascetical life, where vocal prayer, meditation, and acquired recollection are the most common forms of prayer. From the fourth mansions on, she describes the various states of mystical prayer. In these stages of prayer, Teresa sees an ever-deepening presence in the soul of the penetrating light of the Holy Spirit. In the infused recollection of the fourth mansions, this divine light penetrates the understanding. In the prayer of quiet (also of the fourth mansions), it penetrates the will. In the prayer of union of the fifth mansions, it penetrates the interior senses of memory and imagination. Now in the state of spiritual betrothal of the sixth mansions, it takes hold of the exterior senses and gives the person the experience of mystical ecstasy, of being "outside of one's senses." Her presentation of the mystical life is thus a process whereby the Holy Spirit gradually takes over more and more of the soul's inner recesses and eventually has measurable (albeit fleeting) effects on the bodily senses.

When seen in this light, the mystical experiences themselves are not important in the state of spiritual betrothal, but only that Spirit is deepening his penetration of the soul. The experiences themselves are nothing more than effects of this ever-deepening penetration and should be understood and appreciated as such. Teresa advises her readers that these experiences are gifts of God and cannot be obtained through human effort. They are not to be actively sought out and should not be the primary focus of one's prayer. God alone must be the sole object of one's prayer. Teresa's presentation of the mystical life, moreover, is extremely Christ-centered. She asserts that contemplating the mysteries of Christ with a simple penetrating gaze will enable a person to grow in humility and self-knowledge and lead to the most sublime state of prayer. She also asserts that those who consciously try to forget about Christ will fail to make further progress into the heart of the soul's interior castle.

Chapter One

✜

Introduction

In this chapter, Teresa tells her readers of the many trials the soul in the sixth mansions must undergo. Deeply wounded by its love for the beloved, it wants nothing but solitude and seeks to remove itself from anything that will take it away. The soul yearns for its beloved and looks forward to the conclusion of its betrothal. Before it can enter the seventh mansion, however, it must bear many trials and will be able to endure them only by virtue of the courage it gains from its nearness to its beloved. Teresa thinks her readers will benefit from a presentation of what these trials might be and writes them down not in the order of their occurrence, but as they come to her mind.

These trials are of both an exterior and interior nature. She begins with the least important: those in the sixth mansions will suffer from the criticism of others. Many people, even those considered close friends, will level grave accusations against them and talk as though they are going to lose their souls. Since such criticisms will likely last for the rest of their lives, those in the sixth mansions must know how to deal with them. Again referring to herself through a veiled reference, she says she knows someone who was criticized so much that she was afraid she would not be able to find anyone to hear her confession.

Next, there are trials of praise. These are even worse than those of criticism, because those in the sixth mansions understand their poverty before God and find it very painful to hear others heaping undeserved praise on them. In the beginning, such praise is almost unbearable. As time goes on, however, it gets easier to endure. One begins, for example, to see that some people will praise others just as readily as they will criticize them. One also gradually receives a deeper insight into God as the source of all that is good and responds to such praise with even greater praise to God for his great gifts. One also may see that the praise one receives from others may be of help to them and may itself be pleasing to God. Finally, the soul comes to value God's honor and glory so much that it is able to see things in their proper perspective and is no longer bothered by the praise of others. Its only concern is to live for God's glory and praise. Even though a person may find the praises of others easier to bear as time goes on, Teresa insists that they are immeasurably more difficult than dealing with the criticism of others. In fact, once someone in the sixth mansions learns to cope with the praises of others, he or she will care very little about their negative comments.

Next, Teresa says those in the sixth mansions are often given serious illnesses to bear, which are often acute and last for long periods of time, perhaps even for a lifetime. Such illnesses can be very difficult to endure, because they give the person intense pain both interior and exterior. In yet another veiled reference to herself, she says she knows someone who was given a grave illness some forty years ago and has not been a day without pain ever since. Difficult and painful as they are, such illnesses, she claims, give the soul the opportunity to embrace the suffering of the cross in imitation of Christ.

Next, she tells her readers that internal suffering is much more intense and difficult to bear than external sufferings. Although she readily admits that internal suffering is very difficult to describe, she gives her readers some examples of the kinds of things to expect. There are, for example, overly cautious confessors, whose lack of experience causes them to condemn those who have arrived at the sixth mansions because they display some small imperfections. Such confessors torture these souls by forcing them to second-guess their experiences and to strive for a state of angelic purity that is simply beyond their grasp. They are even more difficult to bear when those in the sixth mansions find themselves in a state of spiritual aridity, when God seems very far away from them and they do not have the support of learned and experienced guides in the spiritual life.

Teresa likens the torments such souls suffer at the hands of inexperienced confessors to the pains of hell. In another veiled reference to herself, she tells of an experience of sharing her difficulties with one such confessor, who ended up making matters much worse for her. By enduring such pain, Teresa believes that the soul begins to recognize its utter powerlessness before God. In the end, she claims, all one can do is call upon God's mercy. God is capable of righting even the most difficult situations and, in a single moment, can bring clarity and insight out of the most darkened confusion. From such trying situations, he wants the soul to learn not only of his great power, but also of its smallness before him.

As she draws the first chapter to a close, Teresa says that other trials exist, but are less serious and do not occur often enough to warrant saying anything about them. She then briefly prepares her readers for the next chapter, which deals with favors granted by the Lord that trouble the soul internally before its entrance into the seventh mansion.

✢

Text

Shows how, when the Lord begins to grant the soul greater favors, it has also to endure greater trials. Enumerates some of these and describes how those who are in this Mansion must conduct themselves. This is a good chapter for any that suffer interior trials.

L et us now, with the help of the Holy Spirit, come to speak of the sixth Mansions, in which the soul has been wounded with love for the Spouse and seeks more opportunity of being alone, trying, so far as is possible to one in its state, to renounce everything that can disturb it in this its solitude. That sight of Him that it has had is so deeply impressed upon it that its whole desire is to enjoy it once more. Nothing, I must repeat, is seen in this state of prayer that can be said to be really seen, even by the imagination; I use the word "sight" because of the comparison I made.

The soul is now completely determined to take no other spouse; but the Spouse disregards its yearnings for the conclusion of the Betrothal, desiring that they should become still deeper and that this greatest of all blessings should be won by the soul at some cost to itself. And although everything is of but slight importance by comparison with the greatness of this gain, I assure you, daughters, that, if the soul is to bear its trials, it has no less need of the sign and token of this gain that it now holds. Oh, my God, how great are these trials, which the soul will suffer, both within and without, before it enters the seventh Mansion![1] Really, when I think of them, I am sometimes afraid that, if we realized their intensity beforehand, it would be most difficult for us, naturally weak as we are, to muster determination enough to enable us to suffer them or resolution enough for enduring them, however attractively the advantage of so doing might be presented to us, until we reached the seventh Mansion, where there is nothing more to be feared, and the soul will plunge deep into suffering for God's sake. The reason for this is that the soul is almost continuously near His Majesty, and its nearness brings it fortitude. I think it will be well if I tell you about some of the things that I know are certain to happen here. Not all souls, perhaps, will be led along this path, though I doubt very much if souls that from time to time really taste the things of Heaven can live in freedom from earthly trials, in one way or in another.

Although I had not intended to treat of this, it has occurred to me that some soul finding itself in this state might be very much comforted if it knew what happens to those whom God grants such favors, at a time when everything really seems to be lost I shall not take these experiences in the order in which they happen, but as each one presents itself to my memory. I will begin with the least of them. An outcry is made by people with whom such a person is acquainted, and even by those with whom she is not acquainted and who she never in her life supposed would think about her at all. "How holy she's getting!" they exclaim, or "She's only going to these extremes to deceive the world and to make other people look sinful, when really they are better Christians than she is without any of these goings-on!" (Notice, by the way, that she is not really indulging in any "goings-on" at all: she is only trying to live up to her profession.) Then people whom she had thought her friends abandon, her and it is they who say the worst things of all and express the deepest regret that (as they put it) she is "going to perdition" and "obviously being deluded," that "this is the devil's work," that "she's going the way of So-and-so and So-and-so, who ruined their own lives and dragged good people down with them," and that "she takes in all her confessors." And they actually go to her confessors and tell them so, illustrating what they say by stories of some who ruined their lives in this way: and they scoff at the poor creature and talk about her like this times without number.

I know of a person[2] to whom these things were happening and who was terribly afraid that there would be nobody willing to hear her confession; but there is so much I could say about that that I will not stop to tell it here. The worst of it is, these things are not soon over—they last all one's life long. People warn each other to be careful not to have anything to do with persons like oneself. You will tell me that there are also those who speak well of one. But oh, daughters, how few there are who believe the good things they say by comparison with the many who dislike us! In any case, to be well spoken of is only one trial more and a worse one than those already mentioned. For the soul sees quite clearly that if there is any good in it, this is a gift of God, and not in the least due to itself, for only a short time previously it saw itself in dire poverty and plunged deep into sin. So this praise is an intolerable torment to it, at least at the beginning: afterward it is less so, and this for various reasons. The first of these is that experience shows it clearly how people will speak well of others as readily as ill, and so it takes no more notice of the former class than of the latter. The second, that the Lord has given it greater light and shown it that anything good it may have does not come from itself, but is His Majesty's gift; so it breaks into praises of God, but as though He were being gracious to a third person, and forgetting that it is itself concerned at all. The third reason is that, having seen others helped by observing the favors that God is granting it, the soul thinks that His Majesty has been pleased for them to think of it as good, though in fact it is not, so that they may be profited. The fourth is that, as the soul now prizes the honor and glory of God more than its own honor and glory, it no longer suffers from a temptation that beset it at first—namely, to think that these praises will do it harm, as it has seen them do to others. It cares little about being dishonored itself, provided that it can be the cause of God's being even once praised—come afterward what may.

These and other considerations mitigate the great distress caused by such praises, although some distress is nearly always felt, except when a soul takes no notice of such things whatsoever. But to find itself publicly and unmeritedly described as good is an incomparably greater trial than any of those already mentioned. Once the soul has learned to care little about this, it cares very much less about the other, which, indeed, makes it rejoice and sounds to it like sweetest music. This is absolutely true. The soul is fortified rather than daunted by censure, for experience has shown how great are the benefits it can bring, and it seems to the soul that its persecutors are not offending God, but that His Majesty is permitting this for its great advantage. Being quite clear about this, it conceives a special and most tender love for them and thinks of them as truer friends and greater benefactors than those who speak well of it.

The Lord is also in the habit of sending the most grievous infirmities. This is a much greater trial, especially if the pains are severe; in some ways, when they are very acute, I think they are the greatest earthly trial that exists—the greatest of exterior trials, I mean—however many a soul may suffer: I repeat that it is only to very acute pains that I am referring. For they affect the soul both outwardly and inwardly, till it becomes so much oppressed as not to know what to do with itself, and would much rather suffer any martyrdom than these pains. Still, at the very worst, they do not last so long—no longer, as a rule, than other bad illnesses do. For, after all, God gives us no more than we can bear, and He gives patience first.

I know a person of whom, since the Lord began to grant her this favor aforementioned, forty years ago,[3] it cannot be truly said that she has been a day without pains and other kinds of suffering; I mean because of her poor physical health, to say nothing of other great trials. It is true that she had been very wicked and it was all very slight by comparison with the hell that she had merited. Others, who have not so greatly offended Our Lord, will be led by Him along another way, but I should always choose the way of suffering, if only to imitate Our Lord Jesus Christ, and even were there no other special benefit to be obtained from it—and there are always a great many. But oh, when we come to interior sufferings! If these could be described they would make all physical sufferings seem very slight, but it is impossible to describe interior sufferings and how they happen.

Let us begin with the torture that it costs us to have to do with a confessor so scrupulous and inexperienced that he thinks nothing safe: he is afraid of everything, and doubtful about everything, as soon as he sees that he is dealing with anything out of the ordinary. This is particularly so if he sees any imperfection in the soul that is undergoing these experiences. He thinks that people to whom God grants these favors must be angels; and, as this is impossible while they are in the body, he attributes the whole thing to melancholy or to the devil. The world is so full of melancholy that this certainly does not surprise me;

for there is so much abroad just now, and the devil makes so much use of it to work harm, that confessors have very good cause to be afraid of it and to watch for it very carefully. But, when the poor soul, harassed by the same fear, goes to the confessor as to a judge, and he condemns her, she cannot fail to be upset and tortured by what he says—and only a person who has passed through such a trial will know how great it is. For this is another of the great trials suffered by these souls, especially if they have been wicked—namely, to think that because of their sins God will permit them to be deceived—and although, when His Majesty grants them this favor, they feel secure and cannot believe that it comes from any other spirit than a spirit of God, yet, as it is a state which passes quickly, and the soul is ever mindful of its sins, and it sees faults in itself—for these are never lacking—it then begins to suffer this torture. When the confessor reassures the soul, it becomes calm, though in due course it gets troubled again; but when all he can do is to make it still more fearful the thing grows almost intolerable, especially when on top of everything else come periods of aridity, during which the soul feels as if it has never known God and never will know Him, and as if to hear His Majesty spoken of is like hearing of a person from a great distance away.

All this would be nothing to the person concerned were it not followed immediately by the thought that she cannot be describing her case properly to her confessor and has been deceiving him; and, although when she thinks about it she feels sure she has not kept back even the first movement of her mind, it is of no use. For her understanding is so dim that it is incapable of seeing the truth, but believes what the imagination (now mistress of the understanding) presents to it and the nonsense that the devil attempts to present to it, when Our Lord gives him leave to test her soul, and even to make her think herself cast off by God. For there are many things that assault her soul with an interior oppression so keenly felt and so intolerable that I do not know to what it can be compared, save to the torment of those who suffer in hell, for in this spiritual tempest no consolation is possible.

If she decides to take up the matter with her confessor, it would look as if the devils have come to his aid so that he may torture her soul the more. A certain confessor, dealing with a person who had been in this state of torment, after it had passed away, thought that the oppression must have been of a dangerous type, since it had involved her in so many trials; so he told her, whenever she was in this state, to report to him; but this made her so much worse that he came to realize that he could no longer do anything with her. For, although she was quite able to read, she found that, if she took up a book written in the vernacular, she could understand no more of it than if she had not known her alphabet; her understanding was not capable of taking it in.

Briefly, in this tempest, there is no help for it but to wait upon the mercy of God, Who suddenly, at the most unlooked-for hour, with a single word, or on some chance occasion, lifts the whole of this burden from the soul, so that it seems as if it has never been clouded over, but is full of sunshine and far happier than it was before. Then, like one who has escaped from a perilous battle and gained the victory, the soul keeps praising Our Lord, for it is He Who has fought and enabled it to conquer. It knows very well that it did not itself do the fighting. For it saw that all the weapons with which it could defend itself were in the hands of its enemy, and was thus clearly aware of its misery and realized how little we can do of ourselves if the Lord should forsake us.

We have no need of reflection to enable us to understand this, for the soul's experience of enduring it, and of having found itself completely powerless, has made it realize that it is utterly helpless and that we are but miserable creatures. For, though it cannot be devoid of grace, since despite all this torment it does not offend God, and would not do so for anything upon earth, yet this grace is buried so deeply that the soul seems not to feel the smallest spark of any love for God, nor has it ever done so. If it has done anything good, or His Majesty has granted it any favor, the whole thing seems to it like a dream or a fancy: all it knows for certain is that it has sinned.

Oh, Jesus! How sad it is to see a soul thus forsaken, and how little, as I have said, can it gain from any earthly consolation! So do not suppose, sisters, if you ever find yourselves in this condition, that people who are wealthy, or free to do as they like, have any better remedy for such times. No, no; to offer them earthly consolations would be like telling criminals condemned to death about all the joys that there are in the world; not only would this fail to comfort them—it would but increase their torment; comfort must come to them from above, for earthly things are of no value to them any more. This great God desires us to know that He is a King and we are miserable creatures—a point of great importance for what follows.

Now what will a poor creature like that do if such a thing goes on for a very long time?[4] If she prays, she might as well not be doing so at all—I mean for all the comfort it will bring her, for interiorly she is incapable of receiving any comfort, nor, even when her prayer is vocal, can she understand what she is saying; while mental prayer at such a time is certainly impossible—her faculties are not capable of it. Solitude is still worse for her, though it is also torture for her to be in anyone's company or to be spoken to; and so, despite all her efforts to conceal the fact, she becomes outwardly upset and despondent, to a very noticeable extent. Is it credible that she will be able to say what is the matter with her? The thing is inexpressible, for this distress and oppression are spiritual troubles and cannot be given a name. The best medicine—I do not say for removing the trouble, for I know of none for that, but for enabling the soul to endure it—is to occupy oneself with external affairs and works of charity and to hope in God's mercy, which never fails those who hope in Him. May He be blessed forever. Amen.[5]

Other trials caused by devils, which are of an exterior kind, will not occur so commonly, and thus there is no reason to speak of them, nor are they anything so grievous. For, whatever these devils do, they cannot, in my opinion, go so far as to inhibit the working of the faculties or to disturb the soul, in the way already described. After all, it thinks (and rightly), they cannot do more than the Lord permits, and, so long as it is not lost, nothing matters much by comparison with what has been described above.

We shall next deal with other interior troubles that occur in these Mansions, treating of the different kinds of prayer and favors of the Lord; for, although a few are still harder to bear than those referred to, as will be seen by the effects that they leave upon the body, they do not merit the name of trial, nor is it right that we should give them that name, since they are such great favors of the Lord and the soul understands them to be so, and far beyond its deservings. This severe distress comes just before the soul's entrance into the seventh Mansion, together with many more, only a few of which I shall describe, as it would be impossible to speak of them all, or even to explain their nature. For they are of another type than those already mentioned, and a much higher one; and if, in dealing with those of a lower kind, I have not been able to explain myself in greater detail, still less shall I be able to explain these others. The Lord give me His help in everything I do, through the merits of His Son. Amen.

Exploring the Interior Castle

- Do you love solitude? If so, do you actively seek it out? Have you ever felt so drawn to God that all you want is to be alone with him? Why is solitude so necessary for the spiritual life? Is it possible to maintain solitude of heart in the midst of one's daily activities? If so, how is it done?

- How do you deal with the criticism of others? Does it bother you when you hear it? Does it make you angry? Hurt? Depressed? Do you ignore it? Does it change your behavior? Why does Teresa say that bearing with the criticism of others is a trial for those in the sixth mansions? What danger or threat do they pose?

- How do you deal with the praise of others? Does it make you feel good? Do you seek it out? Do you accept it gracefully? Do you question it? Do you give God credit for it? What dangers does the praise of others present to those in search of an intimate relationship with God? Do you agree with the way Teresa presents these dangers?

- Have you ever had difficulty with an overly scrupulous confessor or spiritual guide? If so, what was the nature of the difficulty? Did he or she place unreal expectations on you? Did he or she listen to you carefully? How did you deal with the situation? Do you think the role of confessor or spiritual guide has changed much since the time of Teresa? If so, how would you describe the change?

Chapter Two

✛

Introduction

In this chapter, Teresa speaks of the various ways in which the Lord enlivens the soul of his beloved. She says that all previous trials were a means of preparation for helping the soul to live in even deeper intimacy with the divine. She admits her difficulty in describing these next experiences, since they come from deep within the heart and are so sensitive and elusive. She also says that it is very difficult for her to find a fitting image or metaphor to help her readers understand.

For Teresa, there is no earthly comparison to describe what the Lord is doing in the soul of his beloved. At times, he rushes in without warning, even when the person is not thinking of him. At such moments, the soul is shaken and experiences a pleasurable wound deep within its core. This delectable pain is more satisfying than the silent absorption it feels in the prayer of quiet. Teresa says she has no way of adequately describing this experience. All she can say is that the soul is certain the Lord is calling it to enter the seventh mansion and be at his side.

This ravishing wound comes not from the senses, the imagination, or the faculties, but directly from the Lord from deep within the soul. The feeling is something like having one's bowels pierced by an arrow and having one's guts come out with it when it is removed. This pain lasts for varying intervals of time. She uses the image of a lighted torch that heats up the soul and kindles within it a burning spark. The soul feels the heat of this spark but not long enough to be set ablaze. The experience, she asserts, is too deep and real to be a product of fancy or melancholy. Nor is it brought on by the evil one, since he is not capable of causing something that is at one and the same time both pleasing and painful. It comes, moreover, from a place within the soul over which he has no jurisdiction and gives the soul something he would not think of giving, a deep determination to embrace the cross of suffering and endure many trials out of love for God.

Teresa concludes the chapter by humbly admitting that she might be mistaken about the experiences she has described. She refuses to change her opinion, however, until she hears convincing arguments from learned counselors that prove otherwise. She says that she knows someone (herself, one presumes) who was terribly afraid of being deceived in these experiences. She maintains that these experiences grant certitude to the soul by their very nature and that to doubt them would itself be a sign of their falsehood. She also admits that the Lord uses other means of enlivening the soul and tells her readers that they have nothing to fear, if they have had the good fortune to receive the favors from God she has just described. If they find themselves in such a state, they should simply accept it as a gift of the Lord and give him thanks.

✢

Text

Treats of several ways in which Our Lord awakens the soul; there appears to be nothing in these to be feared, although the experience is most sublime and the favors are great ones.

We seem to have left the little dove a long way behind, but we have not done so in reality, for these very trials enable it to make a higher flight. So let us now begin to treat of the way in which the Spouse deals with it, and see how, before it is wholly one with Him, He fills it with fervent desire, by means so delicate that the soul itself does not understand them, nor do I think I shall succeed in describing them in such a way as to be understood, except by those who have experienced it; for these are influences so delicate and subtle that they proceed from the very depth of the heart and I know no comparison that I can make that will fit the case.

All this is very different from what one can achieve in earthly matters, and even from the consolations that have been described. For often when a person is quite unprepared for such a thing, and is not even thinking of God, he is awakened by His Majesty, as though by a rushing comet or a thunderclap. Although no sound is heard,[1] the soul is very well aware that it has been called by God, so much so that sometimes, especially at first, it begins to tremble and complain, though it feels nothing that causes it affliction. It is conscious of having been most delectably wounded, but cannot say how or by whom; but it is certain that this is a precious experience and it would be glad if it were never to be healed of that wound. It complains to its Spouse with words of love, and even cries aloud, being unable to help itself, for it realizes that He is present but will not manifest Himself in such a way as to allow it to enjoy Him, and this is a great grief, though a sweet and delectable one; even if it should desire not to suffer it, it would have no choice—but in any case it never would so desire. It is much more satisfying to a soul than is the delectable absorption, devoid of distress, which occurs in the Prayer of Quiet.

I am straining every nerve,[2] sisters, to explain to you this operation of love, yet I do not know any way of doing so. For it seems a contradiction to say that the Beloved is making it very clear that He is with the soul and seems to be giving it such a clear sign that He is calling it that it cannot doubt the fact, and that the call is so penetrating that it cannot fail to hear Him. For the Spouse, Who is in the seventh Mansion, seems to be calling the soul in a way that involves no clear utterance of speech, and none of the inhabitants of the other Mansions—the senses, the imagination, or the faculties—dares to stir. Oh, my powerful God, how great are Thy secrets, and how different are spiritual things from any that can be seen or understood here below. There is no way of describing this favor, small though it is by comparison with the signal favors that souls are granted by Thee.

So powerful is the effect of this upon the soul that it becomes consumed with desire, yet cannot think what to ask, so clearly conscious is it of the presence of its God. Now, if this is so, you will ask me what it desires or what causes it distress. What greater blessing can it wish for? I cannot say; I know that this distress seems to penetrate to its very bowels; and that, when He that has wounded it draws out the arrow, the bowels seem to come with it, so deeply does it feel this love. I have just been wondering if my God could be described as the fire in a lighted brazier, from which some spark will fly out and touch the soul, in such a way that it will be able to feel the burning heat of the fire; but, as the fire is not hot enough to burn it up, and the experience is very delectable, the soul continues to feel that pain and the mere touch suffices to produce that effect in it. This seems the best comparison that I have been able to find, for this delectable pain, which is not really pain, is not continuous: sometimes it lasts for a long time, while sometimes it comes suddenly to an end, according to the way in which the Lord is pleased to bestow it, for it is a thing that no human means can procure. Although occasionally the experience lasts for a certain length of time, it goes and comes again; it is, in short, never permanent, and for that reason it never completely enkindles the soul; for, just as the soul is about to become enkindled, the spark dies, and leaves the soul yearning once again to suffer that loving pain of which it is the cause.

It cannot for a moment be supposed that this is a phenomenon that has its source in the physical nature, or that it is caused by melancholy, or that it is a deception of the devil, or a mere fancy. It is perfectly clear that it is a movement of which the source is the Lord, Who is unchangeable; and its effects are not like those of other devotions whose genuineness we doubt because of the intense absorption of the joy that we experience. Here all the senses and faculties are active, and there is no absorption; they are on the alert to discover what can be happening, and, so far as I can see, they cause no disturbance, and can neither increase this delectable pain nor remove it. Anyone to whom Our Lord has granted this favor will recognize the fact on reading this; he must give Him most heartfelt thanks and must not fear that it may be deception; let his chief fear be rather lest he show ingratitude for so great a favor, and let him endeavor to serve God and to grow better all his life long and he will see the result of this and find himself receiving more and more. One person who was granted this favor spent several years in the enjoyment of it and so completely did it satisfy her that, if she had served the Lord for very many years by suffering great trials, she would have felt well rewarded. May He be blessed forever and ever. Amen.

It may be that you wonder why greater security can be felt about this than about other things. For the following reasons, I think. First, because so delectable a pain can never be bestowed upon the soul by the devil: he can give pleasures and delights which seem to be spiritual, but it is beyond his power to unite pain—and such a great pain!—with tranquility and joy in the soul; for all his powers are in the external sphere, and, when he causes pain, it is never, to my mind, delectable or peaceful, but restless and combative. Secondly, this delectable tempest comes from another region than those over which he has authority. Thirdly, great advantages accrue to the soul, which, as a general rule, becomes filled with a determination to suffer for God's sake and to desire to have many trials to endure, and to be very much more resolute in withdrawing from the pleasures and intercourse of this world, and other things like them.

That this is no fancy is very evident; on other occasions the devil may create fancies of the kind, but he will never be able to counterfeit this. It is so wonderful a thing that it cannot possibly be created by the fancy (I mean, one cannot think it is there when it is not) nor can the soul doubt that it is there; if any doubt about it remains—I mean, if the soul doubts whether or not it has experienced it—it can be sure that the impulses are not genuine, for we perceive it as clearly as we hear a loud voice with our ears. Nor is there any possible way in which it can be due to melancholy, for the fancies created by melancholy exist only in the imagination, whereas this proceeds from the interior of the soul. I may conceivably be mistaken; but, until I hear arguments to the contrary from someone who understands the matter, I shall always be of this opinion; I know, for example, of a person who was terribly afraid of being deceived in this way, and yet who never had any fears about this kind of prayer.

Our Lord, too, has other methods of awakening the soul. Quite unexpectedly, when engaged in vocal prayer and not thinking of interior things, it seems, in some wonderful way, to catch fire. It is just as though there suddenly assailed it a fragrance so powerful that it diffused itself through all the senses or something of that kind (I do not say it is a fragrance; I merely make the comparison) in order to convey to it the consciousness that the Spouse is there. The soul is moved by a delectable desire to enjoy Him, and this disposes it to make many acts and to sing praises to Our Lord. The source of this favor is that already referred to; but there is nothing here that causes pain, nor are the soul's desires to enjoy God in any way painful. This is what is most usually felt by the soul. For several of the reasons already alleged, I do

176 ÷ Interior Castle

not think there is much reason here for fear; one must endeavor to receive this favor and give thanks for it.

Exploring the Interior Castle

- Have you ever experienced something that was at one and the same time both pleasurable and painful? If so, how else would you describe it? Do any particular images or metaphors come to mind?

- What does Teresa mean when she says that the experience of delectable pain comes not from the senses, imagination, or faculties, but directly from God from deep within the soul? Do you believe that God can communicate with a soul in this way? Have you ever felt this way yourself?

- Have you ever been so certain of something that you did not even entertain the possibility of its being untrue? If so, where did this certainty come from? Is it possible to be certain of something and afraid of being mistaken about it at the same time?

- Teresa repeatedly says that she finds this mystical state difficult to describe, yet eventually comes up with images or metaphors to convey that experience. What, in your opinion, is the relationship between a mystical experience and the language used to express it? How great is the gap between word and experience? Is it possible to have one without the other?

Chapter Three

✣

Introduction

In this chapter, Teresa describes another way that God speaks to someone in the state of spiritual betrothal. It is not uncommon for such a person to receive direct messages from God, experienced through one's ears, imagination, or spirit (intellect). Although God can speak to a person as he pleases, care should be taken to determine the authenticity of these locutions, especially since they could simply be the work of one's fancy, a product of melancholy, or the work of the evil one. In these last-mentioned cases, Teresa tells her readers that the best thing to do is not to make these people anxious or upset, but to calm them down, get them to spend less time in prayer, and help them to focus their attention elsewhere. She reminds her readers that, if care is not taken, the evil one can mislead such people and cause them to do great damage to themselves and others.

Teresa offers a number of guidelines for discerning whether the locutions come from the Lord. For example, one should not pay any attention to what one has heard unless it conforms strictly to what the Lord has revealed in the Scriptures. Regardless of whether the Lord speaks to the soul from without (through one's ears), from within (through one's imagination), or from above (through one's spirit or intellect), authentic locutions from God possess power and authority in themselves, give peace to the soul, remain in one's memory for quite some time, and eventually come true. They will remain with a person in the midst of great turmoil, even when trusted counselors implore them to pay no attention to them.

These signs of discernment apply to all three types of authentic locutions. Those that are not from God, however, are mere products of a person's imagination and possess none of these traits. Teresa admits that a person in the spiritual sleep common to the prayer of quiet may sometimes think he or she is experiencing a locution from God in a dream. In such a case, the person has asked something of God out of love and attributes to these dreamlike voices what he or she is hoping to hear. Teresa points out that those with any experience in authentic locutions from God will not be fooled by their imagination in this way.

Teresa goes on to say that those locutions caused by the evil one, who masquerades as an angel of light and is a master of deception, are much more dangerous than those that come from the imagination. For this reason, she tells her readers to submit everything to the judgment of a learned confessor or spiritual guide, even those about which one has certitude of their authenticity. One must put one's confessor in God's place and follow his instructions at all times. She says it is very dangerous for a person to ignore or disregard counsel received from one's confessor or spiritual guide.

As stated earlier, authentic locutions come from without, within, or above. In the final case, the person hears no audible words and receives no impressions through the imagination, but has a direct communication from God in the highest part of the soul. Teresa tells her readers how one can be certain that such a spiritual or intellectual locution has taken place. They possess an uncommon clarity, come unexpectedly, require spiritual listening, contain great depths of meaning, and convey much more than the words themselves.

Locutions from the evil one, by way of contrast, stir confusion and anxiety in the soul. Even though he can appear as an angel of light and is capable of great deception, he cannot produce the effects in the soul of the authentic locutions enumerated above. What is more, authentic locutions give a person a deep sense of one's smallness and sinfulness before God. Teresa concludes by saying that, if God blesses a soul with authentic corporeal, imaginative, or spiritual locutions, one must listen to and act on them. One's sole concern should be to please God by forgetting oneself and doing his will.

✛

Text

Treats of the same subject and describes the way in which, when He is pleased to do so, God speaks to the soul. Gives instructions as to how we should behave in such a case: we must not be guided by our own opinions. Sets down a few signs by which we may know when this favor is, and when it is not, a deception. This chapter is very profitable.

There is another way in which God awakens the soul, and which, although in some respects it seems a greater favor than the others, may also be more perilous. For this reason I will spend a short time in describing it. This awakening of the soul is effected by means of locutions, which are of many kinds.[1] Some of them seem to come from without; others from the innermost depths of the soul; others from its higher part; while others, again, are so completely outside the soul that they can be heard with the ears, and seem to be uttered by a human voice. Sometimes—often, indeed—this may be a fancy, especially in persons who are melancholy—I mean, are affected by real melancholy—or have feeble imaginations.

Of persons of these two kinds no notice should be taken, in my view, even if they say they see or hear or are given to understand things, nor should one upset them by telling them that their experiences come from the devil. One should listen to them as one would to sick persons; and the prioress, or the confessor, or whatever person they confide in, should advise them to pay no heed to the matter, because the service of God does not consist in things like these, over which many have been deceived by the devil, although this may not be so with them. One should humor such people so as not to distress them further. If one tells them they are suffering from melancholy, there will be no end to it. They will simply swear they see and hear things, and really believe that they do.

The real solution is to see that such people have less time for prayer, and also that, as far as is possible, they attach no importance to these fancies. For the devil is apt to take advantage of the infirmity of these souls, to the injury of others, if not to their own as well. Both with infirm and with healthy souls there is invariably cause for misgivings about these things until it becomes clear what kind of spirit is responsible. I believe, too, that it is always better for them to dispense with such things at first, for, if they are of God, dispensing with them will help us all the more to advance, since, when put to the proof in this way, they will tend to increase. Yet the soul should not be allowed to become depressed or disquieted, for it really cannot help itself.

Returning now to what I was saying about locutions, these may come from God, in any of the ways I have mentioned, or they may equally well come from the devil or from one's own imagination. I will describe, if I can, with the Lord's help, the signs by which these locutions differ from one another and when they are dangerous. For there are many people given to prayer who experience them, and I would not have you think you are doing wrong, sisters, whether or not you give them credence, when they are only for your own benefit, to comfort you or to warn you of your faults. In such cases it matters little from whom they proceed or if they are only fancies. But of one thing I will warn you: do not think that, even if your locutions come from God, you will for that reason be any the better. After all, He talked a great deal with the Pharisees: any good you may gain will depend upon how you profit by what you hear. Unless it agrees strictly with the Scriptures, take no more notice of it than you would if it came from the devil himself. The words may, in fact, come only from your weak imagination, but they must be taken as a temptation against things pertaining to the Faith and must therefore invariably be resisted so that they may gradually cease; and cease they will, because they will have little power of their own.

To return, then, to our first point: whether they come from within, from above or from without, has nothing to do with their coming from God. The surest signs that one can have of their doing this are, in my opinion, as follows. The first and truest is the sense of power and authority that they bear with them, both in themselves and in the actions that follow them. I will explain myself further. A soul is experiencing all the interior disturbances and tribulations that have been described, and all the aridity and darkness of the understanding. A single word of this kind—just a "Be not troubled"—is sufficient to calm it. No other word need be spoken; a great light comes to it; and all its trouble is lifted from it, although it had been thinking that, if the whole world, and all the learned men in the world, were to combine to give it reasons for not being troubled, they could not relieve it from its distress, however hard they might strive to do so. Or a soul is distressed because its confessor, and others, have told it that what it has is a spirit sent by the devil, and it is full of fear. Yet that single word that it hears: "It is I, fear not,"[2] takes all its fear from it, and it is most marvelously comforted, and believes that no one will ever be able to make it feel otherwise. Or it is greatly exercised because of some important piece of business and it has no idea how this will turn out. It is then given to understand that it must be, and all will turn out well; and it acquires a new confidence and is no longer troubled. And so with many other things.

The second sign is that a great tranquility dwells in the soul, which becomes peacefully and devoutly recollected, and ready to sing praises to God. Oh, Lord, if there is such power in a word sent by one of Thy messengers (for they say that, in this Mansion, at least, such words are uttered, not by the Lord Himself, but by some angel), what power wilt Thou not leave in the soul that is bound to Thee, as art Thou to it, by love.

The third sign is that these words do not vanish from the memory for a very long time: some, indeed, never vanish at all. Words that we hear on earth—I mean, from men, however weighty and learned they may be—we do not bear so deeply engraved upon our memory, nor, if they refer to the future, do we give credence to them as we do to these locutions. For these last impress us by their complete certainty, in such a way that, although sometimes they seem quite impossible of fulfillment, and we cannot help wondering if they will come true or not, and although our understanding may hesitate about it, yet within the soul itself there is a certainty which cannot be overcome. It may seem to the soul that everything is moving in the contrary direction to what it had been led to expect, and yet, even if many years go by, it never loses its belief that, though God may use other means incomprehensible to men, in the end what He has said will come true; as in fact it does. Nonetheless, as I say, the soul is distressed when it sees things going badly astray. It may be some time since it heard the words; and both their working within it and the certainty that it had at the time that they came from God have passed away. So these doubts arise, and the soul wonders if the whole thing came from the devil, or can have been the work of the imagination. Yet at the time it had no such doubts and it would have died in defense of their veracity. But, as I say, all these imaginings must be put into our minds by the devil in order to distress us and make us fearful, especially if the matter is one in which obeying the locutions will bring others many blessings,

or produce good works tending greatly to the honor and service of
God but presenting considerable difficulties. What will the devil not
do in this case by encouraging such misgivings? At the very least he
will weaken the soul's faith, for it is most harmful not to believe that
God is powerful and can do works that are incomprehensible to our
understanding.

Despite all these conflicts, despite the assertions of some (I refer to
confessors) that these locutions are pure nonsense; and despite all the
unfortunate happenings that may persuade the soul that they cannot
come true, there still remains within it such a living spark of conviction that they will come true (whence this arises I cannot tell) that,
though all other hopes may be dead, this spark of certainty could not
fail to remain alive, even if the soul wished it to die. And in the end,
as I have said, the Lord's word is fulfilled, and the soul is so happy
and glad that it would like to do nothing but praise His Majesty
everlastingly—much more, however, because it has seen His assurances
come true than because of the occurrence itself, even though this may
be of very great consequence to it.

I do not know why it is, but the soul is so anxious for these assurances to be proved true that it would not, I think, feel it so much if it
were itself caught in the act of lying—as though it could do anything
more in the matter than repeat what is said to it! In this connection
a certain person used continually to recall what happened to the
prophet Jonah, when he feared that Nineveh was not to be destroyed.[3]
Of course, as the locutions come from the Spirit of God, it is right that
we should have this trust in Him, and desire that He should never be
thought false, since He is Supreme Truth. Great, therefore, is the joy
of one who, after a thousand vicissitudes and in the most difficult circumstances, sees His word come true; such a person may himself have
to suffer great trials on that account, but he would rather do this than
that what he holds the Lord most certainly told him should not come
to pass. Not everybody, perhaps, will have this weakness—if weakness
it is, for I cannot myself condemn it as wrong.

If the locutions come from the imagination, none of these signs
occur, nor is there any certainty or peace or interior consolation. It
might, however, happen (and I even know of a few people to whom it
has happened) that, when a person is deeply absorbed in the Prayer of
Quiet and in spiritual sleep (for some, because of the weakness of their
constitution, or of their imagination, or for some other reason, are so

entirely carried out of themselves in this act of deep recollection, that they are unconscious of everything external, and all their senses are in such a state of slumber that they are like a person asleep—at times, indeed, they may even be asleep), he thinks that the locutions come to him in a kind of dream, and sees things and believes that these things are of God, and the effects of these locutions resemble those of a dream. It may also happen that, when such a person asks something of Our Lord with a great love, he thinks that the voices are telling him what he wants to be told; this does in fact sometimes happen. But anyone who has much experience of locutions coming from God will not, I think, be deceived in this way by the imagination.

The devil's locutions are more to be feared than those that come from the imagination; but, if the locutions are accompanied by the signs already described, one may be very confident that they are of God, although not to such an extent that, if what is said is of great importance and involves some action on the part of the hearer, or matters affecting a third person, one should do anything about it, or consider doing anything, without taking the advice of a learned confessor, a man of clear insight and a servant of God, even though one may understand the locutions better and better and it may become evident that they are of God. For this is His Majesty's will, so by carrying it out we are not failing to do what He commands: He has told us that we are to put our confessor in His place, even when it cannot be doubted that the words are His. If the matter is a difficult one, these words will help to give us courage and Our Lord will speak to the confessor and if such is His pleasure will make him recognize the work of His spirit; if He does not, we have no further obligations. I consider it very dangerous for a person to do anything but what he has been told to do and to follow his own opinion in this matter; so I admonish you, sisters, in Our Lord's name, never to act thus.

There is another way in which the Lord speaks to the soul, which for my own part I hold to be very certainly genuine, and that is by a kind of intellectual vision, the nature of which I will explain later. So far down in the depths of the soul does this contact take place, so clearly do the words spoken by the Lord seem to be heard with the soul's own faculty of hearing, and so secretly are they uttered, that the very way in which the soul understands them, together with the effects produced by the vision itself, convinces it and makes it certain that no part in the matter is being played by the devil. The wonderful effects it produces are sufficient to make us believe this; at least one is sure that the locutions do not proceed from the imagination, and, if one reflects upon it, one can always be certain of this, for the following reasons.

The first reason is that some locutions are very much clearer than others. The genuine locution is so clear that, even if it consists of a long exhortation, the hearer notices the omission of a single syllable, as well as the phraseology that is used; but in locutions that are created fancifully by the imagination, the voice will be less clear and the words less distinct; they will be like something heard in a half-dream.

The second reason is that often the soul has not been thinking of what it hears—I mean that the voice comes unexpectedly, sometimes even during a conversation, although it frequently has reference to something that was passing quickly through the mind or to what one was previously thinking of. But often it refers to things that one never thought would or could happen, so that the imagination cannot possibly have invented them, and the soul cannot be deceived about things it has not desired or wished for or that have never been brought to its notice.

The third reason is that in genuine locutions the soul seems to be hearing something, whereas in locutions invented by the imagination someone seems to be composing bit by bit what the soul wishes to hear.

The fourth reason is that there is a great difference in the words themselves: in a genuine locution one single word may contain a world of meaning such as the understanding alone could never put rapidly into human language.

The fifth reason is that frequently, not only can words be heard, but, in a way that I shall never be able to explain, much more can be understood than the words themselves convey and this without any further utterance. Of this way of understanding I shall say more elsewhere; it is a very subtle thing, for which Our Lord should be praised. Some people (especially one person with experience of these things, and no doubt others also) have been very dubious about this way of understanding locutions and about the differences between them, and have been quite unable to get the matter straight. I know that this person has thought it all over very carefully, because the Lord has granted her this favor very frequently indeed; her most serious doubt, which used to occur when she first experienced it, was whether she was not imagining the whole thing. When locutions come from the devil, their source can be more quickly recognized, though his wiles are so numerous that he can readily counterfeit the spirit of light. He will do this, in my view, by pronouncing his words very clearly, so that there will be no more doubt about their being understood than if they were being spoken by the spirit of truth. But he will not be able to counterfeit the effects that have been described, or to leave in the soul this peace or light, but only restlessness and turmoil. He can do little or no harm if the soul is humble and does what I have said—that is, if it refrains from action, whatever the locutions may say.

If gifts and favors come to it from the Lord, the soul should consider carefully and see if they make it think any the better of itself; and if, as the words grow more and more precious, it does not suffer increasing confusion, it can be sure that the spirit is not of God; for it is quite certain that, when it is so, the greater the favor the soul receives, the less by far it esteems itself, the more keenly it remembers its sins, the more forgetful it is of its own interest, the more fervent are the efforts of its will and memory in seeking nothing but the honor of God rather than being mindful of its own profit, and the greater is its fear of departing in the least from the will of God and its certainty that it has never deserved these favors, but only hell. When these are the results of all the experiences and favors that come to the soul in prayer, it need not be afraid, but may rest confidently in the mercy of the Lord, Who is faithful, and will not allow the devil to deceive it, though it always does well to retain its misgivings.

It may be that those whom the Lord does not lead by this road think that such souls need not listen to these words that are addressed to them; that, if they are interior words, they should turn their attention elsewhere so as not to hear them; and that in this way they will run no risk of incurring these perils. My answer is that that is impossible—and I am not referring now to locutions invented by the fancy, a remedy for which is to be less anxious about certain things and to try to take no notice of one's own imaginings. When the locutions come from God there is no such remedy, for the Spirit Himself, as He speaks, inhibits all other thought and compels attention to what He says. So I really think (and I believe this to be true) that it would be easier for someone with excellent hearing not to hear a person who spoke in a very loud voice, because he might simply pay no heed and occupy his thought and understanding with something else. In the case of which we are speaking, however, that is impossible. We have no ears that we can stop nor have we the power to refrain from thought; we can only think of what is being said; for He who was able, at the request of Joshua (I think it was), to make the sun stand still,[4] can still the faculties and all the interior part, of the soul in such a way that the soul becomes fully aware that another Lord, greater than itself, is governing that Castle and renders Him the greatest devotion and humility. So it cannot do other than listen: it has no other choice. May His Divine Majesty grant us to fix our eyes only on pleasing Him and to forget ourselves, as I have said: Amen. May He grant that I have succeeded in explaining what I have attempted to explain and that I may have given some help to any who have experience of these locutions.

Exploring the Interior Castle

- Do you believe that God can communicate directly to a soul? If so, how? Through the senses? Through the imagination? Through the spirit or intellect? If this is true, does God do this often or only in rare instances? Have you ever felt that God has spoken to you in this way?

- Do you agree with the various guidelines Teresa offers for telling the difference between authentic and inauthentic locutions? Do they make sense to you? Are any unclear to you? Is there anything you would add to or subtract from this list?

- What would you do if someone told you that he or she was hearing voices from God? Would you ignore it? Dismiss it outright? Ridicule him or her? Would you listen and take it seriously? What counsel or advice would you offer the person? Would you send him or her to someone more knowledgeable than yourself for another opinion?

- Do you agree with Teresa that one must put one's confessor or spiritual guide in the place of God? What benefit does one gain from doing so? What liabilities are there? To what extent is Teresa's advice to her readers on this point a product of her times? Is her advice valid for all of today's spiritual seekers? If not, why not?

Chapter Four

✣

Introduction

In this chapter, Teresa speaks of the different kinds of rapture one might experience in the state of betrothal. A person needs great courage for these experiences, since human nature is very weak and needs God's help to bear them. Rapture, also known as ecstasy or trance, occurs when the experience of the Lord is so intense that the soul seems to be carried out of the senses. Teresa is quick to point out that she is talking only about genuine raptures and not the kind due to a person's weak disposition. She knows she has written about these experiences elsewhere, but she finds value in repeating herself a little so that everything can be found in one place.

One kind of rapture occurs when a person is not at prayer, but is deeply struck by a word he or she remembers or hears from God. The Lord sees this yearning and ignites a spark within the soul, which cleanses it and lifts it out of itself. The union between the soul and its beloved is so intense that no one can describe it but those experiencing it. One still retains control of one's internal senses of memory and will, except one's external senses are totally absorbed in God, and one will find it difficult to speak about the experience afterwards. The person has never before been so in tune with heavenly things. Teresa also points out that the door between this and the final mansion is not closed and that some people might experience them as one. Since many do not, however, she has decided to keep them separate.

In this state of rapture, God impresses on the soul's memory images of the divine mysteries that it can remember and explain at a later time. Intellectual visions are of another sort and differ greatly from these imaginative visions. They implant no images and are so glorious that words cannot contain them. Difficult though it may be, Teresa still asserts that it may be possible at times to recount them once a person comes back to his or her senses. Even if such intellectual visions cannot be described, they are stamped so deeply in the soul that a memory of them always remains. She cannot explain how such a remembrance can occur when no image is actually recorded in the memory. At this point, she can only refer to God's greatness and his power to implant some truths in the soul at a level even deeper than that of faith. She cites the examples of Jacob's ladder and Moses' experiences of the burning bush to demonstrate God's power to do all things.

Teresa comes up with a metaphor that, in her mind, approximates the soul's capacity to remember the whole experience of ecstasy without any of its particulars. She recalls one day seeing a room full of different kinds of glasswork and pottery. She was amazed by the seemingly infinite variety of vessels, but upon leaving the room could not recall what a single glass or pot looked like. All that remained with her was an overall impression of what she saw. Rapture, she claims, is similar to such an experience. A person becomes absorbed in God and is lifted up into a mansion of divine light found in the depths of the soul. There, many of God's mysteries are revealed, but little is recalled afterward other than a very general impression. Teresa is again talking about intellectual visions. She recognizes that she is employing a very rough analogy and that it fails to exhaust the glorious heights of what takes place in rapture. A soul in this sort of rapture is certain that God is taking it entirely to himself and revealing to it some small part of his kingdom. It possesses a general understanding of this vision at a very deep level of its existence. To be without such an understanding would be a sign of the rapture's lack of authenticity.

Teresa says that God grants these favors to whomever he pleases, but that he would gladly offer them to everyone if they truly loved him. She is deeply saddened by the thought of how many divine favors people lose through no fault but their own. When describing the bodily effects of this state of rapture, she says that the Lord closes all doors throughout the castle. The person cannot breathe and therefore cannot speak, even though some of the other senses may still be operative. The person's extremities become cold, and he or she loses all sensory perception. Ecstasy of this sort does not last very long. When the soul comes back to its senses, however, the effect of the experience can be so strong that its will and understanding may be entirely absorbed in God for several days. When these faculties return to normal, the soul is thrown into confusion, but it is also marked by a burning desire to give itself entirely to the Lord through suffering. It seeks to do penance and gives thanks to God when suffering comes its way. To do otherwise would reveal a lack of humility. The soul betrothed to God has everything it wants and cares nothing for bodily pleasures, honors, or possessions. Teresa has tried her best to describe the various states of rapture but does not know if she has successfully conveyed an adequate description of them. She tells her readers that, although it is not possible to give an exhaustive description, she believes her efforts were worthwhile and would help people distinguish true from false ecstatic experiences.

✢

Text

Treats of occasions when God suspends the soul in prayer by means of rapture, or ecstasy, or trance (for I think these are all the same), and of how great courage is necessary if we are to receive great favors from His Majesty.

How much rest can this poor little butterfly have amid all these trials and other things that I have described? Its whole will is set on desiring to have ever-increasing fruition of its Spouse; and His Majesty, knowing our weakness, continues to grant it the things it wants, and many more, so that it may have the courage to achieve union with so great a Lord and to take Him for its Spouse.

You will laugh at my saying this and call it ridiculous, for you will all think courage is quite unnecessary and suppose there is no woman, however lowly, who would not be brave enough to betroth herself to the King. This would be so, I think, with an earthly king, but for betrothal with the King of Heaven I must warn you that there is more need of courage than you imagine, because our nature is very timid and lowly for so great an undertaking, and I am certain that, unless God granted us strength,[1] it would be impossible. And now you are going to see what His Majesty does to confirm this betrothal, for this, as I understand it, is what happens when He bestows raptures, which carry the soul out of its senses; for if, while still in possession of its senses, the soul saw that it was so near to such great majesty, it might perhaps be unable to remain alive. It must be understood that I am referring to genuine raptures, and not to women's weaknesses, which we all have in this life, so that we are apt to think everything is rapture and ecstasy. And, as I believe I have said, there are some people who have such poor constitutions that one experience of the Prayer of Quiet kills them. I want to enumerate here some different kinds of rapture, which I have got to know about through conversations with spiritual people. I am not sure if I shall succeed in doing so, any more than when I wrote of this before.[2] For various reasons it has been thought immaterial if I should repeat myself in discussing this and other matters connected with it, if for no other object than that of setting down in one place all that there is to be said about each Mansion.

One kind of rapture is this. The soul, though not actually engaged in prayer, is struck by some word, which it either remembers or hears spoken by God. His Majesty is moved with compassion at having seen the soul suffering so long through its yearning for Him, and seems to be causing the spark of which we have already spoken to grow within it, so that, like the phoenix, it catches fire and springs into new life. One may piously believe that the sins of such a soul are pardoned, assuming that it is in the proper disposition and has used the means of grace, as the Church teaches.[3] When it is thus cleansed, God unites it with Himself, in a way that none can understand save it and He, and even the soul itself does not understand this in such a way as to be able to speak of it afterward, though it is not deprived of its interior senses; for it is not like one who suffers a swoon or a paroxysm so that it can understand nothing either within itself or without.

The position, in this case, as I understand it, is that the soul has never before been so fully awake to the things of God or had such light or such knowledge of His Majesty. This may seem impossible; because, if the faculties are so completely absorbed that we might describe them as dead, and the senses are so as well, how can the soul be said to understand this secret? I cannot say, nor perhaps can any creature, but only the Creator Himself, nor can I speak of many other things that happen in this state—I mean in these two Mansions, for this and the last might be fused in one: there is no closed door to separate the one from the other. As, however, there are things in the latter Mansion that are not shown to those who have not yet reached it, I have thought it best to separate them.

When the soul is in this state of suspension and the Lord sees fit to reveal to it certain mysteries, such as heavenly things and imaginary visions, it is able subsequently to describe these, for they are so deeply impressed upon the memory that they can never again be forgotten. But when they are intellectual visions they cannot be so described; for at these times come visions of so sublime a kind that it is not fitting for those who live on earth to understand them in such a way that they can describe them; although after regaining possession of their senses they can often describe many of these intellectual visions.

It may be that some of you do not understand what is meant by a vision, especially by an intellectual vision. I shall explain this in due course, as I have been commanded to do so by him who has authority over me; and although it may seem irrelevant, there may possibly be souls who will find it helpful. "But," you will say to me, "if the soul is not going to remember these sublime favors that the Lord grants it in this state, how can they bring it any profit?" Oh, daughters, the profit is so great that it cannot be exaggerated, for, although one cannot describe these favors, they are clearly imprinted in the very depths of the soul and they are never forgotten. "But," you will say next, "if the soul retains no image of them and the faculties are unable to understand them, how can they be remembered?" This, too, is more than I can understand; but I know that certain truths concerning the greatness of God remain so firmly in the soul that even had it not faith, which will tell it Who He is and that it is bound to believe Him to be God, the soul would adore Him as such from that very moment, just as Jacob adored Him when he saw the ladder.[4] He must, of course, have learned other secrets that he could not describe; for, if he had not had more interior light, he would not have understood such great mysteries merely from seeing a ladder on which angels were descending and ascending.

I do not know if I am right in what I am saying, for, although I have heard of the incident, I am not sure if I remember it correctly. Moses, again, could not describe all that he saw in the bush, but only as much as God willed him to;[5] yet, if God had not revealed secret things to his soul in such a way as to make him sure of their truth, so that he should know and believe Him to be God, he would not have taken upon himself so many and such arduous labors. Amid the thorns of that bush he must have learned marvelous things, for it was these things that gave him courage to do what he did for the people of Israel. Therefore, sisters, we must not seek out reasons for understanding the hidden things of God; rather, believing, as we do, in His great power, we must clearly realize that it is impossible for worms like ourselves, with our limited powers, to understand His greatness. Let us give Him hearty praise for being pleased to allow us to understand some part of it.

I am wishing I could find a suitable comparison that would give some sort of explanation of what I am saying. But I can think of none that will answer my purpose. Let us put it like this, however. You enter a private apartment in the palace of a king or a great lord (I think they call it a *camarín*), where they have an infinite variety of glassware, and earthenware, and all kinds of things, set out in such a way that you can see almost all of them as you enter. I was once taken into a room of this kind in the house of the Duchess of Alba, where I was commanded by obedience to stay[6] in the course of a journey, at her pressing invitation. When I went in I was astounded and began to wonder what all this mass of things could be used for, and then I realized that the sight of so many different things might lead one to glorify the Lord. It occurs to me now how useful an experience it was for my present purpose. Although I was there for some time, there was so much to be seen that I could not remember it all, so that I could no more recall what was in those rooms than if I had never seen them, nor could I say what the things were made of; I can only remember having seen them as a whole.[7] It is just like that here. The soul becomes one with God. It is brought into this mansion of the empyrean Heaven, which we must have in the depths of our souls; for it is clear that, since God dwells in them, He must have one[8] of these mansions. And although while the soul is in ecstasy the Lord will not always wish it to see these secrets (for it is so much absorbed in its fruition of Him that that great blessing suffices it), He is sometimes pleased that it should emerge from its absorption, and then it will at once see what there is in this room; in which case, after coming to itself, it will remember that revelation of the great things it has seen. It will not, however, be able to describe any of them, nor will its nature be able to apprehend more of the supernatural than God has been pleased to reveal to it.

Is this tantamount to an admission on my part that it has really seen something and that this is an imaginary vision? I do not mean that at all, for it is not of imaginary, but of intellectual visions that I am treating; only I have no learning and am too stupid to explain anything; and I am quite clear that, if what I have said so far about this kind of prayer is put correctly, it is not I who have said it. My own belief is that, if the soul to whom God has given these secrets in its raptures never understands any of them, they proceed, not from raptures at all, but from some natural weakness, which is apt to affect people of feeble constitution, such as women. In such cases the spirit, by making a certain effort, can overcome nature and remain in a state of absorption, as I believe I said when dealing with the Prayer of Quiet. Such experiences as these have nothing to do with raptures; for when a person is enraptured you can be sure that God is taking her entire soul to Himself, and that, as she is His own property and has now become His bride, He is showing her some little part of the kingdom that she has gained by becoming so. This part may be only a small one, but everything that is in this great God is very great. He will not allow her to be disturbed either by the faculties or by the senses; so He at once commands that all the doors of these Mansions shall be shut, and only the door of the Mansion in which He dwells remains open so that we may enter. Blessed be such great mercy! Rightly shall those who will not profit by it, and who thus forgo the presence of their Lord, be called accursed.

Oh, my sisters, what nothingness is all that we have given up, and all that we are doing, or can ever do, for a God Who is pleased to communicate Himself in this way to a worm! If we have the hope of enjoying this blessing while we are still in this life, what are we doing about it and why are we waiting? What sufficient reason is there for delaying even a short time instead of seeking this Lord, as the Bride did, through streets and squares?[9] Oh, what a mockery is everything in the world if it does not lead us and help us on the way toward this end—and would be even though all the worldly delights and riches and joys that we can imagine were to last forever! For everything is cloying and degrading by comparison with these treasures, which we shall enjoy eternally. And even these are nothing by comparison with having for our own the Lord of all treasures and of Heaven and earth.

Oh, human blindness! How long, how long shall it be before this dust is removed from our eyes? For although, as far as we ourselves are concerned, it seems not to be bad enough to blind us altogether, I can see some mites and particles which, if we allow them to become more numerous, will be sufficient to do us great harm. For the love of God, then, sisters, let us profit by these faults and learn from them what wretched creatures we are, and may they give us clearer sight, as did the clay to the blind man who was healed by our Spouse;[10] and thus, realizing our own imperfections, we shall beseech Him more and more earnestly to bring good out of our wretchedness, so that we may please His Majesty in everything.

Without realizing it, I have strayed far from my theme. Forgive me, sisters; and believe me, now that I have come to these great things of God (come to write about them, I mean), I cannot help feeling the pity of it when I see how much we are losing, and all through our own fault. For, true though it is that these are things that the Lord gives to whom He will, He would give them to us all if we loved Him as He loves us. For He desires nothing else but to have those to whom He may give them, and His riches are not diminished by His readiness to give.

Returning now to what I was saying, the Spouse orders the doors of the Mansions to be shut, and even those of the Castle and its enclosure. For when He means to enrapture this soul, it loses its power of breathing, with the result that, although its other senses sometimes remain active a little longer, it cannot possibly speak. At other times it loses all its powers at once, and the hands and the body grow so cold that the body seems no longer to have a soul—sometimes it even seems doubtful if there is any breath in the body. This lasts only for a short time (I mean, only for a short period at any one time) because, when this profound suspension lifts a little, the body seems to come partly to itself again, and draws breath, though only to die once more, and, in doing so, to give fuller life to the soul. Complete ecstasy, therefore, does not last long.

But, although relief comes, the ecstasy has the effect of leaving the will so completely absorbed and the understanding so completely transported—for as long as a day, or even for several days—that the soul seems incapable of grasping anything that does not awaken the will to love; to this it is fully awake, while asleep as regards all that concerns attachment to any creature.

Oh, what confusion the soul feels when it comes to itself again and what ardent desires it has to be used for God in any and every way in which He may be pleased to employ it! If such effects as have been described result from the former kinds of prayer, what can be said of a favor as great as this? Such a soul would gladly have a thousand lives so as to use them all for God, and it would like everything on earth to be tongue so that it might praise Him. It has tremendous desires to do penance; and whatever penance it does it counts as very little, for its love is so strong that it feels everything it does to be of very small account and realizes clearly that it was not such a great matter for the martyrs to suffer all their tortures, for with the aid of Our Lord such a thing becomes easy. And thus these souls make complaint to Our Lord when He offers them no means of suffering.

When this favor is granted them secretly they esteem it very highly; for so great are the shame and the confusion caused them by having to suffer before others that to some extent they lessen the soul's absorption in what it was enjoying, because of the distress and the anxiety that arise from its thoughts of what others who have seen it will think. For, knowing the malice of the world, they realize that their suffering may perhaps not be attributed to its proper cause but may be made an occasion for criticism instead of for glorifying the Lord. This distress and shame are no longer within the soul's own power of control, yet they seem to me to denote a lack of humility; for if such a person really desires to be despitefully treated, how can she mind if she is? One who was distressed in this way heard Our Lord say: "Be not afflicted, for either they will praise Me or murmur at thee, and in either case thou wilt be the gainer."[11] I learned afterwards that that person had been greatly cheered and consoled by those words; and I set them down here for the sake of any who find themselves in this affliction. It seems that Our Lord wants everyone to realize that such a person's soul is now His and that no one must touch it. People are welcome to attack her body, her honor, and her possessions, for any of these attacks will be to His Majesty's honor. But her soul they may not attack, for unless, with most blameworthy presumption, it tears itself away from its Spouse, He will protect it from the whole world, and indeed from all hell.

I do not know if I have conveyed any impression of the nature of rapture: to give a full idea of it, as I have said, is impossible. Still, I think there has been no harm in my saying this, so that its nature may be understood, since the effects of feigned raptures are so different. (I do not use the word "feigned" because those who experience them wish to deceive, but because they are deceived themselves.)[12]

As the signs and effects of these last do not harmonize with the reception of this great favor, the favor itself becomes discredited, so that those to whom the Lord grants it later on are not believed. May He be forever blessed and praised. Amen.

Exploring the Interior Castle

- Why does Teresa say that a person needs great courage to enter the state of mystical ecstasy? Where does that courage come from? Is this courage something natural to the individual or a gift from God? How can you tell the difference?

- How would you explain the difference between an imaginative vision and a false vision? How would you explain the difference between an imaginative and an intellectual vision? Is the notion of vision essential to Teresa's presentation of mystical ecstasy?

- How does the soul remember what is not implanted in its memory? How does it gain only a general impression of the experience and not remember any particulars? Where in the soul does God implant an impression of this mystical experience?

- Is ecstasy essential or an accessory to authentic Christian mysticism? Is everyone called to it or only a select few? What are its physical, psychological, intellectual, spiritual, and social effects? Are they the same in everyone?

Chapter Five

✤

Introduction

In this chapter, Teresa discusses another type of rapture, one that she refers to as flight of the spirit. This form of ecstasy is very similar to what she has just described, but the soul experiences it in a different way. It, too, requires help from God and great courage, for the soul experiences considerable fear as it feels itself being carried away very quickly into the very heart of the divinity.

For some, this experience is not only one of the soul, but also of the body. When it occurs, it is useless to resist, for the Lord is showing the soul that it is no longer in control. Teresa uses some metaphors to indicate what this is like, the most powerful of which was one she has used to describe the prayer of quiet, that is, a basin of water filled by a nearby spring. Instead of filling the basin quietly and gently, however, in the flight of spirit, the spring fills the basin quickly and with great force. God controls the flow of water and makes a great wave surge up from deep within to lift the soul upward. Although the soul, its faculties, and interior senses can do nothing to control this raging flow, its external senses seem to be unaffected by it.

Teresa lists a number of reasons why the soul needs so much courage at this point in its spiritual journey. For one thing, it is a greatly disturbing experience for a sane person to undergo such intense mystical experiences. When experiencing them, the soul also becomes very fearful, for it sees how weak and in need of God's grace it is. It yearns for God's mercy and compassion because it has a deep sense of its sinfulness and its inability to make up for its failures. It gradually understands that it is meant to unite its suffering to Christ's and to walk humbly with God, allowing him to shape it as he sees fit. For these reasons, the soul needs great courage when it reaches this state. It is not easy to die to self and become entirely free of self-will. This courage comes from God and is more necessary than ever before.

With regard to the experience of being transported in the spirit, Teresa says that, even though the person is not dead, it seems as though the person's body and soul have separated. The soul feels as though it has entered another world, a realm of light unlike anything experienced before. In this state, it is taught in a single moment things that it normally would have taken many years to understand. God teaches the soul through an intense imaginative vision that enables it to see things much more clearly than if it was in the body. God also communicates his secrets to the soul directly, without the use of words.

In addition to these imaginative visions, God also blesses the soul with intellectual visions, through which even deeper secrets are revealed. In such visions, these secrets are learned not through one's bodily eyes or even through the eyes of the soul, but by communicating with it directly in its deepest depths without any intermediaries. In such visions, Teresa cannot say if the soul has left the body while this happens. She likens the experience to the sun remaining in its place in the heavens yet shining its light on the earth through its powerful rays. In a similar way, she thinks it possible for the soul and spirit (the soul's highest dimension) to remain where they are, yet rise above themselves through the powerful rays of divine light that swell up from deep within themselves. In any case, she affirms that such an experience is clearly not a figment of one's imagination or the work of the evil one.

Teresa believes that God reveals these secrets to the soul so that it can have a foretaste of the heavenly delights awaiting it at the end of its journey. In this state, the soul recognizes God's greatness, grows in self-knowledge and humility, and disdains all earthly things except those that serve the Lord. These experiences, she claims, are implanted deep within the soul and would be impossible to forget. The Lord, moreover, graces the soul so as not to lose them and gives it the courage to bear the pain of ecstasy.

✢

Text

Continues the same subject and gives an example of how God exalts the soul through flights of the spirit in a way different from that described. Gives some reasons why courage is necessary here. Says something of this favor that God grants in a way so delectable. This chapter is highly profitable.

There is another kind of rapture, or flight of the spirit, as I call it, which, though substantially the same, is felt within the soul[1] in a very different way. Sometimes the soul becomes conscious of such rapid motion that the spirit seems to be transported with a speed that, especially at first, fills it with fear, for which reason I told you that great courage is necessary for anyone in whom God is to work these favors, together with faith and confidence and great resignation, so that Our Lord may do with the soul as He wills. Do you suppose it causes but little perturbation to a person in complete possession of his senses when he experiences these transports of the soul? We have even read in some authors that the body is transported as well as the soul, without knowing whither it is going, or who is bearing it away, or how, for when this sudden motion begins the soul has no certainty that it is caused by God.

Can any means of resisting this be found? None whatever: on the contrary, resistance only makes matters worse. This I know from a certain person who said that God's will seems to be to show the soul that, since it has so often and so unconditionally placed itself in His hands, and has offered itself to Him with such complete willingness, it must realize that it is no longer its own master, and so the violence with which it is transported becomes markedly greater. This person, therefore, decided to offer no more resistance than a straw does when it is lifted up by amber (if you have ever observed this) and to commit herself into the hands of Him Who is so powerful, seeing that it is but to make a virtue of necessity. And, speaking of straw, it is a fact that a powerful man cannot bear away a straw more easily than this great and powerful Giant of ours can bear away the spirit.

I think that basin of water, of which we spoke in (I believe) the fourth Mansion (but I do not remember exactly where),[2] was being filled at that stage gently and quietly—I mean without any movement. But now this great God, Who controls the sources of the waters and forbids the sea to move beyond its bounds, has loosed the sources whence water has been coming into this basin; and with tremendous force there rises up so powerful a wave that this little ship—our soul—is lifted up on high. And if a ship can do nothing, and neither the pilot nor any of the crew has any power over it, when the waves make a furious assault upon it and toss it about at their will, even less able is the interior part of the soul to stop where it likes, while its senses and faculties can do no more than has been commanded them: the exterior senses, however, are quite unaffected by this.

Really, sisters, the mere writing of this makes me astounded when I reflect how the great power of this great King and Emperor manifests itself here. What, then, must be the feelings of anyone who experiences it? For my own part I believe that, if His Majesty were to reveal Himself to those who journey through the world to their perdition as He does to these souls, they would not dare—out of very fear, though not perhaps out of love—to offend Him. Oh, how great, then, are the obligations attending souls who have been warned in so sublime a way to strive with all their might so as not to offend this Lord! For His sake, sisters, I beseech you, to whom His Majesty has granted these favors or others like them, not merely to receive them and then grow careless, but to remember that anyone who owes much has much to pay.[3]

This is another reason why the soul needs great courage, for the thought is one that makes it very fearful, and, did Our Lord not give it courage, it would continually be in great affliction. When it reflects what His Majesty is doing with it, and then turns to reflect upon itself, it realizes what a little it is doing toward the fulfillment of its obligations and how feeble is that little that it does do and how full of faults and failures. If it does any good action, rather than remember how imperfect this action is, it thinks best to try to forget it, to keep nothing in mind but its sins, and to throw itself upon the mercy of God; and, since it has nothing with which to pay, it craves the compassion and mercy that He has always shown to sinners.

He may perhaps answer it as He answered someone who was very much distressed about this, and was looking at a crucifix and thinking that she had never had anything to offer God or to give up for His sake. The Crucified Himself comforted her by saying that He was giving her all the pains and trials that He had suffered in His Passion, so that she should have them for her own to offer to His Father.[4] That soul, as I have understood from her, was so much comforted and enriched by this experience that she cannot forget it, and, whenever she feels miserable, she remembers it and it comforts and encourages her. There are several other remarks on this subject that I might add; for, as I have had to do with many saintly and prayerful people, I know of a number of such cases, but I do not want you to think that it is to myself that I am referring, so I pass them over. This incident that I have described seems to me a very apt one for helping you to understand how glad Our Lord is when we get to know ourselves and keep trying all the time to realize our poverty and wretchedness, and to reflect that we possess nothing that we have not been given. Therefore, my sisters, courage is necessary for this and for many other things that happen to a soul which the Lord has brought to this state; and, to my thinking, if the soul is humble, more courage is necessary for this last state than for any other. May the Lord, of His own bounty, grant us humility.

Turning now to this sudden transport of the spirit, it may be said to be of such a kind that the soul really seems to have left the body; on the other hand, it is clear that the person is not dead, though for a few moments he cannot even himself be sure if the soul is in the body or not. He feels as if he has been in another world, very different from this in which we live, and has been shown a fresh light there, so much unlike any to be found in this life that, if he had been imagining it, and similar things, all his life long, it would have been impossible for him to obtain any idea of them. In a single instant he is taught so many things all at once that if he were to labor for years on end in trying to fit them all into his imagination and thought, he could not succeed with a thousandth part of them. This is not an intellectual, but an imaginary vision, which is seen with the eyes of the soul very much more clearly than we can ordinarily see things with the eyes of the body; and some of the revelations are communicated to it without words. If, for example he sees any of the saints, he knows them as well as if he had spent a long time in their company.

Sometimes, in addition to the things that he sees with the eyes of the soul, in intellectual vision, others are revealed to him—in particular, a host of angels, with their Lord; and, though he sees nothing with the eyes of the body or with the eyes of the soul, he is shown the things I am describing and many others that are indescribable, by means of an admirable kind of knowledge. Anyone who has experience of this, and possesses more ability than I, will perhaps know how to express it; to me it seems extremely difficult. If the soul is in the body or not while all this is happening I cannot say; I would not myself swear that the soul is in the body, nor that the body is bereft of the soul.

I have often thought that if the sun can remain in the heavens and yet its rays are so strong that without its moving thence they can none the less reach us here, it must be possible for the soul and the spirit, which are as much the same thing as are the sun and its rays, to remain where they are, and yet, through the power of the heat that comes to them from the true Sun of Justice, for some higher part of them to rise above itself. Really, I hardly know what I am saying; but it is a fact that, as quickly as a bullet leaves a gun when the trigger is pulled, there begins within the soul a flight (I know no other name to give it), which, though no sound is made, is so clearly a movement that it cannot possibly be due to fancy. When the soul, as far as it can understand, is right outside itself, great things are revealed to it; and, when it returns to itself, it finds that it has reaped very great advantages and it has such contempt for earthly things that, in comparison with those it has seen, they seem like dirt to it. Thenceforward to live on earth is a great affliction to it, and, if it sees any of the things that used to give it pleasure, it no longer cares for them. Just as tokens of the nature of the Promised Land were brought back by those whom the Israelites sent on there,[5] so in this case the Lord's wish seems to have been to show the soul something of the country to which it is to travel, so that it may suffer the trials of this trying road,[6] knowing whither it must travel in order to obtain its rest Although you may think that a thing that passes so quickly cannot be of great profit, the help that it gives the soul is so great that only the person familiar with it can understand its worth.

Clearly, then, this is no work of the devil; such an experience could not possibly proceed from the imagination, and the devil could never reveal things that produce such results in the soul and leave it with such peace and tranquility and with so many benefits. There are three things in particular that it enjoys to a very high degree. The first is knowledge of the greatness of God: the more we see of this, the more deeply we are conscious of it. The second is self-knowledge and humility at realizing how a thing like the soul, so base by comparison with One Who is the Creator of such greatness, has dared to offend Him and dares to raise its eyes to Him. The third is a supreme contempt for earthly things, save those that can be employed in the service of so great a God.

These are the jewels that the Spouse is beginning to give to His bride, and so precious are they that she will not fail to keep them with the greatest care. These meetings[7] with the Spouse remain so deeply engraved in the memory that I think it is impossible for the soul to forget them until it is enjoying them forever; if it did so, it would suffer the greatest harm. But the Spouse Who gives them to the soul has power also to give it grace not to lose them.

Returning now to the soul's need of courage, I ask you: Does it seem to you such a trifling thing after all? For the soul really feels that it is leaving the body when it sees the senses leaving it and has no idea why they are going. So He Who gives everything else must needs give courage too. You will say that this fear of the soul's is well-rewarded; so, too, say I. May He Who can give so much be forever praised. And may it please His Majesty to grant us to be worthy to serve Him. Amen.

Exploring the Interior Castle

- When describing the flight of the spirit, Teresa gives the impression that God is entirely in control and the soul is helpless to resist. If this is so, how can the soul still offer its love freely to God? Is it possible to be free while being ravaged by God in this way?

- Teresa uses the metaphor of a basin filled by a spring whose waters are loosed by God to fill it rapidly and overflowing. Does this image help or blur your understanding of what she means by flight of the spirit? Can you think of any other images that might help to explain this mystical state?

- Teresa offers a number of reasons why courage is so important at this stage of the spiritual journey. Can you name them? Are some more important than others? Can you think of any others that should be added to the list? Are there any you would remove from it?

- Teresa says that the flight of the spirit gives the soul a sense of God's greatness, humble knowledge of oneself, and a desire for greater detachment from earthly things. Are these still valid for today? Would you add or subtract anything? Why are these so important for a person's spiritual growth?

Chapter Six

✛

Introduction

In this chapter, Teresa focuses on the effects on the soul of ecstasy and flights of the spirit on the soul and then introduces her readers to another favor that God bestows on his beloved. At this point in the state of betrothal, the soul yearns for God so deeply that it becomes restless in this life and begs God to be released from its time of exile. It finds life tiresome and full of tears. It experiences mystical ecstasy very frequently—both privately and in public—and can do nothing to prevent its occurrence. It also feels persecuted by others, even by its confessors and spiritual guides. It feels both rooted in God, but also very anxious and afraid that it is being led astray by the evil one. It is not bothered by the criticism of others, except when confessors blame it for not exercising more control over its mystical experiences. It feels guilty for not obeying its confessor, but also unable to do anything to avoid such states. At times, it wishes to flee into the desert to be with God. At other times, it wants nothing but to be in the midst of the world and help others learn to sing God's praises. It desires nothing but to give God praise.

Teresa admits that she does not understand everything that goes on in a soul in this state. She tells her readers that the effects of these ecstasies and flights of the spirit are permanent. The soul has been touched so deeply by God that it wants nothing else but to rest in his presence. To be marked by this deep desire is a sign of the experience's authenticity. The evil one would not and could not produce such an effect in the depths of the soul. Nevertheless, Teresa warns her readers to be careful lest they are led astray by the forces of evil. Sometimes the desire to see God becomes oppressive, and the soul must try to distance itself from it. Teresa believes it might be necessary to do so, at times, since the evil one might encourage such desires to deceive the soul into thinking it is further along the way of perfection than it really is. She also warns her readers not to attempt to induce tears, but simply to let them come when God so desires. Authentic tears from the Lord are not disturbing, but foster a sense of comfort and peace within the soul. The evil one, she maintains, might be able to cause bodily distress, but will not be able to hurt the soul that has remained humble before God. She encourages her readers not to worry about how many tears they shed, but to focus on their efforts to make progress in leading a virtuous life. To do so, it is better to place oneself in God's presence and meditate on his mercy and love. The soul should entrust itself to God and allow him to decide when it will water its soil with tears or when it is better for it to undergo a time of aridity.

After discussing the effects of ecstasy and flights of the spirit on the soul, Teresa briefly describes yet another mystical favor given by the Lord to his betrothed. It is a strange, jubilant kind of prayer that is difficult to describe, one in which the faculties of the soul are so closely united to the Lord that they experience great delight without understanding precisely what they are enjoying or even how they are enjoying it. The soul is so happy that it is unable to contain itself. It cannot enjoy God alone, but must go out to others and tell them of its uncontainable joy. It wishes to do nothing but extol the name of the Lord with everyone it encounters. Teresa uses examples from scripture (e.g., the father of the prodigal son) and the lives of the saints (e.g., Saint Francis, Friar Peter of Alcántara) to describe the holy madness that fills the soul in this state. This prayer comes directly from God and springs up from the depths of the soul. To be in this condition is like being inebriated while still remaining in control of one's senses. Such a state can last for an entire day. This prayer is greatly beneficial to the soul and gives it a deep sense of security. Teresa wishes that the Lord would bestow this prayer often upon his beloved, for it enables it to forget itself entirely and concentrate on nothing other than giving praise to God.

✢

Text

Describes one effect of the prayer referred to in the last chapter, by which it will be known that it is genuine and no deception. Treats of another favor that the Lord grants to the soul so that He may use it to sing His praises.

Having won such great favors, the soul is so anxious to have complete fruition of their Giver that its life becomes sheer, though delectable, torture. It has the keenest longings for death, and so it frequently and tearfully begs God to take it out of this exile. Everything in this life that it sees wearies it; when it finds itself alone it experiences great relief, but immediately this distress returns till it hardly knows itself when it is without it. In short, this little butterfly can find no lasting repose; indeed, her love is so full of tenderness that any occasion whatever that serves to increase the strength of this fire causes the soul to take flight; and thus in this Mansion raptures occur continually and there is no way of avoiding them, even in public. Further, although the soul would fain be free from tears, these persecutions and murmurings never leave her; for these all kinds of persons are responsible, especially confessors.

Although on the one hand she seems to be feeling great interior security, especially when alone with God, on the other hand she is in great distress, for she is afraid that the devil may be going to deceive her so that she shall offend Him for Whom she has such love. She is not hurt by what people say about her except when her own confessor blames her, as though she could prevent these raptures. She does nothing but beg everyone to pray for her and beseech His Majesty to lead her by another road, as she is advised to do, since the road she is on is very dangerous. But she has gained so much from following it (for she cannot help seeing, and she reads and hears and learns from the commandments of God that it leads to Heaven) that, try as she may, she feels unable to desire any other; all she wants to do is to leave herself in His hands. And even this impotence of will distresses her, because she thinks she is not obeying her confessor, for she believes that her only remedy against deception consists in obeying and not offending Our Lord. So she feels that she would not intentionally commit so much as a venial sin, even were she to be cut in pieces; and thus she is greatly distressed to find that, without being aware of the fact, she cannot avoid committing a great many.

God gives these souls the keenest desire not to displease Him in any respect whatsoever, however trivial, or to commit so much as an imperfection if they can avoid doing so. For this reason alone, if for no other, the soul would like to flee from other people, and greatly envies those who live, or have lived, in deserts. On the other hand it would like to plunge right into the heart of the world, to see if by doing this it could help one soul to praise God more; a woman in this state will be distressed at being prevented from doing this by the obstacle of sex and very envious of those who are free to cry aloud and proclaim abroad Who is this great God of Hosts.

Oh, poor little butterfly, bound by so many fetters, which prevent you from flying whithersoever you will! Have pity on her, my God; and dispose things so that she may be able to do something towards fulfilling her desires to Thy honor and glory. Remember not the slightness of her merits and the baseness of her nature. Mighty art Thou, Lord, for Thou didst make the great sea to draw back, and the great Jordan, and didst allow the Children of Israel to pass over them.[1] And yet Thou needest not have pity on her, for, with the aid of Thy strength, she is capable of enduring many trials. And this she is determined to do: to suffer them is her desire. Stretch out Thy mighty arm, O Lord, and let not her life be spent in things so base. Let Thy greatness appear in this creature, womanish and base though she is, so that men may realize that nothing she does comes from herself and may give Thee praise. Cost what it may, it is this that she desires, and she would give a thousand lives, if she had them, so that on her account one soul might praise Thee a little more. She would consider them all well spent, for she knows that in actual fact she deserves not to suffer the very smallest trial for Thy sake, still less to die for Thee.

I do not know why I have said this, sisters, nor to what purpose, for I have not understood it all myself. It should be realized that such, without any kind of doubt, are the effects that remain after these suspensions or ecstasies; the desires they inspire are not fleeting but permanent; and when any opportunity occurs of demonstrating the fact, it becomes evident that the experience was not feigned. You may ask why I use the word "permanent," since sometimes and in the most trifling matters the soul feels cowardly, and is so fearful and devoid of courage that it seems impossible it can be courageous enough to do anything whatsoever. But this, I take it, occurs at a time when the Lord leaves it to its own nature—an experience that is extremely good for it, making it realize that any usefulness it may have had has been a gift bestowed upon it by His Majesty. And this it realizes with a clearness that annihilates any self-interest in it and imbues it with a greater knowledge of the mercy of God and of His greatness, which He has been pleased to demonstrate to it in so small a matter. But more usually it is as we have already said.

Note one thing, sisters, concerning these great desires of the soul to see Our Lord: that they will sometimes oppress you so much that you must not encourage them but put them from you—if you can, I mean; because there are other desires, of which I shall write later, which cannot possibly be so treated, as you will see. These of which I am now speaking it is sometimes possible to put from you, since the reason is free to resign itself to the will of God, and you can echo the words of Saint Martin;[2] in such a case, where the desires are very oppressive, the thoughts may be deflected from them. For, as such desires are apparently found in souls that are very proficient, the devil might encourage them in us, so as to make us think ourselves proficient too; and it is always well to proceed with caution. But I do not myself believe he could ever fill the soul with the quietness and peace caused it by this distress; the feelings he arouses are apt to be passionate ones, like those that we experience when we are troubled about things of the world. Anyone without experience of each kind of distress will not understand that, and, thinking it a great thing to feel like this, will stimulate the feeling as much as possible. To do this, however, may be to injure the health, for the distress is continuous, or, at the least, occurs with great frequency.

Note also that distress of this kind is apt to be caused by weak health, especially in emotional people, who weep for the slightest thing; again and again they will think they are weeping for reasons that have to do with God, but this will not be so in reality. It may even be the case (I mean when they shed floods of tears—and for some time they cannot refrain from doing so whenever they think of God or hear Him spoken of) that some humor has been oppressing the heart, and that it is this, rather than their love of God, that has excited their tears. It seems as if they will never make an end of weeping, having come to believe that tears are good, they make no attempt to control them. In fact, they would not do otherwise than weep even if they could, and they make every effort they can to induce tears. The devil does his best, in such cases, to weaken them, so that they may be unable either to practice prayer or to keep their Rule.

I seem to hear you asking whatever you are to do, as I am telling you there is danger in everything. If I think deception possible in anything as beneficial as shedding tears may I not be deceived myself? Yes, of course I may; but, believe me, I am not talking without having observed this in certain persons. I have never been like it myself, however, for I am not in the least emotional; on the contrary, my hardness of heart sometimes worries me; though, when the fire within my soul is strong, however hard my heart may be, it distills as if in an alembic. You will easily recognize when tears arise from this source, because they are comforting and tranquilizing rather than disturbing, and seldom do any harm. The great thing about this deception, when such it is, will be that, although it may harm the body, it cannot (if the soul is humble, I mean) hurt the soul. If it is not humble, it will do it no harm to keep its suspicions.

Do not let us suppose that if we weep a great deal we have done everything that matters; let us also set to and work hard, and practice the virtues, for these are what we most need. Let the tears come when God is pleased to send them: we ourselves should make no efforts to induce them. They will leave this dry ground of ours well watered and will be of great help in producing fruit; but the less notice we take of them, the more they will do, because they are the water that comes from Heaven.[3] When we ourselves draw water, we tire ourselves by digging for it, and the water we get is not the same; often we dig till we wear ourselves out without having discovered so much as a pool of water, still less a wellspring. For this reason, sisters, I think our best plan is to place ourselves in the Lord's presence, meditate upon His mercy and grace and upon our own lowliness, and leave Him to give us what He wills, whether it be water or aridity. He knows best what is good for us, and in this way we shall walk in tranquility and the devil will have less opportunity to fool us.

Together with these things, which are at once distressing and delectable, Our Lord sometimes bestows upon the soul a jubilation and a strange kind of prayer, the nature of which it cannot ascertain. I set this down here, so that, if He grants you this favor, you may give Him hearty praise and know that such a thing really happens. I think the position is that the faculties are in close union, but that Our Lord leaves both faculties and senses free to enjoy this happiness, without understanding what it is that they are enjoying and how they are enjoying it. That sounds nonsense but it is certainly what happens. The joy of the soul is so exceedingly great that it would like, not to rejoice in God in solitude, but to tell its joy to all, so that they may help it to praise Our Lord, to which end it directs its whole activity. Oh, what high festival such a one would make to this end and how she would show forth her joy, if she could, so that all should understand it! For she seems to have found herself, and, like the father of the Prodigal Son,[4] she would like to invite everybody and have great festivities because she sees her soul in a place that she cannot doubt is a place of safety, at least for a time. And, for my own part, I believe she is right; for such interior joy in the depths of the soul's being, such peace and such happiness that it calls upon all to praise God cannot possibly have come from the devil.

Impelled as it is by this great joy, the soul cannot be expected to keep silence and dissemble: it would find this no light distress. That must have been the state of mind of Saint Francis, when robbers met him as he was going about the countryside crying aloud and he told them that he was the herald of the great King. Other saints retire to desert places, where they proclaim the same thing as Saint Francis—namely, the praises of their God. I knew one of these, called Fray Peter of Alcántara. Judging from the life he led, I think he is certainly a saint, yet those who heard him from time to time called him mad. Oh, what a blessed madness, sisters! If only God would give it to us all! And how good He has been to you in placing you where, if the Lord should grant you this grace and you show others that He has done so, you will not be spoken against as you would be in the world (where there are so few to proclaim God's praise that it is not surprising if they are spoken against,) but will be encouraged to praise Him the more.

Oh, unhappy are the times and miserable is the life that we now live, and happy are those who have had the good fortune to escape from it! Sometimes it makes me specially glad when we are together and I see these sisters of mine so full of inward joy that each vies with the rest in praising Our Lord for bringing her to the convent; it is very evident that those praises come from the inmost depths of the soul. I should like you to praise Him often, sisters, for, when one of you begins to do so, she arouses the rest How can your tongues be better employed, when you are together, than in the praises of God, which we have so many reasons for rendering Him?

May it please His Majesty often to bestow this prayer upon us since it brings us such security and such benefit. For, as it is an entirely supernatural thing, we cannot acquire it. It may last for a whole day, and the soul will then be like one who has drunk a great deal, but not like a person so far inebriated as to be deprived of his senses; nor will it be like a melancholic, who, without being entirely out of his mind, cannot forget a thing that has been impressed upon his imagination, from which no one else can free him either. These are very unskillful comparisons to represent so precious a thing, but I am not clever enough to think out any more: the real truth is that this joy makes the soul so forgetful of itself, and of everything, that it is conscious of nothing, and able to speak of nothing, save of that which proceeds from its joy—namely, the praises of God. Let us join with this soul, my daughters all. Why should we want to be more sensible than she? What can give us greater pleasure than to do as she does? And may all the creatures join with us forever and ever. Amen, amen, amen.

Exploring the Interior Castle

- Teresa says that there comes a point in the state of betrothal when a soul becomes weary with life in this world and begs God to take it home. Have you ever felt weary with life? If so, how did you deal with it? Did this weariness come because of your relationship to the world or to God? Have you ever asked God to take you home?

- According to Teresa, another effect of betrothal is increased persecution, even from one's closest counselors. Does it make sense to you that the closer a person gets to God, the more he or she will suffer hardship at the hands of others? Have you ever experienced anything like this in your own life?

- Teresa says that one should not try to force tears, but simply allow them to come as the Lord so desires. She also says that it is more important to focus on living a life of virtue than on how many tears one has shed. What is she getting at here? Is she saying that the true effect of being betrothed to the Lord has more to do with how one lives one's life than with one's pious display of emotion?

- For Teresa, another favor that the Lord bestows on his beloved is an intense interior joy that moves the soul to praise God in the presence of others. Have you ever met a person who was steeped in such "blessed madness"? Have you ever felt that way yourself?

Chapter Seven

✢

Introduction

In this chapter, Teresa tells of the deep sorrow those betrothed to the Lord have for their past sins. She also tells her readers that those who progress into the higher mansions should not give up their devotion to the Lord's incarnation, life, and paschal mystery, nor should they neglect their devotion to the Blessed Mother and the communion of saints.

Those in the sixth mansions grieve for their sins not out of fear of punishment or being condemned to hell, but simply because they have offended the Lord. They weep for their sins because they have a very keen sense of the Lord's grandeur. They look back on their lives and are horrified by how callous they have been in their actions toward God. They see how much God has done for them over the years and are ashamed at how ungrateful they were to him. Teresa likens these sins to a muddy river bottom that is always present and weighs a person down as he or she tries to get to the other side. These sins are a heavy cross to bear. Although they sometimes burden the soul with thoughts of hell, the only thing that those in the sixth mansions are truly afraid of is the possibility of offending God once more.

Teresa says that the soul should never forget its past sins. The memories of these sins keep one conscious of one's frailty and humble before God. In this mortal life the potential for sin will always be there; no one is totally secure until he or she passes beyond the pale of death and rests in the Lord's hand for all eternity. She cites Saint Peter and Mary Magdalene as examples of great saints who loved the Lord dearly, yet were burdened and deeply troubled by their past sins.

As they progress in the way of perfection, Teresa tells her readers that they should continue to meditate on the Lord's humanity, life, and death. It would be a mistake, she tells them, to think that one can dispense with such practices because one has become more proficient in the practice of love. She is aware that others have contrary opinions on this matter, but is adamant that one's progress in the spiritual life is closely connected to these meditative practices. She says she has learned this from her own hard experience, saying that she had once been deceived by the evil one into thinking that she could leave her devotion to Christ's humanity, life, and passion behind. Teresa assures her readers that if they choose to do so, they will never be able to enter the final two mansions. To stop such meditative practices would be tantamount to losing Jesus, their guide, the way, the truth, and the life.

At the same time, Teresa understands that some souls have been favored with the gift of pure contemplation and find it difficult to give the mental effort necessary for a fruitful meditation on the mysteries of Christ The reason for this difficulty, she says, is because this divine gift bypasses the intellect and enables the soul to enjoy God directly through a union of wills. She understands that souls in this state might wish to set the intellect aside and simply rest in this intimate union. According to Teresa, however, this state of pure contemplation does not last forever (at least in this life), and the soul cannot simply neglect the intellect in this way. During one's earthly sojourn, it is impossible to put aside meditation and lose oneself entirely in love. Meditation on Christ is essential for growth in the spiritual life, especially for the later mansions, where one must be prepared to walk with Christ in both his divine *and* human natures. An individual will be able to follow the Lord's commandments and counsels only if he or she continues to meditate upon them.

By meditation, Teresa means an extended reflection on a mystery of the faith through one's faculty of understanding. One pictures in one's mind an event from Christ's life (e.g., the agony in the garden, the crucifixion). This image imprints itself on the memory and one rests before it in a state of simple regard, which in turn arouses in the will the desire to give something back to God. Teresa understands that those blessed with the gift of pure contemplation will find it difficult to pray to the Lord in a way that involves the understanding and the memory. She advises them, however, to try to do so since she believes there is no inherent contradiction between meditation and contemplation. The former is not an obstacle to the latter, but reinforces it and actually predisposes one for it.

Regardless of what anyone else says, Teresa cannot be persuaded that doing away with meditation on the mysteries of Christ's paschal mystery can benefit the soul. No matter how spiritual one is, it is a mistake to think that one can become so totally absorbed in God that one can leave behind a concern for Christ's humanity, life, and passion or, worse yet, to even think that meditating on them can do one harm. Such an argument is simply erroneous. She cites the example of the Blessed Mother, who most certainly experienced the heights of mystical prayer, yet was always deeply attached to her son's humanity. To be sure, devotion to the Blessed Mother and the communion of saints will strengthen one's devotion to the humanity of Christ, not diminish it. Such an argument is also very dangerous, for it could possibly lead to the loss of one's devotion to the presence of Christ in the Blessed Sacrament. In much of this, Teresa is speaking from her own experience. It is impossible for human beings to remain always at the height of pure contemplation. Since such spiritual consolations do not last, the soul must be sustained by meditation on the mysteries of Christ and the concrete sacramental signs God has given his beloved as proof of his love for them. To do otherwise is to go down the wrong road, and this will hinder one's growth in virtue and progress in prayer.

✣

Text

Treats of the kind of grief felt for their sins by the souls to whom God grants the favors aforementioned. Says that, however spiritual people may be, it is a great mistake for them not to practice keeping in mind the Humanity of Our Lord and Savior Jesus Christ, His most sacred Passion and life, and His glorious Mother and the Saints. This chapter is of great profit.

You will think, sisters, that these souls to whom the Lord communicates Himself in so special a way (I am speaking now particularly to those who have not attained these favors, for if they have been granted the enjoyment of such favors by God, they will know what I am about to say) will by now be so sure that they are to enjoy Him forever that they will have no reason to fear or to weep for their sins. This will be a very great mistake, for, the more they receive from our God, the greater grows their sorrow for sin; I believe myself that this will never leave us until we reach that place where nothing can cause us affliction.

It is true that this sorrow can be more oppressive at one time than at another, and also that it is of different kinds, for the soul does not now think of the pain that it is bound to suffer on account of its sins, but only of how ungrateful it has been to Him Whom it owes so much, and Who so greatly merits our service. For through these manifestations of His greatness that He communicates to it, the soul gains a much deeper knowledge of the greatness of God. It is aghast at having been so bold; it weeps for its lack of reverence; its foolish mistakes in the past seem to it to have been so gross that it cannot stop grieving, when it remembers that it forsook so great a Majesty for things so base. It thinks of this much more than of the favors it receives, great as they are like those that we have described and like those that remain to be described later. It is as if a mighty river were running through the soul and from time to time bringing these favors with it. But its sins are like the river's slimy bed; they are always fresh in its memory, and this is a heavy cross to it.

I know of a person who had ceased wishing she might die so as to see God, but was desiring death in order that she might not suffer such constant distress at the thought of her ingratitude to One to Whom her debts were so great. She thought nobody's evil deeds could equal hers, for she believed there was no one with whom God had borne for so long and to whom He had shown so many favors.

With regard to fear of hell, these souls have none; they are sometimes sorely oppressed by the thought that they may lose God, but this happens seldom. Their sole fear is that God may let them out of His hand and that they may then offend Him, and thus find themselves in as miserable a state as before. They have no anxiety about their own pain or glory. If they desire not to stay long in Purgatory, it is less for the pain that they will have to suffer than because while they are there they will not be with God.

However favored by God a soul may be, I should not think it secure were it to forget the miserable state it was once in, for, distressing though the reflection is, it is often profitable. Perhaps it is because

I myself have been so wicked that I feel like this and for that reason always keep it in mind; those who have been good will have nothing to grieve for, although for as long as we live in this mortal body we shall always have failures. It affords us no relief from this distress to reflect that Our Lord has forgiven and forgotten our sins; in fact the thought of so much goodness and of favors granted to one who has merited only hell makes the distress greater. I think these reflections must have been a regular martyrdom for Saint Peter and for the Magdalene; because, as their love was so great and they had received so many favors and had learned to understand the greatness and majesty of God, they would find them terribly hard to bear, and must have been moved with the deepest emotion.

You will also think that anyone who enjoys such sublime favors will not engage in meditation on the most sacred Humanity of Our Lord Jesus Christ, because by that time he will be wholly proficient in love. This is a thing of which I have written at length elsewhere,[1] and, although I have been contradicted about it and told that I do not understand it, because these are paths along which Our Lord leads us, and that, when we have got over the first stages, we shall do better to occupy ourselves with matters concerning the Godhead and to flee from corporeal things, they will certainly not make me admit that this is a good way. I may be wrong and we may all be meaning the same thing; but it was clear to me that the devil was trying to deceive me in this way, and I have had to learn my lesson. So, although I have often spoken about this,[2] I propose to speak to you about it again, so that you may walk very warily. And observe that I am going so far as to advise you not to believe anyone who tells you otherwise. I will try to explain myself better than I did before. If by any chance a certain person has written about it, as he said he would, it is to be hoped that he has explained it more fully; to write about it in a general way to those of us who are not very intelligent may do a great deal of harm.

Some souls also imagine that they cannot dwell upon the Passion, in which case they will be able still less to meditate upon the most sacred Virgin and the lives of the saints, the remembrance of whom brings us such great profit and encouragement. I cannot conceive what they are thinking of; for, though angelic spirits, freed from everything corporeal, may remain permanently enkindled in love, this is not possible for those of us who live in this mortal body. We need to cultivate, and think upon, and seek the companionship of those who, though living on earth like ourselves, have accomplished such great deeds for God; the last thing we should do is to withdraw of set purpose from our greatest help and blessing, which is the most sacred Humanity of Our Lord Jesus Christ. I cannot believe that people can really do this; it must be that they do not understand themselves and thus do harm to themselves and to others. At any rate, I can assure them that they will not enter these last two Mansions; for, if they lose their Guide, the good Jesus, they will be unable to find their way; they will do well if they are able to remain securely in the other Mansions. For the Lord Himself says that He is the Way;[3] the Lord also says that He is light[4] and that no one can come to the Father save by Him;[5] and "he that seeth Me seeth my Father."[6] It may be said that these words have another meaning. I do not know of any such meaning myself; I have got on very well with the meaning that my soul always feels to be the true one.

There are some people (and a great many of them have spoken to me about this) on whom Our Lord bestows perfect contemplation and who would like to remain in possession of it forever. That is impossible; but they retain something of this Divine favor, with the result that they can no longer meditate upon the mysteries of the Passion and the life of Christ, as they could before. I do not know the reason for this, but it is quite a common experience in such cases for the understanding to be less apt for meditation. I think the reason must be that the whole aim of meditation is to seek God, and once He is found, and the soul grows accustomed to seeking Him again by means of the will, it has no desire to fatigue itself with intellectual labor. It also seems to me that, as the will is now enkindled, this generous faculty would have no desire to make use of that other faculty,[7] even if it could. There would be nothing wrong in its setting it aside, but it is impossible for it to do so, especially before the soul has reached these last Mansions, and it will only lose time by attempting it, for the aid of the understanding is often needed for the enkindling of the will.

Note this point, sisters, for it is important, so I will explain it further. The soul is desirous of employing itself wholly in love and it would be glad if it could meditate on nothing else. But this it cannot do even if it so desires; for, though the will is not dead, the fire that habitually kindles it is going out, and, if it is to give off heat of itself, it needs someone to fan it into flame. Would it be a good thing for the soul to remain in that state of aridity, hoping for fire to come down from Heaven to burn up this sacrifice of itself, which it is making to God as did our father Elias?[8] No, certainly not; nor is it a good thing to expect miracles: the Lord will perform them for this soul when He sees fit to do so, as has been said and as will be said again later. But His Majesty wants us to realize our wickedness, which makes us unworthy of their being wrought, and to do everything we possibly can to come to our own aid. And I believe myself that, however sublime our prayer may be, we shall have to do this until we die.

It is true that anyone whom Our Lord brings to the seventh Mansion very rarely, or never, needs to engage in this activity, for the reason that I shall set down, if I remember to do so, when I come to deal with that Mansion, where in a wonderful way the soul never ceases to walk with Christ our Lord but is ever in the company of both His Divine and His human nature. When, therefore, the aforementioned fire is not kindled in the will, and the presence of God is not felt, we must needs seek it, since this is His Majesty's desire, as the Bride sought it in the *Songs*.[9] Let us ask the creatures who made them, as Saint Augustine says that he did (in his *Meditations* or *Confessions*,[10] I think) and let us not be so foolish as to lose time by waiting to receive what has been given us once already. At first it may be that the Lord will not give it us, for as long as a year, or even for many years: His Majesty knows why; it is not our business to want to know, nor is there any reason why we should. Since we know the way we have to take to please God—namely, that of keeping His commandments and counsels—let us be very diligent in doing this, and in meditating upon His life and death, and upon all that we owe Him; and let the rest come when the Lord wills.

Such people will reply that they cannot stop to meditate upon these things, and here they may to some extent be right, for the reason already given. You know, of course, that it is one thing to reason with the understanding and quite another for the memory to represent truths to the understanding. You will say, perhaps, that you do not understand me, and it may very well be that I do not understand the matter myself sufficiently to be able to explain it; but I will deal with it as well as I can. By meditation I mean prolonged reasoning with the understanding, in this way. We begin by thinking of the favor that God bestowed upon us by giving us His only Son; and we do not stop there but proceed to consider the mysteries of His whole glorious life. Or we begin with the prayer in the Garden and go on rehearsing the events that follow until we come to the Crucifixion. Or we take one episode of the Passion—Christ's arrest, let us say—and go over this mystery in our mind, meditating in detail upon the points in it that we need to think over and to try to realize, such as the treason of Judas, the flight of the Apostles, and so on. This is an admirable and a most meritorious kind of prayer.

This is the kind of prayer I was referring to, which those whom God has raised to supernatural things and to perfect contemplation are right in saying they cannot practice. As I have said, I do not know why this should be the case; but as a rule they are in fact unable to do so. A man will not be right, however, to say that he cannot dwell upon these mysteries, for he often has them in his mind, especially when they are being celebrated by the Catholic Church; nor is it possible that a soul that has received so much from God should forget all these precious signs of His love, for they are living sparks that will enkindle the soul more and more in its love for Our Lord. But these mysteries will not be apprehended by the understanding: the soul will understand them in a more perfect way. First, the understanding will picture them to itself, and then they will be impressed upon the memory, so that the mere sight of the Lord on His knees, in the Garden, covered with that terrible sweat, will suffice us, not merely for an hour, but for many days. We consider, with a simple regard, Who He is and how ungrateful we have been to One Who has borne such pain for us. Then the will is aroused, not perhaps with deep emotion but with a desire to make some kind of return for this great favor, and to suffer something for One Who has suffered so much Himself. And so it is with other subjects, in which both memory and understanding will have a place. This, I think, is why the soul cannot reason properly about the Passion, and it is because of this that it believes itself unable to meditate upon it at all.

But if it does not already meditate in this way, it will be well advised to attempt to do so; for I know that the most sublime kind of prayer will be no obstacle to it and I believe omission to practice it often would be a great mistake. If while the soul is meditating the Lord should suspend it, well and good; for in that case He will make it cease meditation even against its own will. I consider it quite certain that this method of procedure is no hindrance to the soul but a great help to it in everything that is good; whereas, if it labored hard at meditation in the way I have already described, this would indeed be a hindrance—in fact, I believe such labor is impossible for a person who has attained greater heights. This may not be so with everyone, since God leads souls by many ways, but those who are unable to take this road should not be condemned or judged incapable of enjoying the great blessings contained in the mysteries of Jesus Christ our Good. No one, however spiritual, will persuade me that to neglect these mysteries can be profitable for him.

Some souls, at the beginning of the spiritual life, or even when well advanced in it, get as far as the Prayer of Quiet, and are about to enjoy the favors and consolations given by the Lord in that state, and then think it would be a very great thing to be enjoying these gifts all the time. Let them take my advice, and become less absorbed in them, as I have said elsewhere.[11] For life is long and there are many trials in it and we have need to look at Christ our Pattern, and also at His Apostles and Saints, and to reflect how they bore these trials, so that we, too, may bear them perfectly. The good Jesus is too good company for us to forsake Him and His most sacred Mother. He is very glad when we grieve for His afflictions although sometimes we may be forsaking our own pleasures and consolations in order to do so—though for that matter, daughters, consolations in prayer are not so frequent that there is not time for everything. If anyone told me that she experienced them continuously (I mean so continuously that she could never meditate in the way I have described) I should consider it suspicious. Keep on with your meditation, then, and endeavor to be free from this error, and make every effort to avoid this absorption. If your efforts are not sufficient, tell the prioress, in order that she may give you some work that will keep you so busy that this danger will no longer exist Any continuous exposure to it would be very bad for the brain and the head, if nothing worse.

I think I have explained what it is well for you to know—namely that, however spiritual you are, you must not flee so completely from corporeal things as to think that meditation on the most sacred Humanity can actually harm you. We are sometimes reminded that the Lord said to His disciples that it was expedient for them that He should go away:[12] I cannot, however, allow that as an argument. He did not say this to His most sacred Mother, because she was firm in the faith and knew that He was God and Man; and, although she loved Him more than they, her love was so perfect that His being on earth was actually a help to her. The Apostles could not at that time have been as firm in the faith as they were later and as we have reason to be now. I assure you, daughters, that I consider this a perilous road and that if we took it the devil might end by causing us to lose our devotion to the Most Holy Sacrament.

The mistake, I think, which I used to make myself, did not go as far as this; it was only that I would take less pleasure than previously in thinking of Our Lord Jesus Christ and would go about in that state of absorption, expecting to receive spiritual consolation. Then I saw clearly that I was going wrong; for, as it was impossible always to be having consolations, my thoughts would keep passing from one subject to another, until my soul, I think, got like a bird flying round and round in search of a resting place and losing a great deal of time, without advancing in the virtues or making progress in prayer. I could not understand the cause—nor, I believe, should I ever have understood it, because I thought I was on the proper road, until one day, when I was telling a person who was a servant of God about my method of prayer, he gave me some counsel. This showed me clearly how far I had gone astray, and I have never ceased regretting that there was once a time when I failed to realize that so great a loss could not possibly result in gain. Even if I could obtain it, I want no blessing save that which I acquire through Him by Whom all blessings come to us. May He be praised forever. Amen.

Exploring the Interior Castle

- Teresa says that those in the state of betrothal are deeply grieved by their past sins. How does such grief benefit them? Could it hinder them in any way? Is it possible to be overly concerned about them? Have you ever felt deep regret for the sins of your past? Can you grieve over your past sins yet also trust that God has forgiven you for them?

- Teresa says that meditation on the humanity, life, and death of Christ is important even for those in the state of betrothal. Why is this so? What precisely does Teresa mean by meditation? Have you ever prayed to God in this way? Did you find it easy or difficult? Why is meditation on these mysteries so important for growth in the spiritual life, especially in the later stages?

- Why do those in the state of betrothal have such a difficult time meditating on Christ's humanity, life, and paschal mystery? Why might they wish to leave such practices behind? Why does Teresa insist that they continue these practices? Do you agree with her? Have you ever felt that you have progressed far enough in the spiritual life to do away with meditative reflection on the mysteries of Christ? Has reading this chapter changed your thinking on this in any way?

- How would you describe the difference between meditation and mystical contemplation? What is the relationship between them? Are they opposed in any way? Does one predispose a person for the other? Must one be left behind to experience the other? Do they complement one another in any way? Which is the more usual way for a person to pray? Which is closer to the way you pray?

Chapter Eight

✠

Introduction

In this chapter, Teresa discusses the nature of intellectual visions and their effects. She affirms once more the truth that the more a person progresses in the spiritual life, the more he or she grows in friendship with Christ. One sign of this growing intimacy is the way Jesus manifests himself through various kinds of visions. These often happen when a person least expects it.

An intellectual vision comes about when a soul suddenly becomes deeply conscious of Jesus' nearness to it, even though it cannot see him with its bodily eyes (as in an apparition) or the eyes of the soul (as in an imaginative vision). The soul is first disturbed by this deep sense of Jesus' presence, for it does not see anything and does not understand what it is. Eventually, it overcomes its doubts about the vision being there, but will have misgivings about whether or not it comes from God. Such a vision can last a long time—in some cases, as long as an entire year.

Fearful of the vision's source, the soul seeks guidance from its confessor, who helps it to determine if it is authentic. In time, the soul becomes more and more certain that the intellectual vision comes from the Lord himself. It makes this judgment based on the good effects the vision produces in the soul, the most important of which is humility. The soul knows that the vision is neither a product of human effort, nor a work of the evil one. Although it continues to have some misgivings and, at times, even great confusion about what is happening to it, the soul is blessed with a deep sense of Jesus' abiding presence, which enables it to think of him continuously. From this constant companionship, it receives a special knowledge of God and has a deep desire to serve him. Its nearness to Jesus also purifies its conscience and makes it increasingly sensitive to what happens around it. When the vision ends, the soul has a deep sense of loneliness and, because it is a gift from God, can do nothing to regain it.

Teresa says that an intellectual vision may even give the soul a deep sense of the Blessed Mother's nearness or the presence of some other saint. In such cases, the soul intuits that the Lord is sending the saint in question as a helper and companion. As in the visions of Jesus, the soul has a certainty of the authenticity of these visions. Teresa cannot explain how the soul knows that these intellectual visions are of God. She gives thanks to God for the way he communicates to the soul on such a deep level. She also points to the benefits these visions produce in the soul, especially a desire to serve God and deep sense of inner peace. Once again, these effects could not be a product of the imagination or a work of the evil one. Even when the vision comes to an end, the Lord continues to protect the soul from harm.

Teresa advises her readers not to presume to possess such gifts from God, especially if they do not manifest their effects in their lives. She tells them to submit their experiences to a learned confessor or a highly spiritual person. As far as confessors and spiritual directors are concerned, she says it is best to go to someone who is both learned *and* spiritual. If that is not possible, she advises her readers to seek out a learned director, since he will be less apt to discount the authenticity of such visions, while at the same time submitting them to great scrutiny. If one's director is a prayerful man, but not advanced in the way of perfection, he may become alarmed at what he himself has not experienced and possibly condemn it outright. In such a case, she tells her readers (nuns of her Carmelite reform) to ask their superiors for permission to seek out someone who is both learned *and* spiritual. She advises superiors to be cautious in such cases, but to grant permission for their own good and that of the individual in question. Teresa ends by reminding her readers not to think of themselves as better than anyone else should the Lord bless them with such visions. Growth in the virtues is always the key to determining progress in holiness. The saintly person is the one who serves God selflessly, humbly, and with a pure conscience. Only the Lord can look into a person's heart and judge the state of the soul.

✢

Text

Treats of the way in which God communicates Himself to the soul through intellectual vision.[1] *Describes the effects that this produces when genuine. Charges that these favors be kept secret.*

In order, sisters, that you may the better appreciate the accuracy of what I have been saying to you and see that the farther a soul progresses the closer becomes its companionship with this good Jesus, it will be well for us to consider how, when His Majesty so wills, we cannot do otherwise than walk with Him all the times as is clear from the ways and methods whereby His Majesty communicates Himself to us, and reveals His love for us by means of such wonderful appearances and visions. Should the Lord grant you any of the favors that I shall describe (I mean, if He grants me ability to describe any of them), you must not be dismayed. Even though it be not to us that He grants them, we must give Him hearty praise that He should be pleased to commune with a creature—He Who is of such great majesty and power.

It may happen that, while the soul is not in the least expecting Him to be about to grant it this favor, which it has never thought it can possibly deserve, it is conscious that Jesus Christ Our Lord is near to it, though it cannot see Him either with the eyes of the body or with those of the soul. This (I do not know why) is called an intellectual vision. I saw a person to whom God had granted this favor, together with other favors that I shall describe later. At first that person was greatly perturbed, for she could not understand what the vision was, not having seen anything. She realized with such certainty that it was Jesus Christ Our Lord Who had revealed Himself to her in that way that she could not doubt it—I mean, could not doubt that that vision was there. But as to its being from God or not she had great misgivings, although the effects that it produced were so remarkable that they suggested it came from Him. She had never heard of an intellectual vision, or realized that there was any such thing, but she understood quite clearly that it was this Lord Who often spoke to her in the way I have described: until He granted her this favor to which I am referring she never knew Who was speaking to her, although she understood the words.

Being frightened about this vision (for it is not like an imaginary vision, which is quickly gone, but lasts for many days—sometimes for more than a year), she went off to her confessor in a state of great perturbation.[2] "If you see nothing," he asked her, "how do you know it is Our Lord?" Then he told her to tell him what His face was like. She replied that she did not know, that she had seen no face, and that she could not tell him more than she had done already: what she did know was that it was He Who was speaking to her and that it was no fancy. And, although people aroused grievous misgivings in her about it, she felt again and again that she could not doubt its genuineness, especially when He said to her: "Be not afraid: it is I." These words had such power that when she heard them she could not doubt, and she was greatly strengthened and gladdened by such good companionship. For she saw plainly that it was a great help to her to be habitually thinking of God wherever she went and to be taking such care to do nothing that would displease Him because she felt that He was always looking at her. Whenever she wanted to draw near to His Majesty in prayer, and at other times as well, she felt He was so near that He could not fail to hear her, although she was unable to hear Him speaking to her whenever she wished, but did so at quite unexpected times, when it became necessary. She was conscious that He was walking at her right hand, but this consciousness arose, not from those senses that tell us that another person is near us, but in another and a subtler way that is indescribable. It is quite as unmistakable, however, and produces a feeling of equal certainty, or even greater. Other things of the kind might be attributable to fancy, but this thing is not, for it brings such great benefits and produces such effects upon the interior life as could not occur if it were the result of melancholy. The devil, again, could not do so much good: were it his work, the soul would not have such peace and such constant desires to please God and such scorn for everything that does not lead it to Him. Later, this person attained a clear realization that it was not the work of the devil and came to understand it better and better.

Nonetheless, I know she sometimes felt the gravest misgivings, and at other times the greatest confusion,[3] because she had no idea whence such a great blessing had come to her. She and I were so intimate that nothing happened in her soul of which I was ignorant, and thus I can be a good witness and you may be sure that everything I say about it is true. This favor of the Lord brings with it the greatest confusion and humility. If it came from the devil, it would be just the reverse. As it is a thing that can be clearly recognized as the gift of God and such feelings could not possibly be produced by human effort, anyone who has it must know it does not in reality come from him, but is a gift from the hand of God. And although, as I believe, some of the other experiences that have been described are greater favors than this, yet this brings a special knowledge of God, and from this constant companionship is born a most tender love toward His Majesty, and yearnings, even deeper than those already described, to give oneself wholly up to His service, and a great purity of conscience; for the Presence Which the soul has at its side makes it sensitive to everything. For though we know quite well that God is present in all that we do, our nature is such that it makes us lose sight of the fact; but when this favor is granted it can no longer do so, for the Lord, Who is near at hand, awakens it. And even the favors aforementioned occur much more commonly, as the soul experiences a vivid and almost constant love for Him Whom it sees or knows to be at its side.

In short, the greatness and the precious quality of this favor are best seen in what the soul gains from it. It thanks the Lord, Who bestows this favor on one that has not deserved it, and would exchange it for no earthly treasure or joy. When the Lord is pleased to withdraw it, the soul is left in great loneliness; yet all the possible efforts that it might make to regain His companionship are of little avail, for the Lord gives this when He wills and it cannot be acquired. Sometimes, again, the companionship is that of a saint, and this is also a great help to us.

You will ask how, if this Presence cannot be seen, the soul knows that it is that of Christ, or when it is a saint, or His most glorious Mother. This is a question that the soul cannot answer, nor can it understand how it knows what it does; it is perfectly certain, however, that it is right. When it is the Lord, and He speaks, it is natural that He should be easily recognized; but even when it is a saint, and no words are spoken, the soul is able to feel that the Lord is sending him to be a help and a companion to it; and this is more remarkable. There are also other spiritual experiences that cannot be described, but they all help to show us how impotent our nature is, when it comes to understanding the great wonders of God, for we are not capable of understanding these but can only marvel and praise His Majesty for giving them to us. So let us give Him special thanks for them; for, as this is not a favor that is granted to all, it is one that should be highly esteemed and we must try to render the greatest services to God Who has so many ways of helping us. For this reason no one thus favored has any better opinion of himself on that account. On the contrary, he feels that he is serving God less than anyone else on the earth, and yet that no one else has so great an obligation to serve Him. Any fault that he commits, therefore, pierces his very vitals and has every reason to do so.

These above-described effects that such visions cause in the soul may be observed by any one of you whom the Lord leads by this way, and you will then see that they are due neither to deception nor to fancy. For, as I have said, if they are of the devil, I do not think they can possibly last so long or do the soul such a great deal of good, or bring it such inward peace. It is not usual for one who is so evil to do so much good; he could not, in fact, even if he would. The soul would soon become clouded over by the mist of self-esteem and would begin to think itself better than others. But its continual occupation with God and its fixing of the thought on Him would make the devil so furious that, though he might attempt such a thing once, he would not do so often. God is so faithful that He will not allow the devil to have all this power over a soul whose one aim is to please Him and to devote its whole life to His honor and glory; He will see to it that the devil is speedily disillusioned.

My point is, and will continue to be, that, if the soul walks in the manner described above, and these favors of God are withdrawn from it, His Majesty will see that it is the gainer, and if He sometimes allows the devil to attack it, his efforts will be brought to confusion. Therefore, daughters, if any of you travel along this road, as I have said, do not be alarmed. It is well for us to have misgivings and walk the more warily; and you must not presume upon having received these favors and become careless, for if you do not find them producing in you the result already described it will be a sign that they are not of God. It will be well at first for you to communicate this, in confession, to some very learned man (for it is from such men that we must seek illumination) or to any highly spiritual person if you know one. Should your confessor not be a very spiritual man, someone with learning is better; or, if you know such a person, it is best to consult one both spiritual and learned. If he tells you that it is fancy, do not let that trouble you, for fancy can have little effect on your soul, either for good or for evil: commend yourself to the Divine Majesty and pray

Him not to allow you to be deceived. If he tells you that it is the devil, this will be a greater trial to you, though no learned man would say such a thing if you have experienced the effects described; but, if he says it, I know that the Lord Himself, Who is walking at your side, will console you and reassure you, and will continue to give him light, so that he in his turn may give it to you.

If your director, though a man of prayer, has not been led in this way by the Lord, he will at once become alarmed and condemn it; that is why I advise you to go to a man who has both spirituality and great learning if such a one can be found. Your prioress should give you leave to do this; for although, seeing you are leading a good life, she may think your soul is safe, she will be bound to allow you to consult someone for your own safety and for hers as well. When you have finished these consultations, calm yourself and do not go on talking about the matter, for sometimes, when there is no reason for fear, the devil implants such excessive misgivings that they prevent the soul from being content with a single consultation, especially if the confessor has had little experience and treats the matter timorously and enjoins you to go and consult others. In such a case what should by rights be a close secret gets noised abroad and the penitent is persecuted and tormented; for she finds that what she thought was secret has become public, and this leads to many sore trials, which, as things are at present, might affect the Order. Great caution, then, is necessary here and such caution I strongly recommend to prioresses.

And let none of you imagine that, because a sister has had such experiences, she is any better than the rest; the Lord leads each of us as He sees we have need. Such experiences, if we use them aright, prepare us to be better servants of God; but sometimes it is the weakest whom God leads by this road; and so there is no ground here either for approval or for condemnation. We must base our judgments on the virtues. The saintliest will be she who serves Our Lord with the greatest mortification and humility and purity of conscience. Little, however, can be known with any certainty about this on earth, nor until the true Judge gives each his deserts. Then we shall be amazed to see how different His judgment is from the ideas that we have formed on earth. May He be forever praised. Amen.

Exploring the Interior Castle

- Do you believe that God can manifest himself to a person through visions? If not, why not? If no, do you think he does so often? What would the purpose of such visions be? How do others normally perceive such people?

- What is Teresa's understanding of an intellectual vision? How does it differ from a corporeal vision or one seen with the eyes of the soul? How long does it last? What effects does it produce in the soul? How does the soul gain certitude about its authenticity? Can a person do anything to acquire such a vision? Does her description of an intellectual vision seem beyond the reach of most believers?

- Teresa says that a soul may have an intellectual vision of the Blessed Mother or a saint rather than one of Christ Do you believe that such visions are also possible? If so, how often do they occur? What purpose do they serve in the life of the believer? Why would God send an intellectual vision of the Blessed Mother or a saint when he could send one of his only begotten Son?

- Why does Teresa place such a strong emphasis on going to a confessor or spiritual director who is both spiritual and learned? Have you ever discussed your troubles with someone who had no concrete experience of them in his or her own life? If so, how were you received? Did you feel accepted? Were you looked upon with suspicion? What dangers are there in discussing rarefied mystical experiences to someone who has no experience of them?

Chapter Nine

✛

Introduction

In this chapter, Teresa discusses imaginative visions and why one must exercise great caution when dealing with them. Visions are called "imaginary" (as Peers puts it) because they come to the soul through the imagination. They can be of God, self-constructed, or from the evil one. When they are of God, they can be of great help to the soul, since the use of images is a very common feature of human communication. With the exception of the favors the Lord bestows in the seventh mansions, these are more helpful to the soul than most other visions.

To describe what an imaginative vision from God resembles, Teresa uses the image of a golden reliquary with a precious stone hidden in it. Even though the soul has never seen it, it is aware of the stone and greatly treasures it. Only God knows how to open the reliquary and display the stone for the soul to see. When he does, the soul enjoys what it sees and prizes the stone all the more. In an imaginative vision, God uses the imagination to reveal himself to the soul by impressing on its memory in lightening-quick speed a vivid image of what he was like when he walked the earth or how he was transformed after his resurrection. This image is a dynamic, vibrant presence that reveals much to the soul about its beloved. It is so intense that the soul can gaze upon it only for a short while. The vision gives the soul both a deep sense of God's grandeur that fills it with great fear and an increased sense of its own insignificance. In such a vision, God reveals himself directly to the soul, without any intermediary. When the vision passes, its effect on the soul may cause it to remain in ecstasy for a long time.

Teresa spends some time discussing how people can deceive themselves into thinking they have had an imaginative vision when they are only making it up themselves. She is suspicious of people who claim to have such visions for extended periods of time. She also says that when people create such things themselves, what they see with their imagination is usually constructed in stages, whereas visions from God come whole and entire in a sudden flash. In authentic imaginative visions, moreover, the soul experiences deep inner peace and has no doubt whatsoever that the vision comes from God. Such certainty remains even though the soul's faculties and senses themselves have been thrown into disarray. Teresa directs her readers to tell their confessors about these visions in a simple and direct manner. Unless they reveal them honestly to those who are responsible for their spiritual lives, they will never know for sure if they are following the Lord's will. Being certain of having received a vision from the Lord is one thing; doing God's will, quite another.

As far as imaginative visions caused by the evil one are concerned, Teresa likens them to accurate lifelike reproductions of the Lord painted by a skilled artist She draws a distinction between the artist and the beautiful painting he produces. The soul must have nothing to do with the evil one, but must revere the remarkable resemblance to the Lord he has created. Still, one must proceed with great caution. The evil one is the father of lies, can deceive even those experienced in prayer, and is capable of doing grave harm. Even though they resemble them very closely, imaginative visions from the evil one do not have the same effects on the soul's interior life. Increased humility, holy fear, and deep inner peace come only from those imaginative visions caused by God.

Finally, Teresa offers her readers several reasons why they should not desire or seek out imaginative visions. To ask God for such favors signals a lack of humility; doing so opens the door to the deceptions of the evil one. If one desires them enough, moreover, one might actually start imagining them. It is presumptuous to ask for such favors, and one might not be able to bear the trials that accompany them. In the end, the favor might actually incur a loss for the soul instead of a gain. Teresa reaffirms that the most important thing in the spiritual life is to will only what God wills. God loves each person and knows what is best for him or her. She reminds her readers, moreover, that these favors do not last forever and have very little to do with holiness. Rather than focusing on such favors, it would be much better for the soul to dedicate itself to growing in the virtues.

✤

Text

Treats of the way in which the Lord communicates Himself to the soul through imaginary visions and gives an emphatic warning that we should be careful not to desire to walk in this way. Gives reasons for the warning. This chapter is of great profit.

L et us now come to imaginary visions, in which the devil is said to interfere more frequently than in those already described. This may well be the case; but when they come from Our Lord they seem to me in some ways more profitable because they are in closer conformity with our nature, except for those that the Lord bestows in the final Mansion, and with which no others can compare.

Let us now imagine, as I said in the last chapter, that this Lord is here. It is as if in a gold reliquary there were hidden a precious stone of the highest value and the choicest virtues: although we have never seen the stone, we know for certain that it is there and if we carry it about with us we can have the benefit of its virtues. We do not prize it any the less for not having seen it, because we have found by experience that it has cured us of certain illnesses for which it is a sovereign remedy. But we dare not look at it, or open the reliquary in which it is contained, nor are we able to do so; for only the owner of the jewel knows how to open it, and though he has lent it to us so that we may benefit by it, he has kept the key and so it is still his own. He will open it when he wants to show it to us and he will take it back when he sees fit to do so. And that is what God does, too.

And now let us suppose that on some occasion the owner of the reliquary suddenly wants to open it, for the benefit of the person to whom he has lent it. Obviously this person will get much greater pleasure from it if he can recall the wonderful brilliance of the stone, and it will remain the more deeply engraved upon his memory. This is what happens here. When Our Lord is pleased to bestow greater con-solations upon this soul, He grants it, in whatever way He thinks best, a clear revelation of His sacred Humanity, either as He was when He lived in the world, or as He was after His resurrection; and although He does this so quickly that we might liken the action to a flash of lightning, this most glorious image is so deeply engraved upon the imagination that I do not believe it can possibly disappear until it is where it can be enjoyed to all eternity.

I speak of an "image," but it must not be supposed that one looks at it as at a painting; it is really alive, and sometimes even speaks to the soul and shows it things both great and secret. But you must realize that, although the soul sees this for a certain length of time, it can no more be gazing at it all the time than it could keep gazing at the sun. So the vision passes very quickly, though this is not because its brilliance hurts the interior sight—that is, the medium by which all such things are seen—as the brilliance of the sun hurts the eyes. When it is a question of exterior sight, I can say nothing about it, for the person I have mentioned, and of whom I can best speak, had not experienced this; and reason can testify only inadequately to things of which it has no experience. The brilliance of this vision is like that of infused light or of a sun covered with some material of the transparency of a diamond, if such a thing could be woven. This raiment looks like the finest cambric. Almost invariably the soul on which God bestows this favor remains in rapture, because its unworthiness cannot endure so terrible a sight.

I say "terrible" because, though the sight is the loveliest and most delightful imaginable, even by a person who lived and strove to imagine it for a thousand years, because it so far exceeds all that our imagination and understanding can compass, its presence is of such exceeding majesty that it fills the soul with a great terror. It is unnecessary to ask here how, without being told, the soul knows Who it is, for He reveals Himself quite clearly as the Lord of Heaven and earth. This the kings of the earth never do: indeed, they would be thought very little of for what they are, but that they are accompanied by their suites, or heralds proclaim them.

O, Lord, how little do we Christians know Thee! What will that day be like when Thou comest to judge us? If when Thou comest here in such a friendly way to hold converse with Thy bride the sight of Thee causes us such fear, what will it be, O daughters, when with that stern voice He says: "Depart, accursed of My Father"?[1]

Let us keep that in mind when we remember this favor that God grants to the soul, and we shall find it of no small advantage to us. Even Saint Jerome, holy man though he was, did not banish it from his memory. If we do that we shall care nothing for all we have suffered through keeping strictly to the observances of our Order, for, however long this may take us, the time will be but short by comparison with eternity. I can tell you truly that, wicked as I am, I have never feared the torments of hell, for they seem nothing by comparison with the thought of the wrath that the damned will see in the Lord's eyes—those eyes so lovely and tender and benign. I do not think my heart could bear to see that; and I have felt like this all my life. How much more will anyone fear this to whom He has thus revealed Himself, and given such a consciousness of His presence as will produce unconsciousness![2] It must be for this reason that the soul remains in suspension; the Lord helps it in its weakness so that this may be united with His greatness in this sublime communion with God.

When the soul is able to remain for a long time looking upon the Lord, I do not think it can be a vision at all. It must rather be that some striking idea creates a picture in the imagination: but this will be a dead image by comparison with the other.

Some persons—and I know this is the truth, for they have discussed it with me; and not just three or four of them, but a great many—find that their imagination is so weak, or their understanding is so nimble, or for some other reason their imagination becomes so absorbed, that they think they can actually see everything that is in their mind. If they had ever seen a true vision they would realize their error beyond the possibility of doubt. Little by little they build up the picture that they see with their imagination, but this produces no effect upon them and they remain cold—much more so than they are after seeing a sacred image. No attention, of course, should be paid to such a thing, which will be forgotten much more quickly than a dream.

The experience we are discussing here is quite different. The soul is very far from expecting to see anything and the thought of such a thing has never even passed through its mind. All of a sudden the whole vision is revealed to it and all its faculties and senses are thrown into the direst fear and confusion, and then sink into that blessed state of peace. It is just as when Saint Paul was thrown to the ground and there came that storm and tumult in the sky, just so, in this interior world, there is a great commotion; and then all at once, as I have said, everything grows calm, and the soul, completely instructed in such great truths, has no need of another master. True wisdom, without any effort on its own part, has overcome its stupidity and for a certain space of time it enjoys the complete certainty that this favor comes from God. However often it may be told that this is not so it cannot be induced to fear that it may have been mistaken. Later, when the confessor insinuates this fear, God allows the soul to begin to hesitate as to whether He could possibly grant this favor to such a sinner. But that is all; for, as I have said in these other cases, in speaking of temptations in matters of faith, the devil can disturb the soul, but he cannot shake the firmness of its belief. On the contrary, the more fiercely he attacks it, the more certain it becomes that he could never endow it with so many blessings—which is actually true, for over the interior of the soul he wields less power. He may be able to reveal something to it, but not with the same truth and majesty, nor can he produce the same results.

As confessors cannot see all this for themselves, and a soul to whom God has granted such a favor may be unable to describe it, they have misgivings about it, and quite justifiably. So they have to proceed cautiously, and even to wait for some time to see what results these apparitions produce, and to observe gradually how much humility they leave in the soul and to what extent it is strengthened in virtue; if they come from the devil there will soon be signs of the fact, for he will be caught out in a thousand lies. If the confessor is experienced, and has himself been granted such visions, it will not be long before he is able to form a judgment, for the account that the soul gives will at once show him whether they proceed from God or from the imagination or from the devil, especially if His Majesty has granted him the gift of discerning spirits. If he has this and is a learned man, he will be able to form an opinion perfectly well, even though he may be without experience.

The really essential thing, sisters, is that you should speak to your confessor very plainly and candidly—I do not mean here in confessing your sins, for of course you will do so then, but in describing your experiences in prayer. For unless you do this, I cannot assure you that you are proceeding as you should or that it is God Who is teaching you. God is very anxious for us to speak candidly and clearly to those who are in His place, and to desire them to be acquainted with all our thoughts, and still more with our actions, however trivial these may be. If you do this, you need not be disturbed, or worried, for, even if these things be not of God, they will do you no harm if you are humble and have a good conscience. His Majesty is able to bring good out of evil and you will gain by following the road by which the devil hoped to bring you to destruction. For, as you will suppose that it is God Who is granting you these great favors, you will strive to please Him better and keep His image ever in your mind. A very learned man used to say that the devil is a skilful painter, and that, if he were to show him an absolutely lifelike image of the Lord, it would not worry him, because it would quicken his devotion, and so he would be using the devil's own wicked weapons to make war on him. However evil the painter be, one cannot fail to reverence the picture that he paints, if it is of Him Who is our only Good.

This learned man thought that the counsel, given by some people, to treat any vision of this kind with scorn,[3] was very wrong: we must reverence a painting of our King, he said, wherever we see it. I think he is right; even on a worldly plane we should feel that. If a person who had a great friend knew that insulting things were being said about his portrait he would not be pleased. How much more incumbent upon us is it, then, always to be respectful when we see a crucifix or any kind of portrait of our Emperor!

Although I have written this elsewhere, I have been glad to set it down here, for I knew someone who was in great distress because she had been ordered to adopt this derisive remedy. I do not know who can have invented such advice, for, if it came from her confessor, it would have been a torture to her: she would be bound to obey him, and would have thought herself a lost soul unless she had done so. My own advice is that, if you are given such counsel, you should not accept it and should with all humility put forward this argument that I have given you. I was extremely struck by the good reasons against the practice alleged by the person who advised me in this case.

The soul derives great profit from this favor bestowed by the Lord, for thinking upon Him or upon His life and Passion recalls His most meek and lovely face, which is the greatest comfort, just as in the earthly sphere we get much more comfort from seeing a person who is a great help to us than if we had never known him. I assure you that such a delectable remembrance gives the greatest help and comfort. It also brings many other blessings with it, but as so much has been said about the effects caused by these things, and there is more still to come, I will not fatigue myself or you by adding more just now. I will only warn you that, when you learn or hear that God is granting souls these graces, you must never beseech or desire Him to lead you along this road. Even if you think it a very good one, and to be greatly prized and reverenced, there are certain reasons why such a course is not wise.

The first reason is that it shows a lack of humility to ask to be given what you have never deserved, so I think anyone who asks for this cannot be very humble. A peasant of lowly birth would never dream of wishing to be a king; such a thing seems to him impossible because he does not merit it. Anyone who is humble feels just the same about these other things. I think they will never be bestowed on a person devoid of humility, because before the Lord grants a soul these favors He always gives it a high degree of self-knowledge. And how could one who has such ambitions realize that He is doing him a great favor in not casting him into hell?

The second reason is that such a person is quite certain to be deceived, or to be in great peril, because the devil has only to see a door left slightly ajar to enter and play a thousand tricks on us.

The third reason is to be found in the imagination. When a person has a great desire for something, he persuades himself that he is seeing or hearing what he desires, just as those who go about desiring something all day think so much about it that after a time they begin to dream of it.

The fourth reason is that it is very presumptuous in me to wish to choose my path, because I cannot tell which path is best for me. I must leave it to the Lord, Who knows me, to lead me by the path that is best for me, so that in all things His will may be done.

In the fifth place, do you suppose that the trials suffered by those to whom the Lord grants these favors are light ones? No, they are very heavy, and of many kinds. How do you know if you would be able to bear them?

In the sixth place, you may well find that the very thing from which you had expected gain will bring you loss, just as Saul only lost by becoming a king.

And besides these reasons, sisters, there are others. Believe me, the safest thing is to will only what God wills, for He knows us better than we know ourselves, and He loves us. Let us place ourselves in His hands so that His will may be done in us; if we cling firmly to this maxim and our wills are resolute we cannot possibly go astray. And you must note that you will merit no more glory for having received many of these favors; on the contrary, the fact that you are receiving more imposes on you greater obligations to serve. The Lord does not deprive us of anything that adds to our merit, for this remains in our own power. There are many saintly people who have never known what it is to receive a favor of this kind, and there are others who receive a favor of this kind, and there are others who received such favors, although they are not saintly. Do not suppose, again, that they occur continually. Each occasion on which the Lord grants them brings with it a great many trials; and thus the soul does not think about receiving more, but only about how to put those it receives to a good use.

It is true that to have these favors must be the greatest help toward attaining a high degree of perfection in the virtues; but anyone who has attained the virtues at the cost of his own toil has earned much more merit. I know of a person to whom the Lord had granted some of these favors—of two indeed; one was a man. Both were desirous of serving His Majesty, at their own cost, and without being given any of these great consolations; and they were so anxious to suffer that they complained to Our Lord because He bestowed favors on them, which, had it been possible, they would have excused themselves from receiving. I am speaking here, not of these visions, which bring us great gain, and are very much to be prized, but of consolations that the Lord gives in contemplation.

It is true that, in my opinion, these desires are supernatural, and come from souls fired with love, who would like the Lord to see that they are not serving Him for pay; for which reason, as I have said, they never spur themselves to greater efforts in God's service by thinking of the glory that they will receive for anything they do; rather do they serve Him for the satisfaction of their love, for the nature of love invariably finds expression in work of a thousand kinds. If it were able, the soul would invent methods by which to become consumed in Him, and if, for the greater honor of God, it were necessary that it should remain annihilated forever, it would agree to this very willingly. May He be forever praised Who is pleased to show forth His greatness by stooping to commune with such miserable creatures. Amen.

Exploring the Interior Castle

- What is distinctive about imaginative visions? What do they have in common with other types of visions (e.g., corporeal, intellectual)? Does Teresa's image of the reliquary with the precious stone hidden in it help you to understand the nature of imaginative visions any better? Can you think of any other way of describing the nature of such visions?

- For Teresa, how can one tell if an imaginative vision comes from God and not from oneself or the evil one? In what sense is it "imaginary"? In what sense is it not "imaginary"? Does Teresa's description of imaginative visions speak to your experience? What relevance does her teaching have for today's believers?

- Do you think imaginative visions occur today? If so, do you think many people have them? A select few? The rare individual? Do you think the composition of Christian mystical experience changes over time? If so, in what ways? Are imaginative visions essential or merely accidental to Christian mysticism? What would Teresa say?

- Teresa once again emphasizes wanting what God wants and doing his will as the key to growth in holiness. If this is so important, however, then why does she spend so much time examining rarefied mystical states such as imaginative visions, which, by her own admission, have very little to do with saintliness? Does the fact that she is writing out of obedience have any bearing on the matter?

Chapter Ten

✛

Introduction

In this chapter, Teresa discusses how God uses other kinds of visions to speak to the soul. She does not go into great detail in her treatment of them. She wishes only to give enough description so that her readers might be able to understand their nature and the effects they have on the soul. She also wishes to give them a way of determining whether their own visions are authentic or simply their own imaginings. In doing so, she hopes to lessen their anxiety and help them to love and praise God with even greater fervor.

According to Teresa, the Lord sends these special visions at various times and for different reasons. They might come to a soul when it is troubled, about to undergo a difficult ordeal, or perhaps because God desires to enjoy the soul and put it at ease. Unlike imaginative visions, they are difficult to describe and the evil one cannot imitate them.

Teresa gives an example of what might happen. While the soul is at prayer and fully alert, the Lord might suddenly suspend it and reveal to it some of his innermost secrets. He gives it a special intellectual vision that enables it to see how all things are seen and contained in God. Such a vision lasts for only a moment, but is very helpful to the soul, for it shows it the seriousness of its actions when it chooses to offend him. Teresa uses an image to explain. God, in her mind, is like a very large palace that houses the universe. Since no one can go outside, sinners must commit their sins within the palace walls. It is impossible to do something without

God being present. Despite the grave offenses committed against him, however, the Lord still shows great mercy and compassion to the soul. Teresa exhorts her readers to forgive others in a similar way.

At other times, Teresa says, God might all of a sudden manifest an indescribable truth to the soul that far exceeds all human knowledge. He makes it very evident that he alone is Truth and that the soul must walk in this Truth if it wishes to enter into the fullness of life. To walk in the Truth is not simply a matter of refraining from telling lies. It means walking humbly in God's presence and in the presence of others. One must seek the Truth in all things. Humility is so important in the spiritual life because it helps one recognize that God alone is Truth and that nothing within a person is good unless it comes from God. Teresa concludes by saying that God bestows special gifts on the soul because he loves it like his beloved spouse. Rather than fear them, she says, one should praise God if they come. They are unmistakably from God, since there is no way they can be the work of the imagination or the evil one.

Text

Speaks of other favors that God grants to the soul in a different way from those already mentioned, and of the great profit that they bring.

There are many ways in which the Lord communicates Himself to the soul by means of these apparitions. Some of them come when the soul is afflicted; others, when it is about to be visited by some heavy trial; others, so that His Majesty may take His delight in it and at the same time may comfort it. There is no need to particularize about each of these; my intention is only to explain in turn the different experiences that occur on this road, as far as I understand them, so that you, sisters, may understand their nature and the effects that they cause. And I am doing this so that you may not suppose everything you imagine to be a vision, and so that, when you do see a vision, you will know that such a thing is possible and will not be disturbed or distressed. For, when you are, it is a great gain for the devil; he is delighted to see a soul distressed and uneasy, because he knows that this will hinder it from employing itself in loving and praising God. His Majesty also communicates Himself in other ways, which are much more sublime, and are also less dangerous, because, I think, the devil cannot counterfeit them. But, being very secret things, they are difficult to describe, whereas imaginary visions can be explained more readily.

When the Lord so wills, it may happen that the soul will be at prayer, and in possession of all its senses, and that then there will suddenly come to it a suspension in which the Lord communicates most secret things to it, which it seems to see within God Himself. These are not visions of the most sacred Humanity; although I say that the soul "sees" Him, it really sees nothing, for this is not an imaginary, but a notably intellectual, vision, in which is revealed to the soul how all things are seen in God, and how within Himself He contains them all. Such a vision is highly profitable because, although it passes in a moment, it remains engraved upon the soul. It causes us the greatest confusion, by showing us clearly how wrongly we are acting when we offend God, since it is within God Himself—because we dwell within Him, I mean—that we are committing these great sins. I want, if I can, to draw a comparison to explain this, for, although it is a fact and we hear it stated frequently, we either pay no heed to it or refuse to understand it; if we really understood it, I do not think we could possibly be so presumptuous.

Let us imagine that God is like a very large and beautiful mansion or palace. This palace, then, as I say, is God Himself. Now can the sinner go away from it in order to commit his misdeeds? Certainly not, these abominations and dishonorable actions and evil deeds that we sinners commit are done within the palace itself—that is, within God. Oh, fearful thought, worthy of deep consideration and very profitable for us who are ignorant and unable to understand these truths—for if we could understand them we could not possibly be guilty of such foolish presumption! Let us consider, sisters, the great mercy and long-suffering of God in not casting us straight into the depths, and let us render Him the heartiest thanks and be ashamed of worrying over anything that is done or said against us. It is the most dreadful thing in the world that God our Creator should suffer so many misdeeds to be committed by His creatures within Himself, while we ourselves are sometimes worried about a single word uttered in our absence and perhaps not even with a wrong intention.

Oh, human misery! How long will it be, daughters, before we imitate this great God in any way? Oh, let us not deceive ourselves into thinking that we are doing anything whatever by merely putting up with insults! Let us endure everything, and be very glad to do so, and love those who do us wrong; for, greatly as we have offended this great God, He has not ceased loving us, and so He has very good reason for desiring us all to forgive those who have wronged us. I assure you, daughters, that, although this vision passes quickly, it is a great favor for the Lord to bestow it upon those to whom He grants it if they will try to profit by having it habitually present in their minds.

It may also happen that, very suddenly and in a way that cannot be described, God will reveal a truth that is in Himself and that makes any truth to be found in the creatures seem like thick darkness; He will also manifest very clearly that He alone is truth and cannot lie. This is a very good explanation of David's meaning in that Psalm where he says that every man is a liar.[1] One would never take those words in that sense of one's own accord, however many times one heard them, but they express a truth that is infallible. I remember that story about Pilate, who asked Our Lord so many questions, and at the time of His Passion said to Him: "'What is truth?'"[2] And then I reflect how little we understand of this Sovereign Truth here on earth.

I should like to be able to say more about this matter, but it is impossible. Let us learn from this, sisters, that if we are in any way to grow like our God and Spouse, we shall do well always to study earnestly to walk in this truth. I do not mean simply that we must not tell falsehoods, for as far as that is concerned—glory be to God!—I know that in these convents of ours you take very great care never to lie about anything for any reason whatsoever. I mean that we must walk in truth, in the presence of God and man, in every way possible to us. In particular we must not desire to be reputed better than we are and in all we do we must attribute to God what is His, and to ourselves what is ours, and try to seek after truth in everything. If we do that, we shall make small account of this world, for it is all lying and falsehood and for that reason cannot endure.

I was wondering once why Our Lord so dearly loved this virtue of humility; and all of a sudden—without, I believe, my having previously thought of it—the following reason came into my mind: that it is because God is Sovereign Truth and to be humble is to walk in truth, for it is absolutely true to say that we have no good thing in ourselves, but only misery and nothingness; and anyone who fails to understand this is walking in falsehood. He who best understands it is most pleasing to Sovereign Truth because he is walking in truth. May it please God, sisters, to grant us grace never to fail to have this knowledge of ourselves. Amen.

Our Lord grants the soul favors like these because He is pleased to treat her like a true bride, who is determined to do His will in all things, and to give her some knowledge of the way in which she can do His will and of His greatness. I need say no more; I have said these two things because they seem to me so helpful; for there is no reason to be afraid of these favors, but only to praise the Lord, because He gives them. In my opinion, there is little scope here either for the devil or for the soul's own imagination, and when it knows this the soul experiences a great and lasting happiness.

Exploring the Interior Castle

- Teresa says that there are many ways in which the Lord speaks to the soul. Do you think she is trying to describe all of them? Most of them? Only the more important ones? Do you think she is speaking primarily out of her own personal experience? Do any of the mystical experiences she has spoken about thus far resonate with your own experience?

- Does Teresa's use of the image of God as a very large and beautiful palace that no one can leave work as a way of describing how all things are seen and contained in God? What are the analogy's strengths? Does it fall apart in any way? Can you think of another way of getting her idea across?

- Teresa says that to be humble is to walk in truth. If this is so, then pride is to walk in a lie or at least a false truth. Which walk do you find easier? Which are you better at? What are the lies or false truths that keep you from walking in truth? What does it mean to you to seek the truth in everything?

- Teresa says that God bestows special favors on a soul because he wishes to treat it as his beloved spouse. Does God have favorites? Does he love all people with the same degree of intensity? If not, why not? If so, why does he not bestow special favors on everyone?

Chapter Eleven

✠

Introduction

In this chapter, Teresa speaks of the soul's growing desire for God. This desire increases as the soul nears the final mansions and learns more about God's majesty. It also causes it a great deal of suffering, since each new vision brings fresh pain and anxiety that even a seasoned mystic cannot ward off. Referring obliquely to her own experience, she says that the soul's anxiety increases over the years. She recognizes, however, that God acts as he pleases and can accomplish in a single instant in one soul what he takes years to do in another.

At this point in its journey, Teresa says, the soul's deep yearning for God manifests itself in sighs and weeping. These come from its deep burning love for its beloved, which, at time, feels as though it has been struck by a burning arrow in its innermost depths. This pain passes very quickly, yet it purifies the soul of all that is not oriented toward God. The soul's powers and senses are suspended in rapture, but in a way that increases the soul's yearning for its beloved. The soul's pain is more intense than that of the body and resembles that of the souls in purgatory. Its distress is so deep that it does not take notice of physical pain. Even if it were cut to pieces, it would feel nothing at all.

The soul, Teresa continues, has an unquenchable thirst and yearns for God so deeply that it finds the company of others unbearable. At this point, it cannot think about doing God's will, because it has lost control of its reason and can only focus on the root of its pain. Only God can quench its thirst and ease its torments. Yet it is God who afflicts it in this way, because it must be purified by suffering before it can enter the seventh mansion. The soul loves this pain, for it understands that it will bring it closer to its beloved. Unlike the suffering of those in hell, its torments do not last forever and actually give it great delight. This pain is different from corporeal pain and can last anywhere from fifteen minutes to three or four hours. It comes upon the soul suddenly and with great violence. The soul can do nothing to ward it off or conceal its inner torment. Its pain is so great that it may, at times, even desire death. Only the Lord can relieve it, and he often does so by granting it a deep vision or ecstasy that strengthens and comforts it.

Despite its great suffering, Teresa says, the soul would gladly go through it all again out of love for God. At this point in its journey, it is extremely detached from earthly things and very afraid of doing something that will offend him. In addition to this danger, it must be careful not to rejoice in the Lord so much that it will become faint or appear to leave its senses over every little thing. Teresa concludes by telling her readers that this stage of the spiritual journey requires great courage and that the Lord gives it to those who need it.

✠

Text

Treats of the desires to enjoy God that He gives the soul and that are so great and impetuous that they endanger its life. Treats also of the profit that comes from this favor granted by the Lord.

Have all these favors that the Spouse has granted the soul been sufficient to satisfy this little dove or butterfly (do not suppose that I have forgotten her) and to make her settle down in the place where she is to die? Certainly not; she is in a much worse state than before; for, although she may have been receiving these favors for many years, she is still sighing and weeping, and each of them causes her fresh pain. The reason for this is that, the more she learns about the greatness of her God, while finding herself so far from Him and unable to enjoy Him, the more her desire increases. For the more is revealed to her of how much this great God and Lord deserves to be loved, the more does her love for Him grow. And gradually, during these years, her desire increases, so that she comes to experience great distress, as I will now explain. I have spoken of years, because I am writing about the experiences of the particular person about whom I have been speaking here. But it must be clearly understood that no limitations can be set to God's acts, and that He can raise a soul to the highest point here mentioned in a single moment. His Majesty has the power to do all that He wishes, and He is desirous of doing a great deal for us.

The soul, then, has these yearnings and tears and sighs, together with the strong impulses that have already been described. They all seem to arise from our love, and are accompanied by great emotion, but they are all as nothing by comparison with this other, for they are like a smoldering fire, the heat of which is quite bearable, though it causes pain. While the soul is in this condition, and interiorly burning, it often happens that a mere fleeting thought of some kind (there is no way of telling whence it comes, or how) or some remark that the soul hears about death's long tarrying, deals it, as it were, a blow, or, as one might say, wounds it with an arrow of fire. I do not mean that there actually is such an arrow, but, whatever it is, it obviously could not have come from our own nature. Nor is it actually a blow, though I have spoken of it as such; but it makes a deep wound, not, I think, in any region where physical pain can be felt, but in the soul's most intimate depths. It passes as quickly as a flash of lightning and leaves everything in our nature that is earthly reduced to powder. During the time that it lasts we cannot think of anything that has to do with our own existence: it instantaneously enchains the faculties in such a way that they have no freedom to do anything, except what will increase this pain.

I should not like this to sound exaggerated: in reality I am beginning to see, as I go on, that all I say falls short of the truth, which is indescribable. It is an enrapturing of the senses and faculties, except, as I have said, in ways that enhance this feeling of distress. The understanding is keenly on the alert to discover why this soul feels absent from God, and His Majesty now aids it with so lively a knowledge of Himself that it causes the distress to grow until the sufferer cries out aloud. However patient a sufferer she may be, and however accustomed to enduring great pain, she cannot help doing this, because this pain, as I have said, is not in the body, but deep within the soul. It was in this way that the person I have mentioned discovered how much more sensitive the soul is than the body, and it was revealed to her that this suffering resembles that of souls in purgatory; despite their being no longer in the body they suffer much more than do those who are still in the body and on earth.

I once saw a person in this state who I really believed was dying; and this was not at all surprising, because it does in fact involve great peril of death. Although it lasts only for a short time, it leaves the limbs quite disjointed, and, for as long as it continues, the pulse is as feeble as though the soul were about to render itself up to God. It really is quite as bad as this. For, while the natural heat of the body fails, the soul burns so fiercely within that, if the flame were only a little stronger, God would have fulfilled its desires. It is not that it feels any bodily pain whatsoever, notwithstanding such a dislocation of the limbs that for two or three days afterwards it is in great pain and has not the strength even to write; in fact the body seems to me never to be as strong as it was previously. The reason it feels no pain must be that it is suffering so keenly within that it takes no notice of the body. It is as when we have a very acute pain in one spot; we may have many other pains but we feel them less; this I have conclusively proved. In the present case, the soul feels nothing at all, and I do not believe it would feel anything if it were cut into little pieces.

You will tell me that this is imperfection and ask why such a person does not resign herself to the will of God, since she has surrendered herself to Him so completely. Down to this time she had been able to do so, and indeed had spent her life doing so; but now she no longer can because her reason is in such a state that she is not her own mistress, and can think of nothing but the cause of her suffering. Since she is absent from her Good, why should she wish to live? She is conscious of a strange solitude, since there is not a creature on the whole earth who can be a companion to her—in fact, I do not believe she would find any in Heaven, save Him Whom she loves: on the contrary, all earthly companionship is torment to her. She thinks of herself as of a person suspended aloft, unable either to come down and rest anywhere on earth or to ascend into Heaven. She is parched with thirst, yet cannot reach the water; and the thirst is not a tolerable one but of a kind that nothing can quench, nor does she desire it to be quenched, except with that water of which Our Lord spoke to the Samaritan woman,[1] and that is not given to her.

Ah, God help me! Lord, how Thou dost afflict Thy lovers! Yet all this is very little by comparison with what Thou bestowest upon them later. It is well that great things should cost a great deal, especially if the soul can be purified by suffering and enabled to enter the seventh Mansion, just as those who are to enter Heaven are cleansed in purgatory. If this is possible, its suffering is no more than a drop of water in the sea. So true is this that, despite all its torment and distress, which cannot, I believe, be surpassed by any such things on earth (many of which this person had endured, both bodily and spiritual, and they all seemed to her nothing by comparison), the soul feels this affliction to be so precious that it fully realizes it could never deserve it. But the anguish is of such a kind that nothing can relieve it; none the less the soul suffers it very gladly, and, if God so willed, would suffer it all its life long, although this would be not to die once, but to be always dying, for it is really quite as bad as that.

And now, sisters, let us consider the condition of those who are in hell. They are not resigned, as this soul is, nor have they this contentment and delight that God gives it. They cannot see that their suffering is doing them any good, yet they keep suffering more and more—I mean more and more in respect of accidental pains[2]—for the torment suffered by the soul is much more acute than that suffered by the body and the pains that such souls have to endure are beyond comparison greater than what we have here been describing. These unhappy souls know that they will have to suffer in this way for ever and ever: what, then, will become of them? And what is there that we can do—or even suffer—in so short a life as this that will matter in the slightest if it will free us from these terrible and eternal torments? I assure you it is impossible to explain to anyone who has not experienced it what a grievous thing is the soul's suffering and how different it is from the suffering of the body. The Lord will have us understand this so that we may be more conscious of how much we owe Him for bringing us to a state in which by His mercy we may hope that He will set us free and forgive us our sins.

Let us now return to what we were discussing when we left this soul in such affliction. It remains in this state only for a short time (three or four hours at most, I should say); for, if the pain lasted long, it would be impossible, save by a miracle, for natural weakness to suffer it. On one occasion it lasted only for a quarter of an hour and yet produced complete prostration. On that occasion, as a matter of fact, the sufferer entirely lost consciousness. The violent attack came on through her hearing some words about "life not ending."[3] She was engaged in conversation at the time—it was the last day of Eastertide, and all that Easter she had been affected with such aridity that she hardly knew it was Easter at all. So just imagine anyone thinking that these attacks can be resisted! It is no more possible to resist them than for a person thrown into a fire to make the flames lose their heat and not burn her. She cannot hide her anguish, so all who are present realize the great peril in which she lies, even though they cannot witness what is going on within her. It is true that they can bear her company, but they only seem to her like shadows—as all other earthly things do too.

And now I want you to see that, if at any time you should find yourselves in this condition, it is possible for your human nature, weak as it is, to be of help to you. So let me tell you this. It sometimes happens that, when a person is in this state that you have been considering, and has such yearnings to die,[4] because the pain is more than she can bear, that her soul seems to be on the very point of leaving the body, she is really afraid and would like her distress to be alleviated lest she should in fact die. It is quite evident that this fear comes from natural weakness, and yet, on the other hand, the desire does not leave her, nor can she possibly find any means of dispelling the distress until the Lord Himself dispels it for her. This He does, as a general rule, by granting her a deep rapture or some kind of vision, in which the true Comforter comforts and strengthens her so that she can wish to live for as long as He wills.

This is a distressing thing, but it produces the most wonderful effects and the soul at once loses its fear of any trials that may befall it; for by comparison with the feelings of deep anguish that its spirit has experienced these seem nothing. Having gained so much, the soul would be glad to suffer them all again and again; but it has no means of doing so nor is there any method by which it can reach that state again until the Lord wills, just as there is no way of resisting or escaping it when it comes. The soul has far more contempt for the world than it had previously, for it sees that no worldly thing was of any avail to it in its torment; and it is very much more detached from the creatures, because it sees that it can be comforted and satisfied only by the Creator, and it has the greatest fear and anxiety not to offend Him, because it sees that He can torment as well as comfort.

There are two deadly perils, it seems to me, on this spiritual road. This is one of them—and it is indeed a peril and no light one. The other is the peril of excessive rejoicing and delight, which can be carried to such an extreme that it really seems as if the soul is swooning, and as if the very slightest thing would be enough to drive it out of the body: this would really bring it no little happiness.

Now, sisters, you will see if I was not right in saying that courage is necessary for us here and that if you ask the Lord for these things He will be justified in answering you as He answered the sons of Zebedee: "Can you drink the chalice?"[5] I believe, sisters, that we should all reply: "We can"; and we should be quite right to do so, for His Majesty gives the strength to those who, He sees, have need of it, and He defends these souls in every way and stands up for them if they are persecuted and spoken ill of, as He did for the Magdalene[6]—by His actions if not in words. And in the end—ah, in the end, before they die, He repays them for everything at once, as you are now going to see. May He be forever blessed and may all creatures praise Him. Amen.

Exploring the Interior Castle

- Do you agree with Teresa when she says that no limitations can be set to God's actions? What does she mean by such a statement? Can it be misunderstood in any way? Is God's freedom limited by truth? By goodness? By love? Can God freely choose to limit himself?

- Teresa says that the soul's suffering can be so intense that it feels as though a flaming arrow has touched its very depths. What role does suffering play in the life of faith? What role does it play in one's experience of God? Is it possible to know God without suffering? Why must the soul be purified by suffering before it enters the seventh mansions?

- According to Teresa, as a soul draws closer to God, it becomes more and more detached from worldly concerns. Do you agree with this insight? Does communion with God necessarily mean detachment from ordinary earthly cares? What does Teresa mean by worldly concerns? What does she mean by detachment? Is it possible to share an intimate relationship with God, while still being heavily involved in the affairs of world?

- Teresa once again emphasizes the importance of courage for the spiritual journey. She also states that it comes from the Lord and that he gives it to those who need it. Do you consider yourself courageous? Most of the time? Sometimes? Almost never? Have you ever asked God for courage? If not, why not? If so, how were your prayers answered?

Seventh Mansions

✤

Introduction

Teresa devotes four chapters to the seventh mansions. In them, she explains the difference between what she means by "spiritual betrothal" and "spiritual marriage." For her, there are no closed doors between these sixth and seventh mansions. One flows out of the other and the soul and, while retaining its creaturely status, feels completely absorbed by God.

Teresa describes in detail the soul's experience of spiritual marriage. It is the final stage of mystical contemplation, where the soul reaches the inner sanctum of the interior castle and perceives the quiet indwelling presence of the Holy Trinity. It senses this divine presence apart from any mystical rapture or suspension of the senses. Unlike the soul's experience of union in the fifth mansions and spiritual betrothal in the sixth, the soul is no longer blind and deaf to the communion of divine love within it. In this seventh mansion, God removes the scales from the soul's eyes and enables it to see him face to face.

Illuminated from within, the soul finally understands the mystery of the Trinity and sees the truth with its own eyes. This direct, face-to-face encounter with God immerses it in the community of divine love. This experience heightens its awareness of God in the daily activities of life and enables it to aspire to love even more intensely than before. The soul rests in God, but in a way that makes it more in tune with the needs of others. In the state of spiritual marriage, action and contemplation are intimately related: Martha and Mary work in unison. The soul expresses its love of God through its love of neighbor. The soul has no need of extraordinary mystical experiences, for it knows that it can never again be separated from God. Like Christ, it embraces the cross out of love for the Father and in obedience to his will. It is steeped in happiness even in the midst of great trials and persecution.

Chapter One

✛

Introduction

In this chapter, Teresa discusses the gifts that God gives to those in the seventh mansions. It would be wrong, she says, to think that God could not exceed the wonders he has performed in the soul in the previous mansions. God is infinite and all-powerful and so are his actions. There will never be an end to the stories one can tell of the wonders he has and will continue to perform. The problem with so many people is that they have souls, but fail to recognize God's image in them or appreciate the secrets they hold. She asks the Lord to guide her pen as she sets down the wonders of the seventh mansions. Her only desire in doing so is to make her readers understand their Lord a little more.

Teresa also says that it would be a mistake to think of the soul as a dark and foreboding place. In addition to visible light, by which a person sees exterior objects, there is also an interior light, which lights up the soul. Those who have separated themselves from God through serious sin have blocked out this interior light and wander about as if they are blind and dumb. She asks her readers to pray for such people that their bonds might be loosened and they might enjoy the rich fare just within their reach. Those, however, who have suffered so much in their yearning for God and are about to wed themselves to him, will find that their souls are like a second heaven, a place where the Lord dwells and makes his home. In the state of spiritual marriage, Teresa notes, the Lord takes the soul into his mansion and the soul receives him in its innermost depths.

This mutual indwelling is far different from anything the soul has previously experienced. Unlike prior mystical states, like the prayer of union, the soul now enters into its very center and is keenly aware of the Lord's nearness. Rather than a state of ecstasy, which suspends the faculties and carries the soul out of its senses, making it blind and dumb, the soul's eyes are open and it is able to see things with a clarity it never had before. In the state of spiritual marriage, the Lord grants the soul an intellectual vision of the Blessed Trinity. This vision sets the soul on fire and enables it to see each of the Three Persons both as individuals and as one substance. The soul sees these things not through the eyes of the body or the soul, but in its very core, what Teresa prefers to call the "spirit."

One important quality of the soul in the state of spiritual marriage is that it remains in possession of its senses. Rather than being carried off in a state of rapture or ecstasy, it is more alert than ever and is able to dedicate itself entirely in its service to the Lord. It can do so, because it has an abiding sense of God deep within it. Although the sense of this divine companionship has different degrees of intensity, it never leaves the soul. Regardless of what it is doing, the soul will always have a sense of God's abiding presence deep within it. To describe this experience, Teresa compares the soul to a person who is aware of the other people in a brightly-lighted room even after the shutters are suddenly closed and darkness fills the surrounding space. In a similar way, a soul in the state of spiritual marriage is aware of God's abiding presence within it even if it no longer can see him clearly by the interior light within it. Whatever the soul's trials or difficulties, it will always share in the intimacy of God's friendship. It may feel divided, at times, just as Martha complained of Mary in the gospel stories, but it remains secure in God's close, abiding presence.

Teresa concludes by saying that the soul is one, but may experience itself as divided. She says that this experience is not a work of the imagination, but actually occurs and is, in fact, quite common. To help her readers understand, she draws a distinction between "soul" and "spirit." Although these are both one and the difference between them very nuanced, she believes this understanding of a higher and a lower level of the soul might help her readers understand how the soul might on occasion experience itself as divided. She also affirms that the soul is different from its faculties or powers, but at this point of her exposition does not wish to go into such complicated matters any more than necessary. In her mind, all will come to light in the next life.

✢

Text

Treats of great favors that God bestows on the souls that have attained entrance to the Seventh Mansions. Describes how in the author's opinion there is some difference between the soul and the spirit although both are one. There are notable things in this chapter.

You will think, sisters, that so much has been said about this spiritual road that there cannot possibly be any more to say. It would be a great mistake to think that; just as the greatness of God is without limit, even so are His works. Who will ever come to an end of recounting His mercies and wonders? It is impossible that any should do so; do not be surprised, therefore, at what has been said and at what will be said now, for it is only a fraction of the things that still remain to be related about God. Great is the mercy that He shows us in communicating these things in such a way that we may come to learn of them; for the more we know of His communion with creatures, the more we shall praise His greatness, and we shall strive not to despise a soul in which the Lord takes such delight. Each of us possesses a soul, but we do not prize our souls as creatures made in God's image deserve and so we do not understand the great secrets that they contain. If it be His Majesty's will, may it please Him to guide my pen, and give me to understand how I may tell you some of the many things that there are to be said and that God reveals to every soul that He brings into this Mansion. Earnestly have I besought His Majesty, since He knows my intention is that His mercies be not hidden, to the greater praise and glory of His name.

I am hopeful, sisters, that, not for my sake but for your sakes, He will grant me this favor, so that you may understand how important it is that no fault of yours should hinder the celebration of His Spiritual Marriage with your souls, which, as you will see, brings with it so many blessings. O great God! Surely a creature as miserable as I must tremble to treat of anything so far beyond what I deserve to understand. And indeed I have been in a state of great confusion and have wondered if it will not be better for me in a few words to bring my account of this Mansion to an end. I am so much afraid it will be thought that my knowledge of it comes from experience, and this makes me very much ashamed; for, knowing myself as I do for what

I am, such a thought is terrible. On the other hand, whatever your judgment about it may be, it has seemed to me that this shame is due to temptation and weakness. Let the whole world cry out upon me, so long as God is praised and understood a little better. At all events I may perhaps be dead when this comes to be seen. Blessed be He Who lives and shall live forever. Amen.

When Our Lord is pleased to have pity upon this soul, which suffers and has suffered so much out of desire for Him, and which He has now taken spiritually to be His bride, He brings her into this Mansion of His, which is the seventh, before consummating the Spiritual Marriage. For He must needs have an abiding-place in the soul, just as He has one in Heaven, where His Majesty alone dwells: so let us call this a second Heaven. It is very important, sisters, that we should not think of the soul as of something dark. It must seem dark to most of us, as we cannot see it, for we forget that there is not only a light that we can see, but also an interior light, and so we think that within our soul there is some kind of darkness. Of the soul that is not in grace, I grant you, that is true—not, however, from any defect in the Sun of Justice, Who is within it and is giving it being, but because, as I think I said in describing the first Mansion, this soul is not capable[1] of receiving the light. A certain person came to see that these unhappy souls are, as it were, in a dark prison, with their feet and hands bound so that they can do no good thing that will help them to win merit.[2] They are both blind and dumb. We do well to take pity on them, realizing that there was a time when we were ourselves like them and that the Lord may have mercy on them also.

Let us take especial care, sisters, to pray to Him for them, and not be negligent. To pray for those who are in mortal sin is the best kind of almsgiving—a much better thing than it would be to loose a Christian whom we saw with his hands tied behind him, bound with a stout chain, made fast to a post and dying of hunger, not for lack of food, since he has beside him the most delicious things to eat, but because he cannot take them and put them into his mouth although he is weary to death and actually knows that he is on the point of dying, and not merely a death of the body, but one that is eternal. Would it not be extremely cruel to stand looking at such a man and not give him this food to eat? And supposing you could loose his chains by means of your prayers? You see now what I mean. For the love of God, I beg you always to remember such souls when you pray.[3]

However, it is not of these that we are now speaking, but of those who, by God's mercy, have done penance for their sins and are in grace. We must not think of souls like theirs as mean and insignificant; for each is an interior world, wherein are the many and beauteous Mansions that you have seen; it is reasonable that this should be so, since within each soul there is a mansion for God. Now, when His Majesty is pleased to grant the soul the aforementioned favor of this Divine Marriage, He first of all brings it into His own Mansion. And His Majesty is pleased that it should not be as on other occasions, when He has granted it raptures, in which I certainly think it is united with Him, as it is in the above-mentioned Prayer of Union, although the soul does not feel called to enter into its own center, as here in this Mansion, but is affected only in its higher part. Actually it matters little what happens: whatever it does, the Lord unites it with Himself, but He makes it blind and dumb, as He made Saint Paul at his conversion,[4] and so prevents it from having any sense of how or in what way that favor comes that it is enjoying; the great delight of which the soul is then conscious is the realization of its nearness to God. But when He unites it with Him, it understands nothing; the faculties are all lost

But in this Mansion everything is different. Our good God now desires to remove the scales from the eyes of the soul,[5] so that it may see and understand something of the favor that He is granting it, although He is doing this in a strange manner. It is brought into this Mansion by means of an intellectual vision,[6] in which, by a representation of the truth in a particular way, the Most Holy Trinity reveals Itself, in all three Persons.[7] First of all the spirit becomes enkindled and is illumined, as it were, by a cloud of the greatest brightness. It sees these three Persons, individually, and yet, by a wonderful kind of knowledge that is given to it, the soul realizes that most certainly and truly all these three Persons are one Substance and one Power and one Knowledge and one God alone; so that what we hold by faith the soul may be said here to grasp[8] by sight, although nothing is seen by the eyes, either of the body or of the soul,[9] for it is no imaginary vision. Here all three Persons communicate Themselves to the soul and speak to the soul and explain to it those words which the Gospel attributes to the Lord—namely, that He and the Father and the Holy Spirit will come to dwell with the soul that loves Him and keeps His commandments.[10]

Oh, God help me! What a difference there is between hearing and believing these words[11] and being led in this way to realize how true they are! Each day this soul wonders more, for she feels that they have never left her, and perceives quite clearly, in the way I have described, that They are in the interior of her heart—in the most interior place of all and in its greatest depths. So although, not being a learned person, she cannot say how this is, she feels within herself this Divine companionship.

This may lead you to think that such a person will not remain in possession of her senses but will be so completely absorbed that she will be able to fix her mind upon nothing. But no: in all that belongs to the service of God she is more alert than before; and, when not otherwise occupied, she rests in that happy companionship. Unless her soul fails God, He will never fail, I believe, to give her the most certain assurance of His Presence. She has great confidence that God will not leave her, and that, having granted her this favor, He will not allow her to lose it. For this belief the soul has good reason, though all the time she is walking more carefully than ever, so that she may displease Him in nothing.

This Presence is not of course always realized so fully—I mean so clearly—as it is when it first comes, or on certain other occasions when God grants the soul this consolation; if it were, it would be impossible for the soul to think of anything else, or even to live among men. But although the light that accompanies it may not be so clear, the soul is always aware that it is experiencing this companionship. We might compare the soul to a person who is with others in a very bright room; and then suppose that the shutters are closed so that the people are all in darkness. The light by which they can be seen has been taken away, and, until it comes back, we shall be unable to see them, yet we are nonetheless aware that they are there. It may be asked if, when the light returns, and this person looks for them again, she will be able to see them. To do this is not in her power; it depends on when Our Lord is pleased that the shutters of the understanding shall be opened. Great is the mercy that He grants the soul in never going away from her and in willing that she shall understand this so clearly.

It seems that the Divine Majesty, by means of this wonderful companionship, is desirous of preparing the soul for yet more. that clearly she will be greatly assisted to go onward in perfection and to lose the fear which previously she sometimes had of the other favors that were granted to her, as has been said above. The person already referred to found herself better in every way, however numerous were her trials and business worries, the essential part of her soul seemed never to move from that dwelling-place. So in a sense she felt that her soul was divided; and when she was going through great trials, shortly after God had granted her this favor, she complained of her soul, just as Martha complained of Mary.[12] Sometimes she would say that it was doing nothing but enjoying itself in that quietness, while she herself was left with all her trials and occupations so that she could not keep it company.

You will think this absurd, daughters, but it is what actually happens. Although of course the soul is not really divided, what I have said is not fancy, but a very common experience. As I was saying, it is possible to make observations concerning interior matters and in this way we know that there is some kind of difference, and a very definite one, between the soul and the spirit, although they are both one. So subtle is the division perceptible between them that sometimes the operation of the one seems as different from that of the other as are the respective joys that the Lord is pleased to give them. It seems to me, too, that the soul is a different thing from the faculties and that they are not all one and the same. There are so many and such subtle things in the interior life that it would be presumptuous for me to begin to expound them. But we shall see everything in the life to come if the Lord, of His mercy, grants us the favor of bringing us to the place where we shall understand these secrets.

Exploring the Interior Castle

- Teresa asks her readers to pray for those who have sinned and separated themselves from God's grace. How often do you find yourself praying on behalf of others? Have you witnessed blessings resulting from this? Have you felt the blessing of others' prayers for you? Do you pray for others enough? Too much?

- Teresa describes the soul as a "second heaven," because the Lord abides there when the soul reaches the state of spiritual marriage. Does this image speak to you? Do you believe God wishes to live in others in this way? In what ways does this "second heaven" differ from the first? In what ways is it different?

- Teresa says that a soul in the state of spiritual marriage sees things with a clarity it never before had. Where does this clarity come from? What does it see? How does the state of spiritual marriage differ from prior mystical states? How is it the same? What, in your opinion, are the main characteristics of a soul in the state of spiritual marriage?

- How does Teresa distinguish between the soul and the spirit? How do they differ? In what sense are they the same? Do you accept this distinction? If the two are one, what purpose could such a distinction serve? Which of the two is deeper or more profound?

Chapter Two

✣

Introduction

In this chapter, Teresa continues her discussion of spiritual marriage. Because the soul can still reject God, she says this gift cannot be bestowed completely during this life. To help the soul understand what is happening to it, God may at first reveal himself to the soul through an imaginative vision of his sacred humanity. To other souls, he may reveal himself in a different way. She cites the example of a person (possibly herself) who saw him in his glorified state shortly after having received the Eucharist. However the Lord reveals himself, this mystical state is completely different from the prior ones. It comes with great power and authority; the soul has never before experienced the words it hears and the visions it sees.

Teresa states that, apart from the obvious bodily concerns, the difference between spiritual betrothal and spiritual marriage is the same as that between persons betrothed to each other and those united in holy matrimony. She readily admits that the analogy limps, but says that she can find no more appropriate metaphor for describing these mystical states. Spiritual marriage, she claims, has even less of a tie to the concerns of the body than spiritual betrothal. In this state, the Lord himself dwells in the very heart of the soul and reveals himself in a rarefied intellectual vision without having to engage the soul's senses or faculties. Through this vision, the Lord reveals his sublime secrets directly and instantaneously.

Through it, the spirit, the higher part of the soul, becomes one with the Lord. God, for his part, will not separate himself from the soul.

In an attempt to explain herself even more clearly, Teresa offers another possible image for understanding the difference between spiritual betrothal and spiritual marriage. Those betrothed to one another are like two wax candles, the wicks of which have been joined to give off a single flame. Although the light they project is one, they can still be separated. Those married to one another however, are like rain that falls into a river or spring or like a small stream of water that flows into the sea. The water is one and cannot be sorted out or separated. Those married to one another are also like light that enters a room from two different windows. The light enters from different directions, but fills the room as one. Inadequate though they may be, Teresa uses such images to demonstrate the radical difference between the two states. Even if it cannot be perfectly bestowed in this life, spiritual marriage is unlike anything the soul has ever before experienced.

This difference, Teresa notes, becomes increasingly apparent as the effects of spiritual marriage manifest themselves in the soul. At times it receives words and aspirations, the authenticity of which cannot be doubted and which move it to utter heartfelt prayers to the Lord. It feels as though it were receiving sustenance directly from God. At other times, it is like a small spring that has been swallowed up and totally absorbed by a mighty river. It experiences this river flowing deep within it and knows that this deep flow comes from a divine source. All during this time, the soul communes with the Lord and never moves from its center. The divine light, moreover, spills out into the soul's interior faculties and gives it a deep sense of peace.

In the state of spiritual marriage, Teresa notes, the Lord speaks efficacious words that do not return to him in vain. These words move the soul to remove itself from all earthly and corporeal concerns. The more the soul empties itself in this way, the more the Lord fills it with his love. Jesus' words to the soul are like actions that effect what they signify. He brings the soul into his mansion located in the very center of the soul. Despite this intimate union, Teresa does not wish to give the impression that the soul is absolutely certain of its salvation and thus incapable of falling away. On the contrary, it understands that everything depends on God and is more concerned than ever not to offend him even in small matters. Through God's words, the soul also receives a great desire to serve him in all things. Teresa points out that even though the soul is deeply at peace, its faculties, senses, and passions may, at times, be thrown into deep confusion and turmoil. Despite such times of trial and conflict, nothing can disturb its peace. It is like a king in a fortified castle who is not worried about the wars raging without, or a person of sound mind whose body is deeply in pain.

✥

Text

Continues the same subject. Describes the difference between spiritual union and spiritual marriage. Explains this by subtle comparisons.

L et us now come to treat of the Divine and Spiritual Marriage, although this great Favor cannot be fulfilled perfectly in us during our lifetime, for if we were to withdraw ourselves from God this great blessing would be lost When granting this favor for the first time, His Majesty is pleased to reveal Himself to the soul through an imaginary vision of His most sacred Humanity, so that it may clearly understand what is taking place and not be ignorant of the fact that it is receiving so sovereign a gift. To other people the experience will come in a different way. To the person of whom we have been speaking the Lord revealed Himself one day, when she had just received Communion, in great splendor and beauty and majesty, as He did after His resurrection, and told her that it was time she took upon her His affairs as if they were her own and that He would take her affairs upon Himself; and He added other words that are easier to understand than to repeat.[1]

This, you will think, was nothing new, since on other occasions the Lord had revealed Himself to that soul in this way. But it was so different that it left her quite confused and dismayed: for one reason, because this vision came with great force; for another, because of the words that He spoke to her, and also because, in the interior of her soul, where He revealed Himself to her, she had never seen any visions but this. For you must understand that there is the greatest difference between all the other visions we have mentioned and those belonging to this Mansion, and there is the same difference between the Spiritual Betrothal and the Spiritual Marriage as there is between two betrothed persons and two who are united so that they cannot be separated any more.

As I have already said, one makes these comparisons because there are no other appropriate ones, yet it must be realized that the Betrothal has no more to do with the body than if the soul were not in the body, and were nothing but spirit. Between the Spiritual Marriage and the body there is even less connection, for this secret union takes place in the deepest center of the soul, which must be where God Himself dwells, and I do not think there is any need of a door by which to enter it. I say there is no need of a door because all that has so far been described seems to have come through the medium of the senses and faculties and this appearance of the Humanity of the Lord must do so too. But what passes in the union of the Spiritual Marriage is very different. The Lord appears in the center of the soul, not through an imaginary, but through an intellectual vision (although this is a subtler one than that already mentioned),[2] just as He appeared to the Apostles, without entering through the door, when He said to them: "*Pax vobis.*"[3] This instantaneous communication of God to the soul is so great a secret and so sublime a favor, and such delight is felt by the soul, that I do not know with what to compare it, beyond saying that the Lord is pleased to manifest to the soul at that moment the glory that is in Heaven, in a more sublime manner than is possible through any vision or spiritual consolation. It is impossible to say more than that, as far as one can understand, the soul (I mean the spirit of this soul) is made one with God, Who, being likewise a Spirit, has been pleased to reveal the love that He has for us by showing to certain persons the extent of that love, so that we may praise His greatness. For He has been pleased to unite Himself with His creature in such a way that they have become like two who cannot be separated from one another: even so He will not separate Himself from her.

The Spiritual Betrothal is different: here the two persons are frequently separated, as is the case with union, for, although by union is meant the joining of two things into one, each of the two, as is a matter of common observation, can be separated and remain a thing by itself. This favor of the Lord passes quickly and afterwards the soul is deprived of that companionship—I mean so far as it can understand. In this other favor of the Lord it is not so: the soul remains all the time in that center with its God. We might say that union is as if the ends of two wax candles were joined so that the light they give is one:

the wicks and the wax and the light are all one, yet afterwards the one candle can be perfectly well separated from the other and the candles become two again, or the wick may be withdrawn from the wax. But here it is like rain falling from the heavens into a river or a spring; there is nothing but water there and it is impossible to divide or separate the water belonging to the river from that which fell from the heavens. Or it is as if a tiny streamlet enters the sea, from which it will find no way of separating itself, or as if in a room there were two large windows through which the light streamed in: it enters in different places but it all becomes one.

Perhaps when Saint Paul says: "He who is joined to God becomes one spirit with Him,"[4] he is referring to this sovereign Marriage, which presupposes the entrance of His Majesty into the soul by union. And he also says: *Mihi vivere Christus est, mori lucrum.*[5] This, I think, the soul may say here, for it is here that the little butterfly to which we have referred dies, and with the greatest joy, because Christ is now its life.

This, with the passage of time, becomes more evident through its effects; for the soul clearly understands, by certain secret aspirations, that it is endowed with life by God. Very often these aspirations are so vehement that what they teach cannot[6] possibly be doubted: though they cannot be described, the soul experiences them very forcibly. One can only say that this feeling is produced at times by certain delectable words, which, it seems, the soul cannot help uttering, such as: "O life of my life, and sustenance that sustaineth me!" and things of that kind. For from those Divine breasts, where it seems that God is ever sustaining the soul, flow streams of milk, which solace all who dwell in the Castle; it seems that it is the Lord's will for them to enjoy all that the soul enjoys, so that, from time to time, there should flow from this mighty river, in which this tiny little spring is swallowed up, a stream of this water, to sustain those who in bodily matters have to serve the Bridegroom and the bride. And just as a person suddenly plunged into such water would become aware of it, and, however unobservant he might be, could not fail to become so, the same thing may be said, with even greater confidence, of these operations to which I refer. For just as a great stream of water could never fall on us without having an origin somewhere, as I have said, just so it becomes evident that there is someone in the interior of the soul who sends forth these arrows and thus gives life to this life, and that there is a sun whence this great light proceeds, which is transmitted to the faculties in the interior part of the soul. The soul, as I have said, neither moves from that center nor loses its peace, for He Who gave His peace to the Apostles when they were all together[7] can give peace to the soul.

It has occurred to me that this salutation of the Lord must mean much more than the mere words suggest, as must also His telling the glorious Magdalene to go in peace;[8] for the words of the Lord are like acts wrought in us, and so they must have produced some effect in those who were already prepared to put away from them everything corporeal and to leave the soul in a state of pure spirituality, so that it might be joined with Uncreated Spirit in this celestial union. For it is quite certain that, when we empty ourselves of all that is creature and rid ourselves of it for the love of God, that same Lord will fill our souls with Himself. Thus, one day, when Jesus Christ was praying for His Apostles (I do not know where this occurs),[9] He asked that they might become one with the Father and with Him, even as Jesus Christ our Lord is in the Father and the Father is in Him. I do not know what greater love there can be than this. And we shall none of us fail to be included here, for His Majesty went on to say: "Not for them alone do I pray, but also for all who believe in Me,"[10] and again: "I am in them."[11]

Oh, God help me! How true are these words and how well the soul understands them, for in this state it can actually see their truth for itself. And how well we should all understand them were it not for our own fault! The words of Jesus Christ our King and Lord cannot fail; but, because we ourselves fail by not preparing ourselves and departing from all that can shut out this light, we do not see ourselves in this mirror into which we are gazing and in which our image is engraved.[12]

Let us now return to what we were saying. When Our Lord brings the soul into this Mansion of His, which is the center of the soul itself (for they say that the empyrean heaven, where Our Lord is, does not move like the other heavens), it seems, on entering, to be subject to none of the usual movements of the faculties and the imagination, which injure it and take away its peace. I may seem to be giving the impression that, when the soul reaches the state in which God grants it this favor, it is sure of its salvation and free from the risk of backsliding. But that is not my meaning, and whenever I treat of this matter and say that the soul seems to be in safety I should be understood as meaning for so long as the Divine Majesty holds it thus by the hand

and it does not offend Him. At all events, I know for certain that, even when it finds itself in this state, and even if the state has lasted for years, it does not consider itself safe, but goes on its way with much greater misgiving than before and refrains more carefully from committing the smallest offence against God. It is also strongly desirous of serving Him, as will be explained later on, and is habitually afflicted and confused when it sees how little it is able to do and how great is the extent of its obligations, which is no small cross to it and a very grievous penance; for the harder the penance that this soul performs, the greater is its delight. Its real penance comes when God takes away its health and strength so that it can no longer perform any. I have described elsewhere the great distress that this brings, but it is much greater here. This must be due to the nature of the ground in which the soul is planted, for a tree planted by the streams of water is fresher and gives more fruit,[13] so how can we marvel at the desires of this soul, since its spirit is verily made one with the celestial water of which we have been speaking?

Returning to what I was saying, it must not be thought that the faculties and senses and passions are always in this state of peace, though the soul itself is. In the other Mansions there are always times of conflict and trial and weariness, but they are not of such a kind as to rob the soul of its peace and stability—at least, not as a rule. This "center" of our soul, or "spirit," is something so difficult to describe, and indeed to believe, that I think, sisters, as I am so bad at explaining myself, I will not subject you to the temptation of disbelieving what I say, for it is difficult to understand how the soul can have trials and afflictions and yet be in peace. I want to put before you one or two comparisons: God grant they may be of some value, but, if they are not, I know that what I have said is the truth.

A king is living in His palace: many wars are waged in his kingdom and many other distressing things happen there, but he remains where he is despite them all. So it is here: although in the other Mansions there are many disturbances and poisonous creatures, and the noise of all this can be heard, nobody enters this Mansion and forces the soul to leave it; and, although the things that the soul hears cause it some distress, they are not of a kind to disturb it or to take away its peace, for the passions are already vanquished, and thus are afraid to enter there because to do so would only exhaust them further. Our whole body may be in pain, yet if our head is sound the fact that the body is in pain will not cause it to ache as well. These comparisons make me smile and I do not like them at all, but I know no others. Think what you will; what I have said is the truth.

Exploring the Interior Castle

- Teresa says that the Lord introduces the soul to the state of spiritual marriage in different ways. Does this surprise you? What does spiritual marriage mean to you? Is it an image that speaks to your experience? Can you think of a better way of expressing the height of intimate union with God?

- Teresa uses a number of images to explain the difference between the states of spiritual betrothal and spiritual marriage. Do you agree with her selection? Which image can you relate to most easily? Which is the most difficult for you? Can you think of any other images that convey the distinction?

- Teresa upholds the distinction between the Creator and his creation, yet describes a state of union in which the soul seems to become literally lost or absorbed in God. How can one reconcile this tension? Is Teresa speaking on a different level? Is it possible for one to experience complete and utter absorption into God, while remaining all the while metaphysically distinct from him? If so, can you think of an image that could communicate this truth?

- Teresa says that the soul can rest in peace, while the faculties, senses, and passions are in a state of conflict and trial. Have you ever experienced such a state? Have you felt at peace on one level, while being in utter confusion on another? If so, how can you explain this discrepancy? Does God work in a person at different times and on different levels?

Chapter Three

✣

Introduction

In this chapter, Teresa looks at what spiritual marriage does to the soul. With Christ dwelling in its center, the soul has a peace and joy it has never before experienced. It has died to itself and leads an entirely different life. Teresa describes what this new life is like by looking at its effects.

For Teresa, the first great effect of spiritual marriage is the soul's capacity to forget itself. In this state, the soul cares nothing for itself and desires only to give honor and glory to God. It has no knowledge or memory of having a life apart from God; it exists not for itself, but for God. That is not to say that it neglects to take care of its bodily concerns or responsibilities relating to its profession. Teresa is not talking about external matters, but about the interior life of the soul. In all that it does, its sole motivation is to promote God's honor and glory. It seeks to carry out God's will in all things and is deeply saddened when it sees how little it can do for God on its own. The soul in this state wishes to serve God and to be about his business.

The second great effect of spiritual marriage on the soul is a longing to suffer for God. This longing, however, does not distress the soul as in previous mystical states. The soul wills only what God wills. It readily embraces suffering when it comes, but does not become overly anxious when it does not. It has no ill feelings toward those who mistreat it and even fosters a tender love for them. Its desire to serve God is so great that it wants to live a long life so that it might suffer many hardships for God and thus give him praise. Thoughts about heaven or saintly glory do not change its desire to suffer for God. It may forget this desire at times and be taken up with thoughts of death and the afterlife. It soon realizes, however, that Christ dwells within it continuously and that this presence is all it needs. Because of its close union with Christ, it no longer fears death and is ready to do whatever the Lord asks of it.

Because it enjoys such close intimacy with God, the soul no longer longs for consolations and gifts as it did in previous mystical states. Christ is shaping the soul's desires to reflect his own life, which was marked by an embrace of suffering and a desire to do God's will. The soul has detached itself from all things and focuses all of its energies on helping others draw closer to Christ. It experiences little dryness or aridity when at prayer and is keenly attuned to the Lord's inner promptings. Like the upward movement of a flaming fire, God works in the soul from its center to awaken its faculties. The Lord manifests his special care for the soul by communing with it and imploring it to live with him. Teresa tells her readers that the Lord begins to manifest this special care already when the soul enters the prayer of union to give it a sense of delights still to come.

The soul in the state of spiritual marriage has few inner disturbances and is almost always at peace. It is certain of the authenticity of its experiences and trusts that God would not allow the evil one so deeply within it to deceive it. The Lord works peacefully and quietly within the soul as they commune with each other in the deepest silence. The Lord calms the understanding and gives it small glimpses of what is happening to the soul. The soul retains control of its faculties, but they now move in unison with the Lord's inner promptings. The soul has only occasional experiences of rapture. These never occur in public as they did in the past and have no connection to external displays of devotion (e.g., images, sermons, and music). Nor do they carry with them the same transports and flights of spirit as in the past. As the Lord reveals the seventh mansion to the soul, it is tranquil and no longer anxious about being carried off into ecstasy. Teresa lists a number of scriptural images that describe the peace the soul has found in the state of spiritual marriage. The thought of losing this peace enkindles in the soul an even greater desire to please God. It is sometimes overcome by all the blessings it has received. Whatever trials come its way do not disturb its deep inner peace.

✣

Text

Treats of the striking effects produced by this prayer aforementioned. It is necessary to observe and remember the effects it produces, for the difference between them and those already described is remarkable.

A s we are saying, then, this little butterfly has now died, full of joy at having found rest, and within her lives Christ Let us see what her new life is like, and how different it is from her earlier one, for it is by the effects that result from this prayer that we shall know if what has been said is true. As far as I can understand, the effects are these.

First, there is a self-forgetfulness that is so complete that it really seems as though the soul no longer existed, because it is such that she has neither knowledge nor remembrance that there is either heaven or life or honor for her, so entirely is she employed in seeking the honor of God. It appears that the words that His Majesty addressed to her have produced their effect—namely, that she must take care of His business and He will take care of hers.[1] And thus, happen what may, she does not mind in the least, but lives in so strange a state of forgetfulness that, as I say, she seems no longer to exist, and has no desire to exist—no, absolutely none—save when she realizes that she can do something to advance the glory and honor of God, for which she would gladly lay down her life.

Do not understand by this, daughters, that she neglects to eat and sleep (though having to do this is no little torment to her), or to do anything which is made incumbent upon her by her profession. We are talking of interior matters: as regards exterior ones there is little to be said. Her great grief is to see that all she can do of her own strength is as nothing. Anything that she is capable of doing and knows to be of service to Our Lord she would not fail to do for any reason upon earth.

The second effect produced is a great desire to suffer, but this is not of such a kind as to disturb the soul, as it did previously. So extreme is her longing for the will of God to be done in her that whatever His Majesty does she considers to be for the best: if He wills that she should suffer, well and good; if not, she does not worry herself to death as she did before.

When these souls are persecuted again, they have a great interior joy, and much more peace than in the state described above. They bear no enmity to those who ill-treat them, or desire to do so. Indeed they conceive a special love for them, so that, if they see them in some trouble, they are deeply grieved and would do anything possible to relieve them; they love to commend them to God, and they would rejoice at not being given some of the honors that His Majesty bestows upon them if their enemies might have them instead and thus be prevented from offending Our Lord.

What surprises me most is this. You have already seen what trials and afflictions these souls have suffered because of their desire to die and thus to enjoy Our Lord. They have now an equally strong desire to serve Him, and to sing His praise, and to help some soul if they can. So what they desire now is not merely not to die but to live for a great many years and to suffer the severest trials, if by so doing they can become the means whereby the Lord is praised, even in the smallest thing. If they knew for certain that, on leaving the body, they would have fruition of God, their attitude would not be affected, nor is it altered when they think of the glory that belongs to the saints, for they do not desire as yet to attain this. Their conception of glory is of being able in some way to help the Crucified, especially when they see how often people offend Him and how few there are who really care about His honor and are detached from everything else.

True, they sometimes forget this, turn with tender longing to the thought of enjoying God and desire to escape from this exile, especially when they see how little they are doing to serve Him. But then they turn back and look within themselves and remember that they have Him with them continually; and they are content with this and offer His Majesty their will to live as the most costly oblation they can give Him. They are no more afraid of death than they would be of gentle rapture. The explanation of this is that it is He Who gave the soul those earlier desires, accompanied by such excessive torment that now gives it these others. May He be blessed and praised forever.

In short, the desires of these souls are no longer for consolations or favors, for they have with them the Lord Himself and it is His Majesty Who now lives in them. His life, of course, was nothing but a continual torment and so He is making our life the same, at least as far as our desires go. In other respects, He treats us as weaklings, though He has ample fortitude to give us when He sees that we need it. These souls have a marked detachment from everything and a desire to be always either alone or busy with something that is to some soul's advantage. They have no aridities or interior trials but a remembrance of Our Lord and a tender love for Him, so that they would like never to be doing anything but giving Him praise. When the soul is negligent, the Lord Himself awakens it in the way that has been described, so that it sees quite clearly that this impulse, or whatever it is called, proceeds from the interior of the soul, as we said when discussing these impulses. It is now felt very gently, but it proceeds neither from the thought nor from the memory, nor can it be supposed that the soul has had any part in it. This is so usual and occurs so frequently that it has been observed with special care: just as the flames of a fire, however great, never travel downward, but always upward, so here it is evident that this interior movement proceeds from the center of the soul and awakens the faculties.

Really, were there nothing else to be gained from this way of prayer but our realization of God's special care for us in His communing with us and of the way He keeps begging us to dwell with Him (for He seems to be doing nothing less), I believe that all trials would be well endured if they led to the enjoyment of these gentle yet penetrating touches of His love. This, sisters, you will have experienced, for I think that, when the soul reaches the Prayer of Union, the Lord begins to exercise this care over us if we do not neglect the keeping of His commandments. When this experience comes to you, remember that it belongs to this innermost Mansion, where God dwells in our souls, and give Him fervent praise, for it is He who sends it to you, like a message, or a letter, written very lovingly and in such a way that He would have you alone be able to understand what He has written and what He is asking of you in it.[2] On no account must you fail to answer His Majesty, even if you are busy with exterior affairs and engaged in conversation. It may often happen that Our Lord will be pleased to bestow this secret favor upon you in public, as your reply must needs be an interior one, it will be very easy for you to do what I say and make an act of love or exclaim with Saint Paul: "Lord, what wilt Thou have me to do?"[3] Then He will show you many ways of pleasing Him. For now is the accepted time: He seems indeed to be listening to us and this delicate touch almost always prepares the soul to be able to do, with a resolute will, what He has commanded it.

The difference between this Mansion and the rest has already been explained. There are hardly any of the periods of aridity or interior disturbance in it, which at one time or another have occurred in all the rest, but the soul is almost always in tranquility. It is not afraid that this sublime favor may be counterfeited by the devil but retains the unwavering certainty that it comes from God. For, as has been said, the senses and faculties have no part in this: His Majesty has revealed Himself to the soul and taken it with Him into a place where, as I believe, the devil will not enter, because the Lord will not allow him to do so; and all the favors that the Lord grants the soul here, as I have said, come quite independently of the acts of the soul itself, apart from that of its having committed itself wholly to God.

So tranquilly and noiselessly does the Lord teach the soul in this state and do it good that I am reminded of the building of Solomon's temple, during which no noise could be heard; just so, in this temple of God, in this Mansion of His, He and the soul alone have fruition of each other in the deepest silence. There is no reason now for the understanding to stir, or to seek out anything, for the Lord Who created the soul is now pleased to calm it and would have it look, as it were, through a little chink, at what is passing. Now and then it loses sight of it and is unable to see anything; but this is only for a very brief time. The faculties, I think, are not lost here; it is merely that they do not work but seem to be dazed.

And I am quite dazed myself when I observe that, on reaching this state, the soul has no more raptures (accompanied, that is to say, by the suspension of the senses),[4] save very occasionally, and even then it has not the same transports and flights of the spirit. These raptures, too, happen only rarely, and hardly ever in public as they very often did before.[5] Nor have they any connection, as they had before, with great occasions of devotion; if we see a devotional image or hear a sermon, it is almost as if we had heard nothing, and it is the same with music. Previously, the poor little butterfly was always so worried that everything frightened her and made her fly away. But it is not so now, whether because she has found her rest, or because the soul has seen so much in this Mansion that it can be frightened at nothing, or because it no longer has that solitude that it was wont to have, now that it is enjoying such companionship. Well, sisters, I do not know what the reason may be, but, when the Lord begins to reveal the contents of this Mansion and brings souls into it, they lose the great weakness that was such a trial to them and of which previously they could not rid themselves. Perhaps the reason is that the Lord has so greatly strengthened and dilated and equipped the soul, or it may be that, for reasons that His Majesty alone knows, He was anxious to make a public revelation of His secret dealings with such souls, for His judgments surpass all that we can imagine here on earth.

These effects God bestows, together with all those other good effects already described in the above-mentioned degrees of prayer, when the soul approaches Him, and He also gives the soul that kiss for which the Bride besought Him; for I understand it to be in this Mansion that that petition is fulfilled. Here to this wounded hart are given waters in abundance. Here the soul delights in the tabernacle of God.[6] Here the dove sent out by Noah to see if the storm is over finds the olive-branch[7]—the sign that it has discovered firm ground amidst the waters and storms of this world.

Oh, Jesus! If only one knew how many things there are in Scripture which describe this peace of the soul! My God, since Thou seest how needful it is for us, do Thou inspire Christians to desire to seek it; take it not, by Thy mercy, from those to whom Thou hast given it, and who, until Thou give them true peace and take them where peace will never end, must always live in fear. I say "true" peace, not because I think this peace is not true, but because in this life war might always begin again if we were to withdraw from God.

And what will be the feeling of these souls when they realize that they might lack so great a blessing? The thought makes them walk the more warily and endeavor to bring strength out of their weakness, so as not to be responsible for losing any opportunity that might offer itself to them of pleasing God better. The more they are favored by God, the more timorous and fearful do they become concerning themselves, and as they have learned more about their own wretchedness by comparing it with His greatness and their sins are now so much more serious to them, they often go about, like the Publican, without daring to lift up their eyes.[8] At other times, they long to reach the end of their lives so as to be in safety, though they are soon anxious again to live longer so that they may serve Him because of the love which they bear Him, as has been said, and they trust all that concerns themselves to His mercy. Sometimes the many favors they receive leave them overwhelmed and afraid lest they be like an overladen ship sinking to the bottom of the sea.

I assure you, sisters, that they have no lack of crosses, but these do not unsettle them or deprive them of their peace. The few storms pass quickly, like waves of the sea, and fair weather returns, and then the Presence of the Lord that they have within them makes them forget everything. May He be forever blessed and praised by all His creatures. Amen.

Exploring the Interior Castle

- Teresa says that self-forgetfulness is an important effect of spiritual marriage. What does she mean by self-forgetfulness? How is it manifested in a person's life? What is its connection to the love of God and neighbor? Do you find it easy to forget yourself? Is it possible for someone to be too self-forgetful?

- Teresa says that another important effect of spiritual marriage is a great desire to suffer. Have you ever met anyone with such a desire? If so, did you consider him or her a saintly person? Do you think such a desire can be easily misunderstood? If so, how? Have you ever had a desire to suffer? What distinguishes such a desire from masochism? How can one rectify the love of suffering with genuine self-love based on a person's being created in God's image and likeness?

- Teresa says that the soul's enjoyment of the touches of God's love begins in the prayer of union and reaches its culmination in the state of spiritual marriage. What does this say about the relationship among the later mansions of the mystical life? Are the prayer of union and the states of betrothal and spiritual marriage closely related? How does Teresa describe the differences among them? Have you ever felt deeply touched by God's love in the way Teresa describes?

- Teresa says that the soul in the state of spiritual marriage is deeply at peace. Where does this peace come from? How long does it last? What are its symptoms? What is its opposite? Why is the soul not disturbed by surrounding trials? How does one know one is at peace? Have you ever met someone who seemed fully at peace? Have you ever felt this way?

Chapter Four

✢

Introduction

In this chapter, Teresa talks about the Lord's motivation for giving the soul the supernatural gifts associated with spiritual marriage and also of the importance of integrating the active and contemplative life.

She begins by saying that the effects of spiritual marriage are habitually present in the soul, but vary in their manifestations and degrees of intensity. For a short while, the soul may experience some trial arising from its surroundings, but soon regains its sense of God's presence. In the midst of such trials, its firm desire to serve God in all circumstances never wavers and its resolve even deepens. The Lord permits them to keep the soul humble and to help it see its need for God, appreciate the great gifts it has received, and give God praise.

Teresa does not wish to give her readers the impression that the soul in the state of spiritual marriage is free from all imperfections. Although it is generally free from serious sins, the potential to commit them always remains. What is more, the soul is capable of committing many smaller offenses against God. These are usually done unintentionally but bring great grief to the soul whenever they occur. Its potential for sin prevents it from presuming too much of God and helps it to appreciate the importance of walking in fear of the Lord.

Teresa goes on to say that God gives the soul so many favors in the state of spiritual marriage, not simply to give it pleasure, but to enable it to imitate Christ more closely, especially with respect to his great suffering.

Teresa goes on to say that those who were closest to Christ (the Blessed Mother, Saints Peter and Paul, the other apostles) also suffered the greatest trials. The Lord dwells in the soul and makes his abode there not to give it rest or great esteem, but to make it selfless and to concentrate all of its efforts on finding ways to please and love him. The purpose of spiritual marriage is that good works might flow from the intimacy that the soul shares with its Lord. It profits the soul very little to spend time in recollection and to be resolved to be of service to others and then do nothing when the occasion arises. One must supplement prayer and promises with concrete deeds, even if they be small and represent but little progress.

Teresa underscores the importance of keeping one's eyes fixed on the suffering Christ. If one can do that, everything else will seem insignificant. To be a spiritual person means becoming a slave of God by giving one's freedom to God and being marked by the sign of the cross in one's life. Doing so enables a person to walk in humility and to be a true servant to others. For Teresa, the whole spiritual edifice is built on humility. It enables one to make great progress in the spiritual life, for it helps one see the importance of relying on God and doing his will in all things. Love of God and neighbor are very close for Teresa. In doing his will, the slave of God seeks to please and to serve all of his or her companions on the journey through life.

Teresa then emphasizes the importance of integrating the life of prayer and contemplation with the cultivation of and the practice of the virtues. She is not referring to beginners in the spiritual life, but even to those who have progressed far into the mansions of the interior castle. It is a mistake to try to rest on one's spiritual laurels. While the soul in the state of spiritual marriage enjoys an interior repose, its external life becomes increasingly active. The two are obviously connected: the soul's internal rest in the Lord overflows into its body and gives it the strength to lead a vigorous life of virtue. Teresa cites Mary Magdalene, Elias, and Saints Dominic and Francis as examples of people who received great outward strength from their intimate relationship with the Lord.

Teresa also cites Martha and Mary as an example of how the life of contemplation and action must work together. To the observation that Mary was said to have chosen the better part, she responds that this greater part came to her only after a life of much suffering that resulted from her close friendship with Christ. To the observation of her readers that they cannot integrate contemplation and action like the apostles because they do not know how to teach and preach, she responds that they should not try to do the impossible, but only what is within their means and only to those within their reach. Teresa adds that it is impossible to serve everyone, and one must do what one can with the talents God has given. While her readers may not be converting others to the faith as the apostles did, they are certainly doing the Lord's work simply by helping others to love God more. She concludes by saying that God does not look at the greatness of one's deeds, but at the love with which one does them. If the soul does what it can, the Lord will strengthen it each day and help it improve.

✣

Text

Concludes by describing what appears to be Our Lord's aim in granting the soul such great favors and says how necessary it is for Martha and Mary to walk in each other's company. This chapter is very profitable.

You must not take it, sisters, that the effects that I have described as occurring in these souls are invariably present all the time; it is for this reason that, whenever I have remembered to do so, I have referred to them as being present "habitually." Sometimes Our Lord leaves such souls to their own nature, and when that happens, all the poisonous things in the environs and mansions of this castle seem to come together to avenge themselves on them for the time during which they have not been able to have them in their power.

It is true that this lasts only for a short time—for a single day, or a little longer, at the most—and in the course of the ensuing turmoil, which as a rule is the result of some chance happening, it becomes clear what the soul is gaining from the good Companion Who is with it. For the Lord gives it great determination, so that it will on no account turn aside from His service and from its own good resolutions. On the contrary, these resolutions seem to increase, and so the soul will not make the slightest move that may deflect it from its resolve. This, as I say, happens rarely, but Our Lord's will is for the soul not to forget what it is—for one reason, so that it may always be humble; for another, so that it may the better realize what it owes to His Majesty and what a great favor it is receiving, and may praise Him.

Do not, of course, for one moment imagine that, because these souls have such vehement desires and are so determined not to commit a single imperfection for anything in the world, they do not in fact commit many imperfections, and even sins. Not intentionally, it is true, for the Lord will give such persons very special aid as to this: I am referring to venial sins, for from mortal sins, as far as they know, they are free, though they are not completely proof against them; and the thought that they may commit some without knowing it will cause them no small agony. It also distresses them to see so many souls being lost; and, although on the one hand they have great hopes of not being among them, yet, when they remember some whom the Scriptures describe as having been favored of the Lord—like Solomon, who enjoyed such converse with His Majesty[1]—they cannot, as I have said, but be afraid. And let whichever of you feels surest of herself fear most, for, says David, "Blessed is the man that feareth God."[2] May His Majesty always protect us; let us beseech Him to do so, that we may not offend Him; this is the greatest security that we can have. May He be forever praised. Amen.

It will be a good thing, sisters, if I tell you why it is that the Lord grants so many favors in this world. Although you will have learned this from the effects they produce, if you have observed them, I will speak about it further here, so that none of you shall think that He does it simply to give these souls pleasure. That would be to make a great error. For His Majesty can do nothing greater for us than grant us a life that is an imitation of that lived by His Beloved Son. I feel certain, therefore, that these favors are given us to strengthen our weakness, as I have sometimes said here, so that we may be able to imitate Him in His great sufferings.

We always find that those who walked closest to Christ Our Lord were those who had to bear the greatest trials. Consider the trials suffered by His glorious Mother and by the glorious Apostles. How do you suppose Saint Paul could endure such terrible trials? We can see in his life the effects of genuine visions and of contemplation coming from Our Lord and not from human imagination or from the deceit of the devil. Do you imagine that he shut himself up with his visions so as to enjoy those Divine favors and pursue no other occupation? You know very well that, so far as we can learn, he took not a day's rest, nor can he have rested by night, since it was then that he had to earn his living.[3] I am very fond of the story of how, when Saint Peter was fleeing from prison, Our Lord appeared to him and told him to go back to Rome and be crucified. We never recite the Office on his festival, in which this story is found, without my deriving a special consolation from it.[4] How did Saint Peter feel after receiving this favor from the Lord? And what did he do? He went straight to his death; and the Lord showed him no small mercy in providing someone to kill him.

Oh, my sisters, how little one should think about resting, and how little one should care about honors, and how far one ought to be from wishing to be esteemed in the very least if the Lord makes His special abode in the soul. For if the soul is much with Him, as it is right it should be, it will very seldom think of itself; its whole thought will be concentrated upon finding ways to please Him and upon showing Him how it loves Him. This, my daughters, is the aim of prayer: this is the purpose of the Spiritual Marriage, of which are born good works and good works alone.

Such works, as I have told you, are the sign of every genuine favor and of everything else that comes from God. It will profit me a little if I am alone and deeply recollected, and make acts of love to Our Lord and plan and promise to work wonders in His service, and then, as soon as I leave my retreat and some occasion presents itself, I do just the opposite. I was wrong when I said it will profit me little, for any-one who is with God must profit greatly, and, although after making these resolutions we may be too weak to carry them out, His Majesty will sometimes grant us grace to do so, even at great cost to ourselves, as often happens. For, when He sees a very timorous soul, He sends it, much against its own will, some very sore trial, the bearing of which does it a great deal of good; and later, when the soul becomes aware of this, it loses its fear and offers itself to Him the more readily. What I meant was that the profit is small by comparison with the far greater profit that comes from conformity between our deeds on the one hand and our resolutions and the words we use on the other. Anyone who cannot achieve everything at once must progress little by little. If she wishes to find help in prayer, she must learn to subdue her own will and in these little nooks of ours there will be very many occasions when you can do this.

Reflect carefully on this, for it is so important that I can hardly lay too much stress on it. Fix your eyes on the Crucified and nothing else will be of much importance to you. If His Majesty revealed His love to us by doing and suffering such amazing things, how can you expect to please Him by words alone? Do you know when people really become spiritual? It is when they become the slaves of God and are branded with His sign, which is the sign of the Cross, in token that they have given Him their freedom. Then He can sell them as slaves to the whole world, as He Himself was sold, and if He does this He will be doing them no wrong but showing them no slight favor. Unless they resolve to do this, they need not expect to make great progress. For the foundation of this whole edifice, as I have said, is humility, and, if you have not true humility, the Lord will not wish it to reach any great height: in fact, it is for your own good that it should not; if it did, it would fall to the ground. Therefore, sisters, if you wish to lay good foundations, each of you must try to be the least of all, and the slave of God, and must seek a way and means to please and serve all your companions. If you do that, it will be of more value to you than to them and your foundation will be so firmly laid that your Castle will not fall.

I repeat that if you have this in view you must not build upon foundations of prayer and contemplation alone, for, unless you strive after the virtues and practice them, you will never grow to be more than dwarves. God grant that nothing worse than this may happen—for, as you know, anyone who fails to go forward begins to go back, and love, I believe, can never be content to stay for long where it is.

You may think that I am speaking about beginners, and that later on one may rest: but, as I have already told you, the only repose that these souls enjoy is of an interior kind; of outward repose they get less and less, and they have no wish to get more. What is the purpose, do you suppose, of these inspirations—or, more correctly, of these aspirations—that I have described, and of these messages which are sent by the soul from its innermost center to the folk outside the Castle and to the Mansions which are outside that in which it is itself dwelling? Is it to send them to sleep? No, no, no. The soul, where it now is, is fighting harder to keep the faculties and senses and everything to do with the body from being idle than it did when it suffered with them. For it did not then understand what great gain can be derived from trials, which may indeed have been means whereby God has brought it to this state, nor did it realize how the companionship that it now enjoys would give it much greater strength than it ever had before. For if, as David says, with the holy we shall be holy,[5] it cannot be doubted that, if we are made one with the Strong, we shall gain strength through the most sovereign union of spirit with Spirit, and we shall appreciate the strength of the saints that enabled them to suffer and die.

It is quite certain that, with the strength it has gained, the soul comes to the help of all who are in the Castle, and, indeed, succors the body itself. Often the body appears to feel nothing, but the strength derived from the vigor gained by the soul after it has drunk of the wine from this cellar, where its Spouse has brought it and which He will not allow it to leave, overflows into the weak body, just as on the earthly plane the food that is introduced into the stomach gives strength to the head and to the whole body. In this life, then, the soul has a very bad time, for, however much it accomplishes, it is strong enough inwardly to attempt much more and this causes such strife within it that nothing it can do seems to it of any importance. This must be the reason for the great penances done by many saints, especially by the glorious Magdalene, who had been brought up in such luxury all her life long; there was also that hunger for the honor of his God suffered by our father Elias;[6] and the zeal of Saint Dominic and Saint Francis for bringing souls to God, so that He might be praised. I assure you that, forgetful as they were of themselves, they must have endured no little suffering.

This, my sisters, I should like us to strive to attain: we should desire and engage in prayer, not for our enjoyment, but for the sake of acquiring this strength that fits us for service. Let us not try to walk along an untrodden path, or at the best we shall waste our time: it would certainly be a novel idea to think of receiving these favors from God through any other means than those used by Him and by all His saints. Let us not even consider such a thing: believe me, Martha and Mary must work together when they offer the Lord lodging, and must have Him ever with them, and they must not entertain Him badly and give Him nothing to eat. And how can Mary give Him anything, seated as she is at His feet, unless her sister helps her? His food consists in our bringing Him souls, in every possible way, so that they may be saved and may praise Him forever.

You will reply to me by making two observations. The first, that Mary was said to have chosen the better part[7]—and she had already done the work of Martha and shown her love for the Lord by washing His feet and wiping them with her hair.[8] And do you think it would be a trifling mortification to a woman in her position to go through those streets—perhaps alone, for her fervor was such that she cared nothing how she went—to enter a house that she had never entered before and then to have to put up with uncharitable talk from the Pharisee[9] and from very many other people, all of which she was forced to endure? What a sight it must have been in the town to see such a woman as she had been making this change in her life! Such wicked people as we know the Jews to have been would only need to see that she was friendly with the Lord, Whom they so bitterly hated, to call to mind the life that she had lived and to realize that she now wanted to become holy, for she would of course at once have changed her style of dress and everything else. Think how we gossip about people far less notorious than she and then imagine what she must have suffered. I assure you, sisters, that that better part came to her only after sore trials and great mortification—even to see her Master so much hated must have been an intolerable trial to her. And how many such trials did she not endure later, after the Lord's death! I think myself that the reason she was not granted martyrdom was that she had already undergone it through witnessing the Lord's death.[10] The later years of her life, too, during which she was absent from Him, would have been years of terrible torment; so she was not always enjoying the delights of contemplation at the Lord's feet.

The other thing you may say is that you are unable to lead souls to God, and have no means of doing so; that you would gladly do this, but, being unable to teach and preach like the Apostles, you do not know how. That is an objection that I have often answered in writing, though I am not sure if I have done so in discussing this Castle. But, as it is a thing that I think must occur to you, in view of the desires that the Lord implants in you, I will not omit to speak of it here. I told you elsewhere that the devil sometimes puts ambitious desires into our hearts, so that, instead of setting our hand to the work that lies nearest to us, and thus serving Our Lord in ways within our power, we may rest content with having desired the impossible. Apart from praying for people, by which you can do a great deal for them, do not try to help everybody, but limit yourselves to your own companions; your work will then be all the more effective because you have the greater obligation to do it. Do you imagine it is a small advantage that you should have so much humility and mortification, and should be the servants of all and show such great charity towards all, and such fervent love for the Lord that it resembles a fire kindling all their souls, while you constantly awaken their zeal by your other virtues? This would indeed be a great service to the Lord and one very pleasing to Him. By your doing things that you really can do, His Majesty will know that you would like to do many more, and thus He will reward you exactly as if you had won many souls for Him.

"But we shall not be converting anyone," you will say, "for all our sisters are good already." What has that to do with it? If they become still better, their praises will be more pleasing to the Lord, and their prayers of greater value to their neighbors. In a word, my sisters, I will end by saying that we must not build towers without foundations, and that the Lord does not look so much at the magnitude of anything we do as at the love with which we do it. If we accomplish what we can, His Majesty will see to it that we become able to do more each day. We must not begin by growing weary; but during the whole of this short life, which for any one of you may be shorter than you think, we must offer the Lord whatever interior and exterior sacrifice we are able to give Him, and His Majesty will unite it with that which He offered to the Father for us upon the Cross, so that it may have the value won for it by our will, even though our actions in themselves may be trivial.

May it please His Majesty, my sisters and daughters, to bring us all to meet where we may praise Him and to give me grace to do some of the things of which I have told you, through the merits of His Son, Who liveth and reigneth forever, Amen. As I say this to you I am full of shame and by the same Lord I beg you not to forget this poor miserable creature in your prayers.

Exploring the Interior Castle

- Teresa says that a soul in the state of spiritual marriage is afraid of offending the Lord in even the slightest way. How does fear of the Lord help a person progress in the spiritual life? Of what does it make a person aware? In what ways can it be misunderstood? Do you reflect a healthy fear of the Lord in your life? If so, in what ways?

- Teresa says that the best thing God can do for a person is to help him or her imitate Jesus Christ, his beloved son. What does Teresa mean by the imitation of Christ? What is its opposite? Why is it so important in the spiritual life? How do you imitate Christ? In what areas of your life do you fail to imitate him?

- Teresa talks about becoming a "slave of God." What does she mean by this expression? Can one be enslaved and free at the same time? Would this expression get a sympathetic hearing today? If not, can you think of a similar expression that might?

- Teresa underscores the importance of integrating the contemplative life with the life of virtue. How does one do this? What concrete steps does she suggest? Have you integrated these two important aspects of Christian living in your own life? Which of the two do you favor? Which do you need to work on?

Epilogue

✛

Introduction

Teresa concludes with a brief epilogue that tells of her experience in writing the work and what she hopes to accomplish through it. She does not claim to have covered all the mansions in the interior castle; nor does she claim that the work is entirely free of error. All that is good in the work, she attributes to God; all errors are due to her own lack of understanding.

In this epilogue, Teresa offers her readers some practical advice on how to explore the mansions she has just described. She reminds them, for example, that they cannot enter all of the mansions by their own efforts and that admission to the higher ones depends entirely on the Lord. She suggests to her readers that they make no effort at all to gain entrance into these higher mansions, since God loves the humble heart and will be more apt to open them up to those who feel unworthy. Although she was hesitant to begin the work, she says she is now very happy to have finished it. She understands how most of her readers (the nuns of her Carmelite reform) are restricted in their movements and hopes that the interior castle she has laid out before them will bring them great delight and an increasing sense of freedom.

Teresa concludes by asking her readers to pray for the growth of the Church and that those outside of it might receive light. She also submits all of her writing to the authority of the Catholic Church and asks that they pray that her sins may be forgiven and that she might escape Purgatory.

She writes that she has finished the work on the vigil Saint Andrew, in the convent of Saint Joseph in Avila, in the year 1577.

✢

Text

JHS.

Although when I began to write what I have set down here it was with great reluctance, as I said at the beginning, I am very glad I did so now that it is finished, and I think my labor has been well spent, though I confess it has cost me very little. And considering how strictly you are cloistered, my sisters, how few opportunities you have of recreation and how insufficient in number are your houses, I think it will be a great consolation for you, in some of your convents, to take your delight in this *Interior Castle*, for you can enter it and walk about in it at any time without asking leave from your superiors.

It is true that, however strong you may think yourselves, you cannot enter all the Mansions by your own efforts: the Lord of the Castle Himself must admit you to them. So, if you meet with any resistance, I advise you not to make any effort to get in, for if you do you will displease Him so much that He will never admit you. He is a great Lover of humility. If you consider yourselves unworthy of entering even the third Mansions, He will more quickly give you the will to reach the fifth, and thenceforward you may serve Him by going to these Mansions again and again, till He brings you into the Mansion that He reserves as His own and that you will never leave, except when you are called away by the prioress, whose wishes this great Lord is pleased that you should observe as if they were His own. And even if, at her command, you are often outside these Mansions, He will always keep the door open against your return. Once you have been shown how to enjoy this Castle, you will find rest in everything, even in the things that most try you, and you will cherish a hope of returning to it that nobody can take from you.

Although I have spoken here only of seven Mansions, yet in each there are comprised many more, both above and below and around, with lovely gardens and fountains[1] and things so delectable that you will want to lose yourselves in praise of the great God Who created it in His image and likeness. If you find anything good in this book which helps you to learn to know Him better, you can be quite sure that it is His Majesty Who has said it, and if you find anything bad, that it has been said by me.

By the earnest desire that I have to be of some use in helping you to serve this my God and Lord, I beg you, in my own name, whenever you read this, to give great praise to His Majesty and beg Him to multiply His Church and to give light to the Lutherans and to pardon my sins and set me free from Purgatory, where perhaps, by the mercy of God,[2] I shall be when this is given you to read, if, after being revised by learned men, it is ever published. And if there is any error in it, that is due to my lack of understanding, for in all things I submit to what is held by the Holy Roman Catholic Church, in which I live, and protest and promise that I will both live and die. Praised and blessed forever be God our Lord. Amen, Amen.

The writing of this was finished in the convent of Saint Joseph of Avila, in the year one thousand five hundred and seventy seven, on the vigil of Saint Andrew, to the glory of God, Who liveth and reigneth for ever and ever. Amen.

Exploring the Interior Castle

- Teresa hopes that her work will offer her cloistered readers the opportunity to explore great interior spaces without ever having to ask permission from their superiors. The metaphor of an interior castle seems especially suited to cloistered contemplatives, but is it a helpful metaphor for today's spiritual seekers? Does it speak to you?

- Teresa tells her readers that entrance into some mansions of the interior castle depends entirely on God and that it would be better if they did not try to gain access to them. Is it possible to try to do something by not trying? Does such passivity before God border on quietism? How does Teresa defend herself from such a charge?

- Teresa says that there are many other mansions in the interior castle that she has not described. What does such a statement say about her mystical teaching? What does it say about the way her teaching relates to other presentations of Christian mysticism? Is Teresa's presentation just one of many models of authentic Christian mysticism? If so, can you name others?

- Teresa submits everything she has written to the judgment of the authorities of the Catholic Church. She has also submitted her work to the learned men to revise. Why does she take such care to distance herself from any errors in her work? Could it be that the theological climate in which she wrote forced her to take such precautions? Does a similar climate exist today?

Notes

Introduction

1. In the notes to his translation, Peers prefers to use the Spanish version of Gratian's name, "Jerónimo Gracián."
2. See Teresa of Avila, *Interior Castle*, ed. and trans. E. Allison Peers (Garden City, NY: Image Books, by special arrangement with Sheed & Ward, 1961). This translation is based on the critical edition of Silverio de Santa Teresa. (See below no. 11.)
3. The historical information in this section comes from: Marcelle Auclair, *Teresa of Avila: The Vivid Dramatic Life Story of a Great Woman: Organizer, Foundress, Mystic, Saint*, trans. Kathleen Pond (New York: Pantheon Books, 1953), 439–45; *The New Catholic Encyclopedia* (New York: McGraw-Hill, 1967), s.v. "Teresa of Avila, Saint," by O. Steggink; Kieran Kavanaugh, "Introduction," in Teresa of Avila, *The Interior Castle*, The Classics of Western Spirituality, trans. Kieran Kavanaugh and Otilio Rodriguez (New York, Ramsey, Toronto: Paulist Press, 1979), 1–6.
4. For a discussion of these categories, see Romano Guardini, *Prayer in Practice*, trans. Leopold of Loewenstein-Wertheim (New York: Pantheon, 1957), 120–57. For the last two categories, Guardini prefers the terms "inward" and "mystic" prayer.
5. The presentation of the nine grades of prayer is based on the summary of the Teresian teaching found in Jordan Aumann, *Spiritual Theology* (London: Sheed and Ward, 1980; seventh impression, 1993), 316–57, and appears in a slightly different context in Dennis J. Billy, *With Open Heart: Spiritual Direction in the Alphonsian Tradition* (Liguori, MO: Liguori Publications, 2003), 31–36. See also P. Pourrat, *La spiritualité chrétienne*, 3rd ed., vol. 4 (Paris: Librairie Lecoffre, 1928), 485–87; A. Poulain, *The Graces of Interior Prayer*, 10th ed., trans. Leonora L. Yorke Smith (London: Routledge & Keegan Paul, 1950), 7–58; Fabio Giardini, *Pray Without Ceasing: Toward a Systematic Psychotheology of Christian Prayerlife* (Gracewing/Millennium: Leominster, Herefordshire/Rome,

1998), 267-70; Father Ermanno, O.D.C., "The Degrees of Teresian Prayer," in *Saint Teresa of Avila: Studies in Her Life, Doctrine, and Times*, eds. Father Thomas, O.D.C., and Father Gabriel, O.D.C. (Westminster, MD: The Newman Press, 1063), 77-103. In her own works, Teresa's teaching on the various grades of prayer is dispersed throughout her autobiography, *The Way of Perfection*, and *The Interior Castle*. See *The Complete Works of Saint Teresa of Jesus*, ed. and trans. E. Allison Peers, vol. 2 (New York: Sheed & Ward, 1946). (Hereafter cited as *Way* and *The Complete Works*.)

6. Teresa of Avila, *The Life of Teresa of Avila*, chap. 8 in *The Complete Works*, vol. 1, p. 50 (hereafter cited as *Life*).

7. See Aumann, *Spiritual Theology*, 324.

8. "The three stages or degrees of charity are nothing more than divisions that characterize in a general way the infinite variety of aspects in the Christian life. The path of the supernatural life is a winding path, and its stages offer a variety of transitions and levels that will differ with each individual. We must never think that the three basic stages are self-contained compartments, and that those who are at a given time in one stage will never participate in the activities of another stage." See Aumann, *Spiritual Theology*, 115-16.

9. For a brief synthesis of Teresa's teaching, see John Dalton, "Preface," in Teresa of Avila, *The Interior Castle*, trans. John Dalton (London: Cox and Wyman, 1859), 13-21; Father Marcellus, O.D.C., "Friendship with the Blessed Trinity," in *Saint Teresa of Avila: Studies in Her Life, Doctrine, and Times*, 113-38; Teresa of Avila, *The Interior Castle*, The Classics of Western Spirituality, trans. Kieran Kavanaugh and Otilio Rodriguez, with an Introduction by Kieran Kavanaugh (New York, Ramsey, Toronto: Paulist Press, 1979), 21-29; Cathleen Medwick, *Teresa of Avila: The Progress of a Soul* (New York: Image Books, 1999), 205-16.

10. When Teresa completed the work, she submitted it to her confessor, Jerome Gratian, who, along with the Dominican theologian P. Yanguas, went over it very carefully in Teresa's presence in June and July of 1580. Peers tells us that the original manuscript has very few corrections, none of which have any great doctrinal significance. Some years later, another critic, most likely her biographer, P. Francis of Ribera, objected to many of the corrections and restored much of the text to its original form. See E. Allison Peers, "Introduction," in Teresa of Avila, *Interior Castle*, 15-17.

11. See *Obras de Santa Teresa de Jesús*, ed. Silverio de Santa Teresa, *Biblioteca mística Carmelitana*, 9 vols. (Burgos: Monte Carmelo, 1915-24); *Obras Completas de Santa Teresa de Jésus*, eds. Efrén de la Madre de Dios, Otilio del Niño Jesús, and Otger Steggink, 3 vols. (Madrid: Biblioteca de Autores Cristianos, 1951-59); *Obras de Santa Teresa de Jesús*, ed. Tomás de la Cruz (Burgos: El Monte Carmelo, 1971).

12. Other English translations, in addition to that of Peers, include: one by Dalton (see above no. 8); one by Kavanaugh and Rodriguez (see above no. 2), as well as Teresa of Avila, *Interior Castle or The Mansions*, trans. The Benedictines of Stanbrook, ed. F. Benedict Zimmerman (Kila, MT: Kessinger Publishing, 2003);

Teresa of Avila, *Interior Castle*, trans. Mirabei Starr (New York: Riverhead Books, 2004).

13. See Medwick, *Teresa of Avila*, 267.

How to Read Interior Castle

1. The notes of the Peers translation are very good at pointing out the appropriate cross-references to Teresa's other works.
2. See, for example, the Council's teaching on "the universal call to holiness" in *Lumen gentium*, nos. 39–42.
3. See H. Richard Niebuhr, *Christ and Culture* (New York: Harper & Row, 1951; Harper Colophon Books ed., 1975), 39–44.

Interior Castle

1. As a kind of subtitle Saint Teresa wrote on the back of the first page of the autograph: "This treatise, called '*Interior Castle*,' was written by Teresa of Jesus, nun of Our Lady of Carmel to her sisters and daughters the Discalced Carmelite nuns." Below this is a note by P. Ribera (formerly attributed to Fray Luis de León), which asserts [somewhat verbosely, for which reason the full text is not here translated] that the marginal emendations in the autograph are often inconsistent with other parts of the text and in any case are inferior to the author's own words, and begs readers to respect "the words and letters written by that most holy hand." [It is noteworthy that the word "mansions" (*moradas:* Cf. First Mansions, Chap. 1, no. 2), by which the book is generally known in Spain, does not appear in the title or subtitle of the autograph, though it occurs in the title of each of the seven sections of the book.]

Prologue

1. *Lit.*: "literally."
2. June 2, 1577.
3. The words "Roman Catholic" are inserted by the author interlineally.

First Mansion

Chapter One

1. [*Aposentos*—a rather more pretentious word than the English "room": dwelling place, abode, apartment.]
2. [*Moradas*: derived from *morar*, to dwell, and not, therefore, absolute identical in sense with "mansions." The reference, however, is to Saint John 14:2.]
3. Proverbs 8:31
4. Genesis 1:26
5. Here the Saint erased several words and inserted others, leaving the phrase as it is in the text.
6. [*Moradas* (see n. 2, above).]
7. Saint John 9:2
8. Genesis 19:26

9. [*Lit.*, "into such bestiality."] P. Gracián deletes "bestiality" and substitutes "abomination." [I think the translation in the text, however, is a more successful way of expressing what was in Saint Teresa's mind: cf. Saint John of the Cross's observations on "animal penances"—*penitencias de bestias*—in his *Dark Night*, I, vi.

10. P. Gracián corrects this to "thirty-eight years." Saint John 5:5

11. Saint Matthew 6:21

Chapter Two

1. Psalm 1:3
2. *Lit.*: "fruit," for which P. Gracián substitutes "merit."
3. Saint Teresa herself. See Relation XXIV (*The Complete Works*, Vol. I, p. 345).
4. Psalm 126:2 [AV., 127:1]
5. The palmetto is a shrub, common in the south and east of Spain, with thick layers of leaves enclosing a succulent edible kernel.
6. [The autograph has, after the word "room," "Oh, but if it is (*Uh, que si es*) in (the room of) self-knowledge!" Previous editors have altered this difficult Spanish phrase to *aunque sea*, "not even if it is." Saint Teresa's meaning however, seems to me quite clearly the opposite of this, though it is impossible to translate her exclamation literally.]
7. [*Lit.*: "excess is as bad as defect."]
8. [*Ratero*: creeping, flying low, content with a low standard.]
9. *Lit.*, "a million."
10. *Lit*: "and had earth on his eyes."
11. See *Life*, Chapter XIII and *Method for the Visitation of Convents*.

Second Mansions

Chapter One

1. Below this line Saint Teresa wrote "Chapter," to which Luis de León prefixed the word "Only."
2. *Life*, Chaps. XI–XIII; *Way*, Chaps. XX–XXIX.3. [The word (*guisar*: "season," "dress") is a homely one: "dished up" would hardly be too colloquial a translation.]
4. [Saint Luke 15:15–16]
5. Judges vii, 5. "With Gedeon in the Judges," adds P. Gracián in the margin, crossing out the words "I forget with whom."
6. *Life*, Chap. XI.
7. [Probably a conscious reference to Saint Matthew 7:26–27.]
8. Saint Matthew 20:22
9. The autograph has, not *casas* ("homes") but *cosas* ("things"). Luis de León, however, read *casas* and succeeding editors have followed him.
10. Saint John 20:21.
11. *Life*, Chaps. XI, XIX.
12. Ecclesiasticus 3:27
13. Saint John 14:6

14. P. Gracián crossed through the bracketed words and wrote in the margin: "Both are said by Saint John, Chapter 14." [Actually the words are: "No man cometh. . . ."]
15. Saint John 14:9
16. Saint Matthew 10:24
17. Saint Matthew 24:41

Third Mansions

Chapter One

1. Psalm 111:1 (Authorized Version of the Bible, 112:1). (Hereafter the Authorized Version, generally referred to as the King James Version, will be cited as A.V.)
2. Saint John 11:16. The last four words are a marginal addition of the author's.
3. Gracián adds "in Heaven"; the addition is deleted by Ribera.
4. Gracián alters this to: "some who, although they are saints [*a more exact translation would be "are saintly"*], yet fell," but Ribera restores Saint Teresa's reading.
5. Gracián alters this to: "we have no certainty of abandoning them and of doing, etc."
6. The bracketed words, which Saint Teresa wrote in the margin of the autograph, are crossed out with two strokes. But Ribera has written underneath them: "This is not to be deleted."
7. [A striking example of Saint Teresa's untranslatably concise language. The original is: *Recia obediencia ha sido! Lit.:* "Rigorous obedience (it) has been!"]
8. Gracián altered this word to "Absalom" but Ribera wrote in the margin: 'This should read 'Solomon', as the holy Mother said."
9. Psalm 111:1 (A.V., 112:1)
10. The autograph makes this sentence negative, but partially deletes the negative particle. Luis de León, followed by later editors, omits it.
11. Saint Matthew 19:16–22
12. The phrase "like . . . Gospel" was written by Saint Teresa in the margin. [No doubt she recalled the reference to Saint Matthew 19:16–22, which she had made just above.]
13. [Or this clause might mean: "yet a person who gives all that he has thinks that he gives in fullest measure." But the interpretation in the text seems preferable.]
14. [Saint Luke 17:10] Gracián, in a note, gives the correct authorship.
15. "For what He has suffered for us" was substituted for the phrase by Gracián but the original text was restored by Ribera.
16. Gracián deleted the words "I write . . . truth" but Ribera wrote in the margin: "Nothing is to be deleted, for what the Saint says is well said."

Chapter Two

1. [*Lit.:* "drove me silly"—"*me traían tonta*": a typically homely and forcible expression. Cf. *Mansions* 4, Chap. 1, n. 15.]
2. "Very easily," added Gracián, interlinearly, but the addition is crossed out.

3. Saint Luke 22:42
4. [*Lit.*: "the Surgeon."]
5. [The Spanish phrase means, literally, "anyone of their humour," but there is no such "saying" as this in English.]

Fourth Mansions

Chapter One

1. Cf. Saint Teresa's definition of supernatural prayer in Relation V (*The Complete Works*, Vol. I, p. 327).
2. From the outline of Saint Teresa's life, Image Books Edition, (Vol. 1, *The Complete Works*, pp. xxvii–xxxvii), it will be seen that this computation is approximately correct. The reference is to *Life*, Chaps. XI–XXVII.
3. [The word is the same as is used above for "sweetness"—i.e., *contentos*, but in the singular. Such word play, as we have seen, is common in Saint Teresa: in the title of this very chapter we have an identical play on *contentos* ("sweetness") and *contento* ("happiness").]
4. [*contentos*]
5. [*contento*]
6. [*contentos*]
7. [Psalm 118:32: "(I have run the way of thy commandments,) when thou didst enlarge my heart." A.V. 119:32]
8. [*contento*]
9. The remainder of this paragraph was scored through in the autograph by Gracián and are omitted from the Córdoba copy. They are, however, quite legible.
10. [*Lit.*: "from how the disposition is."]
11. *Life*, Chap. XII.
12. The words in brackets were written in the margin by Saint Teresa and lightly scored out. Ribera, however, adds: "Nothing to be deleted." Gracián has added, interlineally, after "imagination": "for so we women generally call it."
13. [*tan tortolito*, an expressive phrase: "so like a little *tórtola* (turtle-dove)"—i.e. not only timid, but irresolute and apparently stupid, like an inexperienced fledgling.]
14. [Here there is a play on words difficult to render in English: the word translated both "restrain" and "uniting" is *atar*—"tie," "bind."]
15. [*Traíame tonta*. Cf. Third Mansions, Chap. 2, n. 1]
16. Gracián scores out this sentence in the autograph.
17. Song 8:1. Gracián has copied in the margin of the autograph the Spanish text of Song 8:1-4.

Chapter Two

1. [The original is quite colloquial: "in the mess I have got into" or "in what I have let myself in for" would be nearer its spirit.]
2. Psalm 118:32 (A.V., 119:32). Cf. Fourth Mansions, Chap. 2, n. 7.

3. Again, as above (Fourth Mansions, Chap. 1, n. 2), the Saint's computation is exactly correct.

4. [A very strong word, *estrujarse*. In its non-reflexive form, the verb means to squeeze, crush or press hard, or to extract something by so doing. The sense is, therefore, that with all our efforts we cannot squeeze out a drop of this water.]

Chapter Three

1. *Life*, Chap. XVI; *Way*, Chaps. XXVIII, XXIX; *Relations*, V.

2. There is little doubt that Saint Teresa is here using Bk. IX, Chap. VII of Francisco de Osuna's *Third Spiritual Alphabet*.

3. *Confessions*, Bk. X, Chap. XXVII [or *Soliloquies*, Chap. XXXI: cf. *The Complete Works of Saint John of the Cross* translated and edited by E. Allison Peers, 3 vols. (London:19341935): II, 33, 196, n. 9.]

4. [*Lit.*: "conscious of a gentle interior shrinking": *encogimiento*, the noun used, means "shrinkage," "contraction"; it should be distinguished from *recogimiento*, a word often used by Saint Teresa and translated "recollection."]

5. Osuna (*op. cit.*, Bk. VI, Chap. IV) uses this simile of the hedgehog in much the same way.

6. The reference is presumably to the famous "Eighth Counsel" of the *Treatise of Prayer and Meditation* [Cf. *Studies of the Spanish Mystics*, E. Allison Peers, 2 vols. (London:19271930), II, 113–14].

7. "With his human skill," adds Gracián, interlinearly.

8. *Way*, Chap. XXXI.

9. Saint Teresa had written "to discuss the effects of'" but deleted the last three words.

10. [The two Spanish words, on which Saint Teresa plays so trenchantly, are added to their English equivalents so as to make the phrase intelligible.]

Fifth Mansions

Chapter One

1. Gracián has scored through part of this sentence in the autograph.

2 Saint Matthew 20:16

3. Gracián substitutes for "are": "follow the rule of being."

4. Gracián inserts the word "perhaps."

5. Luis de León modifies this passage [which has been slightly paraphrased in translation, the construction in the Spanish being rather obscure], reading, after "delight": "for, although it [the soul] is in Him, according to the truth, it appears to have withdrawn so far from the body, in order to come closer to God, that I do not know, etc."

6. "Of the soul alone," inserts Gracián, interlineally.

7. Gracián deletes "the essence of."

8. Gracián substitutes "understanding" for "thoughts" and adds a marginal note: "This is (to be) understood of acts of the understanding and the will, for the thoughts of the imagination are clearly seen by the devil unless God blinds

him in that respect." Luis de León included the marginal note in the text of his edition but Gracián did not reproduce it in either the text or the margin of the Córdoba copy though he altered "thoughts" to "understanding."

9. Gracián inserts the word "nature" here, interlineally.

10 [P. Silverio refers here to *Way*, Chap. XXXI, but I hardly think this can be meant. Perhaps the author's allusion is to the first chapter of the Fourth Mansions or possibly to something she once said *viva voce*.]

11. [*Lit.*: "a something": the Spanish is *un no sé qué*, an expression corresponding to the French *un je ne sais quoi*.]

12. Gracián alters "as" to "as being, I think."

13. Gracián inserts: "it thinks."

14. Gracián amends the following phrase to read: "but that there has since remained with it, as it thinks, a certainty, etc."

15. Gracián alters this phrase to: "which made her understand this in such a way."

16. Saint Teresa refers to this experience of hers in *Life*, Chap. XVIII (Image Books Edition, p. 180). Later, a favor that she received (*Relations*, LIV: Vol. I, p. 361.) enlightened her further on this point. According to Diego de Yepes, *Vida de Santa Teresa* (Madrid:1615) (II, xx), she asked him for theological guidance about it just before she began the *Interior Castle*.

17. The rest of this paragraph was omitted by Luis de León.

18. Song 1:3; 2:4. Gracián deletes the bracketed phrase but writes "put" above "brought."

19. Song 3:2.

20. Here and just below Gracián has crossed out the word "center."

21. Saint John 20:19

Chapter Two

1. "Mustard-seeds," writes Gracián, interlineally, deleting the bracketed sentence which follows and adding the words: "It is so, for I have seen it."

2. Colossians 3:3. Gracián deletes "for that . . . my purpose" and supplies text and source in the margin.

3. [*Lit.*: "Whether this be so or not." But the meaning is clear from the context.]

4. The words "I meant . . . at all" are omitted from the *editio princeps*.

5. A characteristically emphatic phrase—*en fin, fin*.

6. [Cf. Fifth Mansions, Chap. 1. The reference here is clearly to Song 2:4.]

7. Saint Luke 22:15

8. Saint Teresa herself.

Chapter Three

1. Saint Teresa herself. Cf. *Life*, Chap. VII, pp. 37–48.

2. [The phrase is very emphatic: *Harto provecho, harto*—"exceedingly great profit, exceedingly."]

3. Saint John 11:35

4. Saint Teresa added here the word *aculla*, "yonder," which Luis de León altered to *en lo susodicho*, "in what is (said) above." [This affects the sense: Luis de León's alteration suggests that the silkworm is referred to, which seems to me unlikely. I take *aculla* to refer to the end of one's life and *aca* to mean "here and now."]

5. [*Lit.*: "to kill it ourselves." By "it," which in the Spanish can only stand for "life," is presumably meant the Pauline "old man."]

6. Jonah 4:6–7 [The "gourd" of A.V.]

7. Saint John 17:22

8. [*Encapotadas*: *lit.*, covering their faces with a cloak, muffled up. Metaphorically, the word can mean "frowning," "sullen." Here a less reprehensible meaning seems indicated.]

9. Cf. *Way*, Chap. VII.

Chapter Four

1. The words "in . . . souls" were written by Saint Teresa interlineally and "because . . . repose" were added by her in the margin.

2. [*Vengan a vistas*: *lit.*, "have sight of each other," "have an interview with each other"; and, in that sense, "come together" or "meet."]

3. [This sounds contradictory, but the word "take" (*tomar* each time in the Spanish) is of course used in two different senses.]

4. *No fué más de una vista.* [Cf. n. 2, above.]

5. Luis de León omitted the reference to Saint Ignatius of Loyola and the Society of Jesus from his edition, reading: "and other founders of Orders, all of whom, as we read, etc."

6. Gracián deletes, and León omits, the words "and the Holy Spirit."

Sixth Mansions

Chapter One

1. [Saint Teresa is not always consistent in her use of singular and plural in referring to each stage of the Mystic Way. The translation, throughout, follows her here exactly.]

2. Saint Teresa herself: cf. *Life*, Chap. XXVIII.

3. The person referred to is no doubt the author. [It was almost exactly forty years since she had professed at the Incarnation.]

4. [*Lit.*: "for many days"; but, as we have already seen, Saint Teresa often uses that phrase vaguely.]

5. At this point in the autograph, Saint Teresa wrote the word "Chapter," evidently intending to end the first chapter of the Sixth Mansions here, but deleted it again. Luis de León treated the insertion as valid and began the new chapter with the following paragraph: he was followed by other editors until the mid-nineteenth century. The autograph, however, does not support this procedure.

Chapter Two

1. The author had first written: "or a lightning-flash. Although no light is seen"; but she deleted this and substituted the phrase in the text.
2. [The verb used is *deshacerse*, "to undo oneself," implying here the utmost effort.]

Chapter Three

1. A. Francisco de Santo Tomás, O.C.D., in his *Médula mystica* (Trat. VI, Cap. i), has a succinct description of the three types of locution referred to by Saint Teresa, a classification applicable to visions also: "Some are corporeal, some imaginary and some spiritual or intellectual. Corporeal locutions are those actually heard by the physical powers of hearing. . . . Imaginary locutions are not heard in that way but the impression apprehended and received by the imaginative faculty is the same as though they had been. . . . In spiritual or intellectual locutions God imprints what He is about to say in the depth of the spirit: there is no sound, or voice, or either corporeal or imaginary representation of such, but an expression of (certain) concepts in the depth of the spirit and in the faculty of the understanding, and as this is not corporeal, but spiritual, the species, or similitudes, under which it is apprehended are not corporeal, but spiritual." Intellectual locutions, as explained by Saint John of the Cross (*Ascent of Mount Carmel*, Book II, Chaps. XXVI–XXX), are of three kinds: successive, formal and substantial.
2. [Saint Luke 24:36]
3. Jonah 4
4. Joshua 10:12–13

Chapter Four

1. [The original here interpolates two clauses, *con cuanto veis, u que nos está bien*, which, translated literally as "with all that you see or that it is acceptable to us," make no sense. I suspect that, if Saint Teresa had re-read her work, the phrase would have been omitted or clarified. Freely it might be rendered: "wonderful as you see it to be and much as we appreciate it," or, "however many visions you see or however much we desire them," but I am not convinced that either of these translations represents the author's meaning and other paraphrases are admissible.]
2. *Life*, Chap. XX; *Relations*, V.
3. The phrase "assuming . . . teaches" was added by Saint Teresa, in the autograph, as a marginal note.
4. Genesis 28:12
5. Exodus 3:2
6. "Two days" adds the *editio princeps*. The visit was made at the beginning of 1574. See "An Outline of the Lofe of Saint Teresa" (*The Complete Works*, Vol. I, p. xxxi).

7. The sentence "I can . . . whole" was written by Saint Teresa in the margin of the autograph.
8. [Or "some": the Spanish word, *alguna*, can have either a singular or a plural sense.]
9. [The "streets and the broad ways" of Canticles iii, 2.]
10. Saint John 9:6–7
11. Cf. *Life*, Chap. XXXI [Image Books Edition, 292].
12. This is Luis de León's emendation of the sentence in the autograph, which reads: "I do not use the word 'feigned', because those who experience them do not wish to deceive, but because [*sic*] they are deceived themselves." Gracián, in the Córdoba copy, emends similarly, though not identically. Both evidently express what Saint Teresa meant but failed to put clearly.

Chapter Five

1. The mystics concur with Saint Thomas in holding that ecstasy, rapture, transport, flight of the spirit, etc., are in substance one and the same, though there are accidental differences between them, as Saint Teresa explains here, in *Life*, Chap. XX, and in *Relations*, V.
2. IV, chapter ii.
3. Saint Luke 12:28
4. Saint Teresa received this favor at Seville about 1575–76. Cf. *Relations*, LI (*The Complete Works*, Vol. I, p. 360.)
5. Numbers xiii, 18–24.
6. [*Los trabajos de este camino tan trabajoso*: the word play is intentional.]
7. [*Vistas*. Cf. Fifth Mansions, Chap. 4, n. 4.]

Chapter Six

1. Exodus 14:21–2; Joshua 3:13
2. In the office of this Saint the Church recalls these words of his: "Lord, if I am still necessary to Thy people, I do not refuse toil: Thy will be done."
3. [Cf. *Life*, Chap. XVIII (*The Complete Works of Saint Teresa*, Vol. I, pp. 105–111)].
4. Saint Luke 15:11–32

Chapter Seven

1. *Life*, Chap. XXII.
2. *Life*, Chaps. XXII–XXIV.
3. Saint John 14:6
4. The words "the Lord . . . light" [which clearly interrupt the thought of the passage] are in the author's hand, but are marginal.
5. Saint John 14:6
6. Saint John 14:9
7. [I.e., the understanding.]
8. 3 Kings [A.V., 1 Kings] 18:30–39
9. Song 3:3.

10. "Or *Confessions*" is a marginal addition in Saint Teresa's hand. The passage alluded to comes from Chapter XXXI of the *Soliloquies*, a work first published in Spanish at Venice in 1512 and often reprinted in Spain during the sixteenth century. A passage very similar to this will be found in the *Confessions*, Bk. X, Chap. VI.
11. *Foundations*, Chap. VI.
12. Saint John 16:7

Chapter Eight

1. For Saint Teresa's treatment of intellectual vision, see *Life*, Chaps. XXVII, XXVIII.
2. [Cf. *Life*, Chap. XXVII.]
3. Ibid.

Chapter Nine

1. Saint Matthew 25:41 [The abrupt change of pronoun is reproduced exactly from the Spanish.]
2. [This characteristic example of Saint Teresa's word play is allowed to stand in translation, though to English ears it may sound artificial.]
3. [*Dar higas*. Cf. note on this phrase, *Life* (*The Complete Works*, Vol. I, p. 189, n. 1). The theologian referred to was P. Báñez: cf. *Life*, Chap. XXIX, *Foundations*, Chap. VIII.]

Chapter Ten

1. Psalm 115:11 [: "I said in my excess: 'Every man as a liar,'" Cf. A.V., Psalm 116:11.]
2. Saint John 18:38

Chapter Eleven

1. Saint John 4:7–13
2. The words of the parenthesis were inserted by Saint Teresa in the margin of the autograph.
3. Cf. *Relations* XV. [*The Complete Works*, Vol. I., p. 340. This incident took place at Salamanca in 1571. The singer was M. Isabel de Jesús. The song begins: "Let mine eyes behold Thee, Sweetest Jesu, nigh; Let mine eyes behold Thee, And at once I'll die." It has no verbal reference, as our text suggests, to "life not ending," but this is its general theme, as it is also that of several poems by Saint Teresa herself.]
4. [*Lit.*: "and is dying in order to die"—a reference, no doubt, to the poem to be found in *The Complete Works*, Vol. III, pp. 277–79].
5. Saint Matthew 20:22: "'Can you drink the chalice that I shall drink?' They say to Him: 'We can.'"
6. Saint Luke 7:44.

Seventh Mansions

Chapter One

1. Gracián altered "capable" to "prepared."
2. To win merit" is the Saint's marginal addition.
3. This paragraph was considerably altered in the *editio princeps.*
4. Acts 9:8
5. [Acts 9:18]
6. Gracián reads: "vision or knowledge, born of faith."
7. Luis de León added the following note here: "Though man in this life, if so raised by God, may lose the use of his senses and have a fleeting glimpse of the Divine Essence, as was probably the case with Saint Paul and Moses and certain others, the Mother is not speaking here of this kind of vision, which, though fleeting, is intuitive and clear, but of a knowledge of this mystery which God gives to certain souls, through a most powerful light which He infuses into them, not without created species. But as this species is not corporeal, nor figured in the imagination, the Mother says that this vision is intellectual and not imaginary.
8. Gracián reads: "grasp better, it seems."
9. Gracián reads: "either of the body (for God is Spirit) or of the imagination.
10. Saint John 14:23
11. Gracián adds: "as they are commonly believed and heard."
12. Saint Luke 10:40

Chapter Two

1. Cf. Relations, XXXV (*The Complete Works*, Vol. I, pp. 351–52.)
2. The words "but through an intellectual" and "although . . . mentioned" are substituted by Saint Teresa for others which she has deleted.
3. Saint John 20:19, 21
4. 1 Corinthians 6:17. [The Spanish has two verbs, *arrimarse* and *allegarse*, corresponding to "joined," and linked by the word "and." The Scriptural text reads: "He who is joined to the Lord is one spirit."] The whole of the passage "He who . . . by union" is Saint Teresa's interlinear substitution for something deleted.
5. Philippians 1:21: "For to me, to live is Christ; and to die is gain."
6. [*Lit.*: "that they cannot."] The words "that what . . . doubted" are scored through in the original—we suspect by Gracián.
7. Saint John 20:19, 21 [Cf. n. 3, above]
8. Saint Luke 6:50
9. Gracián deletes the bracketed words and substitutes the Scriptural test, giving its source (Saint John 17:21) in the margin.
10. Saint John 17:20
11. Saint John 17:23
12. [Cf. Saint Teresa's poem on this theme (*The Complete Works of Saint Teresa*, Vol. III, pp. 287–88).]
13. Psalm 1:3

Chapter Three

1. [Cf. VII, n. 224, above;] *Relations*, XXXV (*The Complete Works*, Vol. I, p. 352).
2. In the margin of the autograph Saint Teresa wrote at this point: "*Cuando dice aquí: os pide, léase luego este papel.*" ["When you get to the words *asking of you in it*, go straight on to this paper."] "This paper" is no longer extant, but Luis de León evidently had it, as the rest of this paragraph, though not in the autograph, figures in his edition. It is also found, with slight modifications, in early copies.
3. Acts 9:6
4. The bracketed phrase is Saint Teresa's marginal addition.
5. Luis de León modifies this paragraph thus. After "save very occasionally" he adds, in parenthesis: "that is, as I say here, with respect to these exterior epoch of the suspension of the senses and loss of heat; but they tell me that only the accidents disappear and that interiorly there is rather an increase." He then continues: "So the raptures, in the way I describe, cease, and it [the soul] has not these raptures and Bights of the spirit; or, if it has them, only rarely, and hardly ever in public as it very often had before."
6. Revelation 21:3
7. Genesis 8:8-9
8. Luke 18:13

Chapter Four

1. 3 Kings [A.V. 1 Kings] 11
2. Psalm 111:1 [A.V., 112:1]
3. 1 Thessalonians 2:9
4. In the old Carmelite Breviary, which Saint Teresa would have used, the Antiphon of the Magnificat at First Vespers on June 29 runs: "The Blessed Apostle Peter saw Christ coming to meet him. Adoring Him, he said: 'Lord, whither goest Thou?' 'I am going to Rome to be crucified afresh.'" The story has it that Saint Peter returned to Rome and was crucified.
5. Psalm 17:26 [A.V. 18:26]
6. 3 Kings [A.V. 1 Kings] 19:10
7. Saint Luke 10:42
8. Saint Luke 7:37–38
9. Saint Luke 7:39
10. This sentence is authentic but marginal.

Epilogue

1. "And mazes," adds Luis de León. The words also occur in several copies of the autograph, including that of Toledo, but not in the autograph itself. There is reason to suppose, however, that there may have been two autographs of this epilogue.
2. "By the mercy of God" is the Saint's marginal addition.

Suggested Readings

✛

Ahlgren, Gillian, T.W. *Teresa of Avila and the Politics of Sanctity*. Ithaca: Cornell University Press, 1996.

Auclair, Marcelle. *Teresa of Avila: The Vivid Dramatic Life Story of a Great Woman: Organizer, Foundress, Mystic, Saint*. With a Preface by André Maurois. Translated by Kathleen Pond. New York: Pantheon Books, 1953.

Bilinkoff, Jodi. *The Avila of Saint Teresa: Religious Reform in a Sixteenth-Century City*. Ithaca: Cornell University Press, 1989.

Clissold, Stephen. *Saint Teresa of Avila*. New York: The Seabury Press, 1982.

Dickens, E.W.T. *The Crucible of Love: A Study of the Mysticism of Saint Teresa of Avila and Saint John of the Cross*. New York: Sheed and Ward, 1963.

Donze, Mary Terese. *Teresa of Avila*. New York/Ramsey, NJ: Paulist Press, 1982.

Hamilton, Elizabeth. *Saint Teresa: A Journey in Spain*. New York: Charles Scribner's Sons, 1959.

Lincoln, Victoria. *Teresa: A Woman. A Biography of Teresa of Avila*. Edited with Introductions by Elias Rivers and Antonio T. de Nicolás. New York: Paragon House Publishers, 1984.

Mazzoni, Cristina. *Saint Hysteria: Neurosis, Mysticism, and Gender in European Culture*. Ithaca: Cornell University Press, 1996.

Medwick, Cathleen. *Teresa of Avila: The Progress of a Soul*. New York: Image Books, 1999.

Petersson, Robert T. *The Art of Ecstasy: Teresa, Bernini, and Crashaw*. New York: Atheneum, 1970.

Sackville-West, Vita. *The Eagle and the Dove: A Study in Contrasts. Saint Teresa of Avila, Saint Thérese of Lisieux*. New York: Doubleday, Doran & Company, Inc., 1944.

Saint Teresa of Avila: Studies in Her Life, Doctrine and Times. Edited by Father Thomas, O.D.C., and Father Gabriel, O.D.C. Westminster, MD: The Newman Press, 1963.

Slade, Carole. *Saint Teresa of Avila: Author of a Heroic Life*. Berkeley/ Los Angeles/ London: University of California Press, 1995.

Weber, Alison. *Teresa of Avila and the Rhetoric of Femininity*. Princeton: Princeton University Press, 1990.

Dennis J. Billy, C.Ss.R. is a teacher, writer, and poet. Ordained a Redemptorist priest in 1980, he is currently ordinary professor of the history of moral theology and Christian spirituality at the Alphonsian Academy of Rome's Pontifical Lateran University and the Karl Rahner Professor of Catholic Theology at the Graduate Theological Foundation in South Bend, Indiana. He is the author of numerous books and articles, both popular and scholarly. Raised in Staten Island, New York and educated there through high school in local Catholic schools, he graduated from Dartmouth College and went on to receive four master degrees, as well as doctorates from Harvard University, the Pontifical University of St. Thomas, and the Graduate Theological Foundation.

✛

Teresa of Avila (1515–1582) was a contemplative nun, religious reformer, monastic founder, spiritual writer, and gifted poet. One of the greatest Christian mystics of all time, she wrote *Interior Castle* in 1577 at the request of her trusted and learned confessor, Jerome Gratian. This work contains her mature spiritual doctrine, and many consider it to be her masterpiece. She wrote it to explain to the nuns of her Discalced Carmelite reform the various kinds of prayer they might experience on their journey to God. Teresa of Avila was canonized in 1622 and declared a doctor of the Church in 1970.

ℭLASSICS with ℭOMMENTARY series

Interior Castle
The Classic Text with a Spiritual Commentary
Teresa of Avila
Commentary by Dennis Billy, C.Ss.R.
The classic E. Allison Peers translation of this Christian favorite is united with fresh spiritual commentary, making it the only edition of Teresa of Avila's classic to remain faithful to her mystical vision while providing spiritual nourishment.
ISBN: 9780870612312 / 320 pages / $16.95

The Imitation of Christ
A Spiritual Commentary and Reader's Guide
Thomas Á Kempis
Commentary by Dennis Billy, C.Ss.R.
Fr. Billy highlights how today's Christians can interpret and apply *The Imitation* to their own spiritual journeys with the help of William Creasy's accessible translation.
ISBN: 9780870612343 / 272 pages / $15.95

Visits to the Most Holy Sacrament and to Most Holy Mary
A New Translation and Spiritual Commentary
Alphonsus de Liguori
Translation and Commentary by Dennis Billy, C.Ss.R.
The first complete and faithful English translation from its original Italian of *Visits to the Most Holy Sacrament and to Most Holy Mary*, a devotional classic by St. Alphonsus de Liguori.
ISBN: 9780870612442 / 160 pages / $15.95

Spiritual Friendship
The Classic Text with a Spiritual Commentary
Aelred of Rievaulx
Commentary by Dennis Billy, C.Ss.R.
Written in the 12th century by Cistercian abbot Aelred of Rievaulx, *Spiritual Friendship* invites readers to enter into one of the great works of the Christian tradition that sees friendship as a key to spiritual growth and true happiness.
ISBN: 9780870612428 / 160 pages / $15.95

ave maria press®

Available from your local bookstore or from
ave maria press / Notre Dame, IN 46556
www.avemariapress.com / Ph: 800-282-1865
A Ministry of the Indiana Province of Holy Cross

Keycode: FØTØ1Ø7ØØØØ